Faces of Fear

GW01045035

Douglas E. Winter

Faces of Fear

Encounters with the creators of modern horror

Pan Books   London, Sydney and Auckland

First published 1990 by
The Berkeley Publishing Company, New York

First published in Great Britain 1990 by
Pan Books Ltd, Cavaye Place, London SW10 9PG

9 8 7 6 5 4 3 2 1

© Douglas E. Winter 1985, 1990

ISBN 0 330 31246 4

Phototypeset by Input Typesetting Ltd, London SW19 8DR
Printed in England by Clays Ltd, St Ives plc

for my father

"And when he had crossed the bridge,
the phantoms came to meet him."

Nosferatu (1922)

Contents

Introduction

Who writes this stuff?

A man bursts spontaneously into flames. Disembodied voices speak. Something lurks behind the closet door. A victim of religious mania kills his wife and children.

It's the new Stephen King novel, right?

Wrong.

These episodes, as well as other horrific delights, can be found in *Wieland, or The Transformation*, published in 1798 and still available in bookstores today. It is the first American horror novel, written by Charles Brockden Brown, a Philadelphian of Quaker stock who is recognized as the father of American literature. He was, in other words, the first American crazy enough to try to support himself solely by writing fiction.

But in the occupation of telling horror stories, Charles Brockden Brown was a relative late-comer. Despite what you may have heard about Horace Walpole, whose *The Castle of Otranto* (1764) sparked the Gothic flame, the first true horror writer in the English language was probably John Webster, who wrote such plays as *The White Devil* (1912) and *The Duchess of Malfi* (1623). Even what some have called the earliest "novel" of western civilization, *Metamorphoses* by Lucius Apuleius (circa 170 AD), is a fantasy about a man tormented by witchcraft. A ghost haunts Pliny's *Epistles* (100 AD), a werewolf stalks the *Satyricon* of Petronius (60 AD), and, as any high school student knows, horrific elements animate the *Aeneid* (circa 20 BC), the *Iliad* and *Odyssey* (circa 700 BC), and the granddaddy of all western literature, the

Sumerian epic poem *Gilgamesh*, written about 2000 BC. Before the written word, the tale of horror flourished in cave paintings, in religion and ritual, in stories told by firelight as our distant ancestors huddled together against the night . . . and its creatures, real and imagined.

"The oldest and strongest emotion of mankind is fear," wrote H. P. Lovecraft, the early twentieth-century master of horror, and stories evoking fear have thus never lacked for tellers. But the horror story has never been so popular, so visible, so intrinsic to our culture, as it is today. The names that we hold sacred as classic horror writers sell more books now than during their lifetimes. Edgar Allan Poe had to support himself as an editor; his short stories, although admired while he was alive, did not gain him wealth or recognition. When H. P. Lovecraft died in poverty in 1937, only four people attended his funeral; he lived to see but a single book bearing his name on its cover—and it was published in an edition of 150 copies.

Today, more than one hundred million copies of books by Stephen King alone have seen print worldwide. Our bookstores include sections devoted specifically to horror; some, in fact, have sections devoted solely to King. More horror novels have been published in the past twenty years than in the entire previous history of the printed word. The number of horror films produced in that time span is likewise staggering. And the aesthetics of horror have moved beyond fiction and film, invading the very character of our culture. Our grocery stores offer breakfast cereals endorsed by caricatures of vampires and ghosts; rock musicians sky-rocket their careers with videos that feature werewolves and cavorting zombies; Stephen King camps it up for an American Express television commercial. Meanwhile, like a horde of walking corpses battering at our doors and windows, the horror novels and films just won't stop coming. In fact, they seem to be multiplying daily, an irresistible art of darkness concocted from the fears of a fascinated public.

Why? Why do modern readers and film-goers seek so

eagerly to be scared out of their wits? What scares us? What is there in human nature that makes us *like* to be scared?

These are important questions—questions that probably have been asked since that first horror story was told by firelight. But they all pale before the one that readers and film-goers ask most:

Who writes this stuff?

This kind of curiosity is natural, particularly for anyone who reads; after all, reading is an intimate act, a sharing of imagination by writer and reader, and one that is heightened when the subject matter concerns our deepest fears. Just what kind of person would write a book called *Psycho* or *Firestarter* or *Hell House*, or, indeed, *The Doll Who Ate His Mother*?

The books themselves rarely tell us, at least on an explicit level. We do know, from cover credits, that most horror writers are men. Their names are mundane, often monosyllabic—Bloch, Coyne, Grant, Straub—and their dust-jacket biographies seem written either by a census-taker ("He lives in New Jersey") or the headline scribe for the *New York Daily News* ("His other brain-splattering tales of terror include . . .").

Answers will not be found at your local library. Putting aside the tendency of critics and academics to consider fiction in abstract terms, divorced from the personality and motives of the writer—as well as from all commercial realities—the simple fact of the matter is that horror fiction is rarely the subject of serious critical inquiry. Existing biographical sources are almost exclusively retrospective, focused on writers like Poe and Lovecraft and their contemporaries of the 1800s and early 1900s rather than on writers who live and work today. A 1978 reference work entitled *Who's Who in Horror and Fantasy Fiction* included only five of the seventeen writers profiled here. But these seventeen writers account for more than three hundred books, sixty motion pictures, episodes of at least twenty television series, and short stories numbering in the thousands. They are the best and the best-selling of modern horror—the fearmakers of our frightened times—and if answers are to be found, it is in their words and their lives.

That's where I come in. I write about horror fiction, and I also write horror fiction, but I do neither for a living. I know these people—most of them, anyway—and have read virtually everything that they have written. If anyone were to tell their stories, perhaps I would possess the precise balance between an insider's knowledge and distanced objectivity that would assure, rather than obscure, truths. At least Berkley Books, the first publisher that I contacted, agreed. Armed with my tape recorder, I set out to make conversation with the dark.

A life in the day of . . .

The first interview for this book was conducted with Charles L. Grant; he took me to the Manhattan Playboy Club for lunch.

It was not, however, an auspicious beginning. My tape recorder stopped fifteen minutes into our conversation; the batteries, which I had bought that morning, were dead. As I ventured back onto the baking-hot streets of New York City looking for replacements, I had yet to confront my real problem: Charlie Grant and I are friends.

The business of inquiring into anyone's life is a delicate one, but the notion of attempting, on the basis of a single interview, to summarize that life *and* a body of fiction—all in 6,000 words or less—is simply absurd. I had no such delusions. My purpose was to let the writers speak for themselves, airing what was on their minds about their life and work, within a context of knowledgeable questions and mutual trust—and in so doing, to offer an honest look into the writing of modern horror fiction.

Despite the exotic locale of my initial interview, I preferred to visit each writer at his or her home. There we would talk, usually in a conversational manner rather than a formal exchange of questions and answers. I normally avoided the specifics of any given novel, story or film; instead, I offered open-ended comments and questions intended to direct the interviewee's attention inward. Writers talk too often about the public side of their work—storylines, pending projects, potential movie deals—and too little about the private side that I wished to explore.

Although the personalities of both parties affect any interview, I soon realized the danger of relying upon subjective impressions in writing this book. Friends such as Charlie Grant might be favoured; persons whom I had never before met might be disadvantaged if, for example, on the day of my visit, the plumbing in their house had failed and their mood was sour. More important, if I asked the right questions, there would be no need to colour the interviews with commentary; the answers would speak for themselves. I have thus forgone lengthy editorialisation or, worse yet, the sort of superficial lay analysis that characterizes the modern cult of personality. Indeed, other than providing biographic and bibliographic detail, I have limited my commentary—even to the point of excising, wherever possible, the questions that I asked, unless they are necessary to the logic of the discussion. While I have included several anecdotes, and occasional descriptions of lifestyle and environment, clothing and habits, it is from the writers' own words that you will know them.

Editorial matters

Most of the taped conversations lasted about three hours; the verbatim transcriptions, taken together, would fill a book roughly five times the size of the present volume. I arranged for each transcription to be made by a specialist, then replayed each tape, comparing it against the transcription in order to assure complete accuracy.

My next step was to edit these raw materials, deleting irrelevant and redundant passages, and reordering paragraphs, sentences, even phrases, to improve the flow of ideas or to provide grammatical structure. Such editing is a necessary evil, particularly in the colloquial atmosphere that I sought to promote, and it is something which the interviewees heartily approve. As T. E. D. Klein said, in the midst of a digression that had twice been interrupted by a waiter, "I am looking to you the way that Quasimodo would look to a make-up man on the Johnny Carson show. It's like, make me pretty before I go on." But I sought, at all costs, to preserve basic speech patterns, so that reading the words of the writers will be as close as possible to hearing them.

Each writer was given the opportunity to review his or her interview prior to its publication, and to edit, revise, or amend the quoted passages. None of them chose to do so in any substantial fashion.

The faces of fear

Each chapter of this book is devoted to an individual writer. The chapters are organized into rough geographic order, from West Coast to East Coast of the United States; their ordering also has a serendipitous dramatic quality, beginning with the writers whose work helped mould the modern horror field—Robert Bloch, Richard Matheson, William Peter Blatty—and closing with its best-known practitioners, Peter Straub and Stephen King. I have inserted, at appropriate thematic intervals, three chapters profiling Britain's leading horror writers, Ramsey Campbell, James Herbert, and Clive Barker.

The interviewees, as I have suggested, include several personal friends. Some are famous names; others are relative unknowns. My selections were guided by two principles. The first was to assemble the best and best-selling writers working in the field today. The second was commercial reality. A repetitive strain in the interviews is the manner in which commercial considerations affect writers about their work. These considerations affected this book as well; because it was conceived as a trade paperback, it was limited to a certain length—roughly 110,000 words. To work at the depth of inquiry that I desired, this meant that I was restricted to a maximum of seventeen interviewees.

More people are writing horror fiction today than at any point in the history of the field. At least one hundred working writers in the United States and Britain were potential candidates; over the past few years, I have interviewed or corresponded with the majority of them. Some choices were easy: this book could not have gone forward without names like Bloch and Blatty, King and Straub. At the same time, it also could not properly exist without talents like Dennis Etchison and Charles L. Grant, who have garnered almost cult status among hard-core horror fiction fans, but who have never topped the best-seller lists. Other selections were based upon interview content rather than fame or fortune—in other words, because these writers' words or lives made important points about the pleasures and perils of writing horror fiction. I should note that no one refused my request for an interview; my efforts to include Ray Bradbury and Karl Edward Wagner succumbed, however, to the exigencies of my schedule.

I have used the term "horror" throughout this book rather than more socially acceptable—and limiting—phrases such as "supernatural literature". The terminology is intentional. The writers considered here traverse the denotational poles of horror—that "feeling of awe and imaginative fear". In my view, the presence or absence of a fantastic or supernatural element in a story is of little moment, for one of the intrinsic questions posed by the best horror fiction is whether the reality that we perceive is indeed real, or whether it may slip away at any time to reveal even darker landscapes. As made equally clear by Jane Austen's discerning critique of the Gothic, *Northanger Abbey* (1818) and by Stephen King's contemporary *Cujo* (1981), preoccupation with vampires or spirit worlds should not blind us to dangers near at hand. At its best, the horror story acknowledges that warning by expanding our assumptions about where we live to include the dark and frightening regions within ourselves, as well as those hidden beneath the familiar relationships to which we look for support. In assembling my conversations, then, I have considered the explorers of infinite realms of darkness—from those who write of psychotic killers to those who write of creatures that bite in the night.

As you will read, several of these writers prefer terms other than "horror" to describe their work; others have in fact moved on—some only temporarily—to different fields. None of the writers, even those who thrive on being described as horror writers, ultimately deserves categorization; their talents transcend the artificial boundaries of the market-place.

Haunted lives

When I began the interviews, my desire to assure that each writer's story was told uniquely led me to reject the notion of using a standardized set of questions. But during the interviews, patterns inevitably emerged. A few of the more empirical ones deserve summary here, if only as an intriguing set of demographics.

VITAL STATISTICS Although the birth dates of the interviewees span five decades, the predominant force in modern horror has been the generation born in the 1940s—ten of the writers profiled here were born between 1943 and 1947. V. C. Andrews is the only female interviewee, representative of the strikingly small minority of women who write contemporary horror. Thirteen of the writers interviewed here are married, and of this group, all but four are in their first marriage, certainly placing this sample well below the national divorce rate. All of the writers who have been married have had children, which brings us to the question of . . .

UNHAPPY CHILDHOODS Were they warped as children, or were they just born that way?

This question is the horror writer's bane. "Childhood," grumbles Stephen King. "People always want to know what happened in your childhood." In *Danse Macabre*, he wrote of a psychologist who claimed that King had been writing about a bizarre incident in his childhood "ever since it had occurred". As Ramsey Campbell has noted so well, it is a very short step from the conclusion "ah, so *that*'s what your fiction is about" to "that's *all* your fiction is about".

You will read here of some very peculiar childhoods, as well as some that were quite mundane. You will also read the writers' views on the role, if any, that their childhoods played in the fact that they write horror. Were they warped? Judge for yourself; but also ask yourself, as Peter Straub asked me: "Is there such a thing as a happy childhood?"

FIRE AND BRIMSTONE When I began the book, my editor, Susan Allison, offered me a mock wager: "I'll bet that you will find that these guys all came from very conservative religious upbringings—Roman Catholics, Southern Baptists, Methodists." The tally? Seven Catholics, two Jews, one Christian Scientist, one Church of England, one Episcopalian, one Lutheran, one Methodist, one Presbyterian, one Southern Baptist, and one who attended both Lutheran and Presbyterian churches. Perhaps more interesting is the fact that, although many of the interviewees currently have deeply held religious beliefs, none now attends the services of an organized religion.

TINKER, TAILOR, SOLDIER, SPOOK All of the interviewees work full-time as writers. It has not always been that way; indeed, none has worked all of his or her career as a professional writer.

Only Dennis Etchison seems to have fulfilled the romantic notion of a struggling writer as a jack-of-all-trades; before his "retirement" to full-time writing, he worked as, among other things, a dishwasher, shoe salesman, gas-pump jockey. Richard Matheson was a factory labourer before his breakthrough; Ramsey Campbell worked in a tax office and a library; John Coyne served in the Peace Corps and as a college dean. The early careers of most remaining interviewees fall rather neatly into two groups: schoolteachers and advertising/public relations work.

Me? I'm a lawyer. But don't hold that against me; so was Charles Brockden Brown.

A number of people deserve a special word of thanks for their efforts in seeing this book to completion: my editors, Susan Allison (Berkley) and Kathy Gale (Pan), for their confidence and endless patience; my agent, Howard Morhaim; Charles Platt, for his initial advice and encouragement; Mary Sutton, for her work on several transcriptions; Howard Frumes and Gina Kuras, for bed and board in California; Harris Weinstein, lawyer and friend, for the occasional respite from legal horrors; and, as always, my wife, Lynne.

But my greatest appreciation is reserved, of course, for each of the writers who participated in this book. They are, by and large, the nicest people that I know, or would care to know.

So why do they scare us?

Let's find out.

Douglas E. Winter

Alexandria, VA
London, England
Washington, DC

March, 1985

Revised edition
February 1990

Robert Bloch

"The real horror is not in the shadows,
but in that little twisted world inside our own skulls."

My first great scare came, I like to think, from seeing the motion picture *Invasion of the Body Snatchers* soon after its release in 1956. I didn't sleep very well that night: I dreamed that my parents, my brother, my friends were being replaced by pod people, and that, like poor Kevin McCarthy running through the streets of Santa Mira, no one would believe me when I tried to explain. But the next day, safe and secure in the embrace of daylight, there was no doubt that my nightmare had been fun—I had produced, directed, and starred in my own movie, all at age six.

The appeal of the horror story lies, first and foremost, in that element of fantasy: the vicarious thrill of experiencing the worst that could happen and escaping to live again another day, knowing that the scares were imaginary, but wondering, if only for a moment, what it would be like if they were real.

The time comes for all of us, though, when the fantasy becomes too real—when it crosses that thin borderline from the impossible to the probable or, for the sceptic, when it moves in right next door. Vegetable-men from outer space and rubber-suited monsters playing hopscotch on Tokyo are one thing, but what if the creature wears our face, and delivers our mail or fixes our car or . . .

What if he is that nice, soft-spoken fellow who runs the backroads motel?

The reality of horror descended upon me in 1960; I suspect that, upon reflection, many others can point to a similar place, a similar time. I was nine years old, and my Aunt Garnet and Uncle Al had taken my brother and me to the Washington Theater, one of the two indoor movie houses in my hometown of Granite City, Illinois. I was excited; we were going to see a brand-new scary movie with a funny name.

It was called *Psycho*.

Looking back, I wonder just how nervous my aunt must have been, taking two young boys from a good Southern Baptist home to a film whose opening sequence featured a well-proportioned Janet Leigh tossing about on the sack in her skivvies, and soon turned her into a nude pincushion in the shower. Pretty nervous, I suspect; but she was preoccupied, trying to quiet down the two teenage girls sitting behind us. One had seen the film before, and she insisted upon telling her friend, in a loud, gum-popping voice, what was going to happen next. I didn't mind her previews, though — because I, for one, wasn't having a good time. Norman Bates wasn't the kind of monster I had come to love — he was just a man. And I was hunkered down in my seat, scared to even think what might happen next.

Two masters of horror have been immortalized by the motion picture *Psycho* — not simply for that nine-year-old boy, but for the entire popular culture. One, of course, is its director, Alfred Hitchcock; the other is the man who wrote the novel on which it was based. And no one ever said it better than Hitchcock himself: "*Psycho* all came from Robert Bloch's book."

Nearly thirty-five years before my rendezvous with Norman Bates, another nine-year-old boy had also found his first real fear in a motion picture theatre. Robert Bloch, born in Chicago, Illinois, on 5 April 1917, and then living in suburban Maywood, had decided to attend his first movie at night alone.

"I knew nothing in particular about what I was going to see; it was just the idea of being able to be on my own at that age. I went to the Lido, and I was a little put off by the fact that the ushers were wearing masks. I was even more disconcerted when the organist began to play some rather discordant notes, and onto the screen came the title *The Phantom of the Opera*, starring Lon Chaney, a gentleman about whom I knew nothing. But I soon learned a great deal about Mr Chaney: to my surprise, I learned that he wore a mask at all times, that he slept in a coffin because it reminded him of death, that he lived in catacombs five cellars below the Paris Opera House, and that he had some rather antisocial ambitions.

"Then came the unmasking scene: Chaney seated at the organ and Mary Philbin pulling the mask away. And at that point, I paid him the greatest tribute a small child can pay to an actor—I wet my pants.

"I remember running home from that theatre and spending the next three years increasing the family's electric bill by sleeping with the lights on."

Even today, at more than seventy years of age, that frightened child lives in Robert Bloch's wide-eyed face. We sit in the poolside office of his home, high in the Hollywood Hills, overlooking Laurel Canyon. The view, he has assured me, was better when he moved in twenty-six years ago, "before the smog". But Bloch isn't looking out across the sunlit scenery; he sits clutching the arms of his easy chair, smiling uneasily, locked in that childhood memory. And for good reason: although the nine-year-old Robert Bloch had earlier read Edgar Allan Poe and other horror writers, this confrontation with *The Phantom of the Opera* was the making of a horror writer.

"I decided, very wisely, that if you can't lick 'em, join 'em. I began to read more and more of this type of material, and to see more films. I had the impression that I was going to find out not only what fear consisted of, but just what it was that frightened me. That way, I could exorcize my own personal demons. About two or three months later, I discovered *Weird Tales* at the newsstand, and from then on, I was home free."

In those times before paperback books, television, and motion pictures with sound, the only regular forum for the horror story was a pulp magazine, *Weird Tales*. Known as "The Unique Magazine", its roster of authors is now a veritable "Who's Who" of fantasy fiction, and it served as the proving grounds for writers from Bloch to Ray Bradbury, Fritz Leiber, Theodore Sturgeon, and Manly Wade Wellman, as well as the creator of Conan, Robert E. Howard. In its pages, and particularly from the hand of its most influential writer, H. P. Lovecraft, the modern American horror story was born.

Bloch was enthralled by *Weird Tales*, and particularly by Lovecraft's fiction of "cosmic dread"; it filled a need in his young life—a need to overcome "feelings of inadequacy or insecurity" that he believes are possessed by most writers of horror fiction:

"Most of us, I think, would be fully qualified as 'loners' for one reason or another. My family was warm and friendly, and far from intimidating, but in those days, education was not all that progressive. There were no so-called special schools for children who seemed precocious. So when I got into grammar school, the teachers, in their infinite wisdom, decided that they didn't want me throwing spitballs at them because I had already done my lessons before class. I ended up, at the age of nine or ten, sitting with classmates who were eleven and twelve. The physical differences were marked, particularly on the playground, where I couldn't compete with my older classmates in body-contact sports and that sort of thing. I couldn't run as fast; I couldn't throw as far. And I felt a little bit discriminated against.

"I was the one who was always organizing the circuses and the plays and the pirate ships and the World War One trenches—and I had a host of eager and willing participants. But when it came to athletic competition, I felt I wasn't really with it. In that sense, I was alienated."

In 1933, Bloch, sixteen years old and living in Milwaukee, wrote a fan letter to H. P. Lovecraft; he was stunned to receive a reply. Lovecraft began regular correspondence with the young enthusiast, and soon encouraged him to write fiction. "After a few letters, he wrote, in effect, 'There's something about the way you write that tells me that perhaps you would like to try your own hand at it. I would be very glad to read whatever you might turn out.' Of course, I was completely enamoured of Lovecraft and his writing for *Weird Tales*, so I sat down at once and did a few things in emulation. He didn't criticize; he encouraged me, which was what I needed. And when I got out of high school, I didn't need any encouragement; it was sheer economic necessity.

"I graduated at seventeen. The Depression was in full swing. There were no jobs. You couldn't get a job without experience; you couldn't get experience without a job. I had no alternative but to find something to do. So I bought a secondhand typewriter for fifteen dollars and a secondhand card table for one dollar, put the typewriter on top of the card table in my bedroom, went down to the dime store for some paper and carbons, and started working in earnest—learning to type as I went along. Six weeks later, I sold my first story to *Weird Tales*.

"I still don't know what I want to be when I grow up."

Bloch wrote full-time from his high school graduation in 1934 to 1942, when the paper shortage resulting from World War Two began to close down the pulp fiction markets. Horror fiction was also in decline; Lovecraft had died in 1937, his brief writing career ending in virtual poverty. Only after his death, with the founding of a small press, Arkham House, by an admiring fellow writer, August Derleth, was Lovecraft's fiction preserved in book form, enabling it to attain the popular success that it continues to hold today.

"In those days," Block comments, "you didn't write for posterity, you wrote for a penny a word. Your story had a one-month existence in a magazine, and that was the end of it. There were no paperbacks, there were no collections, there were no anthologies. And no critical attention, of course—no reviews, no academic consideration whatsoever. It was more or less taken for granted that what you wrote for this audience had a thirty-day life on the newsstands and then would disappear forever. Lovecraft himself felt that this was going to be his fate, and only a series of fortunate happenstances after his death rescued him."

It should thus come as no surprise that in 1942, Bloch, with a pregnant wife suffering from tuberculosis of the bone, should become concerned with the dwindling economics of writing short stories. He complained of his plight at a meeting of a Milwaukee writers' group, and one of the members, Gus Marx, offered him an apprenticeship in his advertising agency.

"He said, 'Tell you what. I'll give you an office space of your own and a typewriter. You can do your own writing and you can spend as much time with me as you wish, watching what I do, and at the end of six months you can go your own way.' He paid nothing. So I decided to take this gamble and see what I could learn.

"At the end of six months, I was writing any and all of the office's copy. We had increased and expanded the agency. He asked me to stay on at a salary. I stayed on for eleven years.

"It was a strange combination. I put my work on the right-hand side of the typewriter, and the layouts and notes for advertising copy on the left-hand side. And when I exhausted what was on the left-hand side, I would put my material in the typewriter."

Those years were also among Bloch's most productive as a writer, because the time restrictions imposed by his advertising work brought him a sense of discipline. He published more than 150 stories in the horror, science fiction, and detective fields, including a series of humorous fantasies that began with "Time Wounds All Heels" (1942). He also produced the most crucial story of his early career, "Yours Truly, Jack the Ripper" (1943), whose adaptation for radio resulted in Bloch's own radio series, *Stay Tuned for Terror* (1945). An Arkham House edition, *The Opener of the Way* (1945), collected the best of his early short fiction. But the 1947 publication of Bloch's first novel, *The Scarf*, signalled his shift away from the traditional supernatural themes of *Weird Tales* to those on which his lasting fame is based. ("Fetish?" it begins. "You name it. All I know is that I've always had it with me . . .")

Bloch explains: "By the mid-1940s, I had pretty well mined the vein of ordinary supernatural themes until it had become varicose. I realized, as a result of what went on during World War Two and of reading the more widely disseminated work in psychology, that the real horror is not in the shadows, but in that little twisted world inside our own skulls. And that I determined to explore."

Explore he did, fathering—along with Cornell Woolrich, John Franklin Barden, and Jim Thompson—the psychological horror novel, in which the dark corridors of the human mind supplant the supernatural. His early novels—*The Kidnapper, Spiderweb,* and *The Will to Kill,* all published in 1954—provided the groundwork for his most famous novel, and he left advertising that year, moving to Weyauwega, Wisconsin, to write full-time.

In 1957, one of the most bizarre cases in American criminology began to unfold in Plainfield, Wisconsin, less than fifty miles from where Bloch lived. A search for a missing barmaid at the farmhouse of one Edward Gein discovered her corpse hanging by its heels, decapitated and dressed out like a deer. Authorities found preserved human heads, female body parts, a human heart in a coffee can, lampshades fashioned of tanned human skin, and a boarded-up room that had belonged to Gein's mother, who had died twelve years earlier. Intrigued by the case, Bloch wrote the now-classic *Psycho* (1959), with its frightening characterization of Norman Bates.

"I discovered, much to my surprise—and particularly if I was writing in the first person—that I could become a psychopath quite easily. I could think like one and I could devise all manner of unfortunate occurrences. So I probably gave up a flourishing, lucrative career as a mass murderer."

But Bloch feels no affinity for the psychopathic personality: "Again, it's one of those situations—if you can't lick 'em, join 'em. Ever since I was a child, I was unable to explain the callous, casual, careless cruelty of other children, or of adults to one another. My increasing interest in history supplied me with so many thousands of seemingly inexplicable horrors, and I just determined to see what I could learn. I became more and more dissatisfied with the conventional psychiatric explanations.

"I believe that psychotherapy, like meteorology and economics, is an art rather than a science. There are psychiatrists and psychologists who have had some success with a certain type of patient under certain circumstances, but there are an awful lot of impostors, quacks, failures, and just plain incompetents running around in that field, and they exert far too much influence.

"They have become the modern priestcraft. They have supplanted the religious infallibility of previous centuries. A hundred and fifty years ago, phrenologists enjoyed as much status as today's psychiatrists; and yet today, phrenology is dead. I don't know how much longer psychotherapy is going to last."

For many years, Bloch held no religious views, sharing the mechanistic materialism of H. P. Lovecraft:

"My background was German Jewish, without either of my parents or grandparents being devout communicants. They didn't attend temple, they didn't observe the Jewish holidays, they didn't speak or read Hebrew. My mother believed in a Supreme Being, but as a sort of amorphous thing.

"We moved to Maywood when I was five. We found ourselves living in this suburban community outside of Chicago in this friendly neighbourhood atmosphere. After a month or so, it was suggested to my mother that a lot of the social life of our neighbours revolved around the Methodist Church. So why didn't we go to the Methodist Church? Why didn't the kids go to Sunday School? So we did. For the next five years, I would career in the back of a truck with the other kids on the way to the Sunday School picnic, happily singing 'Onward Christian Soldiers'.

"And that's the extent of my formal religious upbringing. I didn't know a word of Hebrew until I got into advertising,

and my education was fine-tuned when I got to Hollywood—
you can imagine the type of words that I picked up."

But with his increasing dissatisfaction with psychiatric
explanations, he has experienced a growing belief in the
supernatural:

"Only in recent years have I ceased being quite so much
of a pragmatist, because I have encountered enough incidents
of what you might call paranormal inexplicabilities to shake
my composure. I now feel that I don't know everything that
there is to be known about the world and that the scientists
who claim to know by means of mathematics and measure-
ments and the ability to repeat experiments are constantly
being confounded as new things come along that force them
to revise their so-called 'laws' and expand their horizons. To
me, a mechanistic explanation is far too simple.

"I have no spiritual view that would coincide with the
dogma of any organized religion. But I do believe that most
of us are mindful of our own subjective definitions of good
and evil. Most people have, even in the absence of a so-
called conscience, knowledge of whether they are doing
something that is harmful or helpful. I don't know whether
any of the conventional legends and mythologies and super-
stitions coincide with my notion of what constitutes good or
evil, although I've read and heard enough about seemingly
inexplicable events in which some of these concepts seem
personified. Cases of so-called possession, that sort of thing.
I am not saying that I am still window-shopping; but I haven't
closed my eyes."

Bloch moved to Hollywood in October, 1959, but not
because of Alfred Hitchcock's acquisition of the film rights
to *Psycho*; he was invited by a friend to attempt writing for
television. His first scripts were for the Macdonald Carey
vehicle, "Lock-Up", but he soon wrote for a number of
classic programmes, including "Thriller", "Star Trek",
"Night Gallery"—and indeed, "Alfred Hitchcock Presents".
Ironically, the fact that he had written *Psycho* was not at all
helpful to his early screenwriting career.

"When I came out here, *Psycho* was just being filmed. One

day I went on the set to look around, and nobody was happy. Paramount, which was to distribute the picture, hated it— they didn't like the title, they didn't like the story, they didn't like anything about it. They put all kinds of obstacles in Hitch's way. He didn't get his usual big budget. He didn't get Technicolor or big stars like Cary Grant or Jimmy Stewart. Then they told him that they had no sound stage for him, and he had to shoot at Universal, using his television cinematographer. But since he had autonomy and he was determined to make his film, they couldn't stop him in the long run.

"At that time, to have announced myself in Hollywood as the author of *Psycho* would have been a negative."

That situation soon changed, of course—to the point that Robert Bloch rarely sees his name in print without the inescapable appendage, "author of *Psycho*". Does the typecasting concern him?

"At first, I resisted the label very much. But people of much greater stature have faced the problem—Maurice Ravel with his Bolero, Serge Rachmaninoff with his Prelude in C Sharp Minor. They used to rail constantly over these things, and in the end, they had to accept them.

"As the years went by, I realized that it was something I couldn't escape, because of the tendency of publishers and publicists to seek some easy identification for the product. And when you've written a book or a teleplay or a motion picture, that's a product. In their minds, it has to be associated with something that is successful.

"Today, the emphasis is entirely on commercial success. You don't talk about the content. You talk about the brand name—this is a Stephen King book or a John Carpenter movie.

"Unfortunately, as the conglomerates take over the film industry and their accountants look more and more at the grosses rather than what goes on the screen, this emphasis is increased. Reliance on the computer to tell you what to do based on mathematical projections is death to the creative impulse. And this is now happening with novels, too. So many publishing houses have been taken over by conglomerates, and there's this terrible intermeshing of film companies and publishing houses and, in some cases, television outlets."

Psycho represented a watershed not only for Bloch, but for the horror story. From the Depression heyday of *Weird Tales* and the evocative Universal film adaptations of *Frankenstein* and *Dracula*, the tale of terror had suffered until the mid-1950s, as if the real horrors of World War Two had snuffed out the human need for fictional confrontation with death. Not until the Eisenhower era did the monsters re-emerge in force: first, in the innocuous science-fictional context of the "big bug" films, then in exuberant American International youth films like *I Was a Teenage Werewolf* (1957), and finally in the serious context of books and films like *Psycho*.

Robert Bloch had evolved as well: after a flurry of books in the early '60s, perfecting the novel of psychological horror—*The Dead Beat* (1960), *Firebug* (1961), *The Couch* (1961)—he devoted most of his time to screenwriting. He penned, among other films, the last great Joan Crawford vehicle, *Strait-Jacket* (1964); *The Night Walker* (1964); and a series of film anthologies based upon his short stories for Britain's Hammer Films, including *The Skull* (1965), *Torture Garden* (1967), *The House That Dripped Blood* (1970), and *Asylum* (1972).

He turned to horror fiction rarely and with a growing sense of concern, expressed in novels like *Night-World* (1972), *American Gothic* (1974), *Strange Eons* (1978), and *There Is a Serpent in Eden* (1979). When he wrote his sequel, *Psycho II* (1982) (which bears no relationship to the film of the same name), and *Night of the Ripper* (1984), it was with a recognition that, in the years since Norman Bates first sprang from Robert Bloch's imagination as a transvestite murderer with a handful of victims, the world had changed: even as Boy George O'Dowd serenades us on television in full drag, a forgettably plain-faced drifter named Henry Lee Lucas claims to have murdered more than three hundred women and children. And Robert Bloch has found that his responsibilities as a horror writer have changed as well.

"Modern horror fiction offers something that present-day society has been seeking for the past twenty years—an abdication of responsibility. It has provided virtually everyone with a Devil theory—as Flip Wilson says, 'The Devil made me do it.' That is the explanation for all of the bad things in the world. No one is individually responsible.

"And it is exactly what we want, because it explains everything from the bomb, the Vietnam war, and corruption in high places, to any individual's actions. What makes such fiction so popular is that it encapsulates this notion and offers a variety of choices, so that the reader may choose from the conventional Devil theory, the psychological Devil theory, and so on.

"We have seen this upsurge of antisocial behaviour and, of course, a concomitant abdication of responsibility. The cop-out, the excuse, is that it's all the result of being underprivileged—poor environment, economic circumstances. But I saw those conditions in the Depression, without such drastic consequences in behaviour patterns.

"It's the permissiveness of our society and the fact that parents have abdicated their responsibilities that create today's problems. You dump it onto the schools; you dump it onto the law enforcement agencies. And they have their own Devil theory about economics or ethnic inequalities."

Bloch is thus disturbed by the graphic depiction of violence in modern horror film and fiction.

"Violence has become not only a cop-out in terms of being presented as self-explanatory—'this is human nature, that's the way it is, folks'—but it is also a drug. When you dose yourself with it, you find that you need increasingly bigger fixes.

"My generation was the product of the library plus silent films and heavily censored talking films. The next generation saw a little more permissiveness in films and a great deal more graphic violence in comic books; so twenty years later, when their members started to write and make films, this was their frame of reference. The permissiveness that saturated films and television offered even more outlets for a still-younger group who are now entering their twenties. And it's apparent that the end is not yet in sight, although I don't know how much further we can actually go. We have just about reached the limit of visual depiction of violence.

"What's going to come out of those people who think that *Night of the Living Dead* isn't enough?"

But it is not the depiction of violence that so much concerns Bloch; it is the attitudes of the audience and the purveyors of violence.

"It's the kind of people who enjoy that type of material that causes me to cringe a little. I really get turned off when I sit in an audience and see what is supposedly an otherwise sane and normal teenager laughing with joy as someone is being eviscerated on the screen. I would much prefer to see him revert to the old enuresis of my childhood and wet his pants when something like that happens.

"What has changed in my work is that I have increasingly felt a sense of responsibility. I feel that it's necessary to take a position. The chief danger, as I have stated in *Psycho II*, is not so much the violent content of today's fiction and film as it is the lack of any attitude on the part of the creator—or, as I like to think of him, the perpetrator—of the material. This business of saying, 'Here it is, folks, a slice of life, raw and bleeding,' without stating any emotional reaction on the part of the writer or director, seems to imply that there is no such thing as moral responsibility—that these actions have to be judged solely on the basis of an individual's interpretation for his or her own convenience.

"I don't believe in turning what I write into preachments, but if the subject matter deals with events that require some value-judgement on the part of the audience, then it is up to the creator to suggest his own views. The audience can accept or reject—that's their privilege. If they don't like the show, they can walk out of the theatre or switch the dial on the TV set. If they don't like the book or story, they can close the pages.

"Horror fiction will rapidly reach a dead end unless there is a revision of structure and concept. I don't think it's going to be possible to continue forever basing horror fiction on notions that are more simply handled in comic books.

"As to whether or not all this is of any importance, I don't know. But it being the sort of thing I have wasted my life on, I continue to be interested in its future."

Late in 1989, Bloch celebrated his fifty-fifth year as a professional writer; far from having "wasted" his life, he has become a true legend of the modern horror field, with a staggering output of more than four hundred published short stories, fifty-five books, and twelve produced screenplays. His best short fiction appeared in *The Selected Stories of Robert Bloch* (1989), and his newest novels are *Lori* (1989) and *Psycho House* (1990). What has kept him going?

"Economic necessity," he laughs. "Aided and abetted by a great deal of good luck. I've been fortunate in knowing people like Buster Keaton and Joan Crawford, Boris Karloff and Fritz Lang, and once one has reached a certain degree of intimacy, you realize that ninety per cent of everyone's career has been luck. Whatever talent you have means nothing unless it is given an opportunity to flourish.

"I've been very lucky. I've been fortunate in my choice of occupation, fortunate that I've survived physically without undue stress or handicap, fortunate in the quiet life that I lead with my lovely wife, and fortunate in the kind of treatment I have received from my fellow writers and readers and fans. When I came out here, I made the acquaintance of a number of people working quite successfully in television and films; and within ten years, ninety per cent of them were out of the business. It's a very fast track, and a lot of people get shoved to one side through no fault of their own—inadvertence, bad breaks, bad timing.

"What would have happened to Boris Karloff if he had not been the fourth or fifth successful candidate for the Frankenstein monster's role?"

But Robert Bloch does not ponder the element of chance; if he has any second thoughts about his career, it is only that he did not become a burlesque comedian. His writing has always been tinged with black humour and outrageous puns, summed up best by his infamous one-liner: "I have the heart of a small boy. I keep it in a jar in my desk."

What is the mutual attraction of humour and horror?

"Comedy and horror are opposite sides of the same coin—a coin that usually ends up in a producer's pocket, by the way. Both deal with the grotesque and the unexpected, but in such a fashion as to provoke two entirely different reactions. Physical comedy is usually fantasy; it's exaggeration, as when W. C. Fields comes out of a small-town pet shop with a live ostrich. There's a willing suspension of disbelief, but we don't generally regard it as fantasy because it's designed to promote laughter rather than tension or fear.

"Comedy is timeless," Bloch says, and notwithstanding his criticism of some aspects of current horror fiction, he is equally certain of its future.

"One of the lures of horror fiction is a constant in the human race—curiosity. It's not fashionable today to speak about emotions except in a knowledgeable way. To confess that one is naive is taboo. But I think that today's youngsters are not much different from those of any previous generation in that they are curious about death and its mysteries, about pain and what happens when one inflicts or undergoes it—about the physiological and psychological symptoms. And the mere fact that it is *verboten* to discuss such matters in ordinary conversation causes them to be even more interested.

"Curiously enough, the attitude toward discussing sex is not as great a barrier to young people as that toward an open, frank discussion of death. It is no longer taboo to avoid all mention of sexual practices. But you still have a hell of a time getting a frank, detailed discussion of the ravages of cancer going in your friendly Sunday afternoon family get-together.

"As long as human beings experience fear, horror will be a timeless emotion. I can scarcely visualize the human being who doesn't have fear, whether it's expressed or secret."

And when I ask Robert Bloch about his darkest fear, he tells me, just as he has written of countless other horrors—with a smile:

"I will admit to fear of extinction. I don't like the idea that I am not going to be around anymore to complain about how rotten life is. I want to live to the year 2000, so I can tell everybody, 'See, I told you it was going to be this bad!' "

Richard Matheson

"People are sitting around the kitchen table having coffee and cakes, and the werewolf is battering at the window."

You're travelling through another dimension, a dimension not only of sight and sound, but of mind; a journey into a wondrous land whose boundaries are that of the imagination.

That's the signpost up ahead...

Something must have been in the air or the water—or in the blood—in that Year of Our Lord 1959. Even as Robert Bloch's *Psycho* hit the bookstands and went into motion picture production, a bright young talent of television, Rod Serling, was preparing a new weekly series that would scare the daylights out of children and adults alike. *The Twilight Zone* would run on CBS-TV from October of 1959 through the summer of 1965, then emerge from burial alive in late-night syndication to ghoulish immortality as a cult classic—spawning, some two decades after its demise, a bimonthly magazine, a nostalgic book (Marc Scott Zicree's *Twilight Zone Companion*), a motion picture, and, inevitably, a new television series.

Each of us has a favourite episode of the original *Twilight Zone*. Mine was "Little Girl Lost": It confirmed my childhood fear that the walls and floors of my bedroom might give way in the night, sending me into a dark otherworld. And then there was "The Invaders", with Agnes Moorehead as a reclusive old woman terrorized by tiny spacemen. Or what about "Nightmare at 20,000 Feet", in which a young William Shatner confronts a strange creature frolicking on an aeroplane's wing?

The author of these and thirteen other *Twilight Zone* episodes, Richard Matheson, is perhaps the most influential writer of horror fiction of his generation. For some twenty years, beginning in the early 1950s, his short stories, novels, teleplays, and motion picture screenplays spoke of a new and uniquely American horror. Along with Rod Serling and two other writers with whom he is intimately associated—Jack Finney and Charles Beaumont—Richard Matheson created the modern landscape of fear.

If Robert Bloch showed us fear in the face of everyday man, it was Matheson who brought that fear from the Gothic landscapes of misty moors and haunted mansions to the American suburbs. He invited terror into our shopping malls and peaceful neighbourhoods—into the house next door.

Then, just before the horror "boom" of the 1970s, he stopped writing horror fiction.

That fact is foremost on my mind as I drive through Laurel Canyon to the Ventura Freeway, then deep into the San Fernando Valley. That's the signpost up ahead, and it reads "Hidden Hills", a name that befits Richard Matheson. He has lived there for twenty years, and clearly revels in his quiet, tree-shrouded home: "I enjoy writing's isolation," he says, his voice a soft, graceful whisper. He is tall, white-bearded, thoroughly gentle—a deceptive personality, given the fiction for which he is famous. But he questions whether it should be called horror fiction.

"I don't think of myself in those terms anymore. I never thought of myself as a horror writer. I thought of myself as a fantasy writer—the most I would admit to is that I wrote terror. It may be just a matter of semantics.

'Horror, to me, is something that is anathema: *Friday the 13th* and axes splitting open skulls and stuff like that; it's visceral. Terror is mental; it's frightening through the mind instead of the guts. If you're going to scare someone, that's the way to do it. I think it was Anatole France who said, 'To see is nothing, to imagine is everything." '

Another *Twilight Zone* writer, George Clayton Johnson, has termed Matheson's fiction as "coffee and cakes" horror.

"You know," smiles Matheson, "where people are sitting around the kitchen table having coffee and cakes, and the werewolf is battering at the window."

He shakes his head with regret. "I don't know whether it was a good thing to do. Now people are afraid of everything."

Richard Matheson was born in New Jersey on 20 February 1926; his parents moved to Brooklyn three years later, where they separated.

"I don't recall that much of my childhood. I was raised mostly—entirely, really—by my mother and my older sister. My older brother stayed with us for a while before he got married.

"I was very withdrawn and introspective, for a number of reasons—the environment certainly among them. It was very ingrown from the standpoint of having a social life. The only people I knew were my family, my uncles, my cousins. They were immigrants from Norway and had a tendency to stay together—for protection, I suppose. Then my mother joined the Christian Science church when I was very young, and the only friends I had were a few friends from church. I have always had a very withdrawn and limited social existence—and still do, for that matter.

"I started reading very early; the first book I recall borrowing from the library was *Pinnochio in Africa*. Not *Pinnochio*. And to this day, I have never met anyone who has even heard of that book, but I *know* I read it. I went for fantasy stories at eight or nine years of age, just these huge collections of fairy tales, and I was very involved in them.

"Obviously, writing was an escape for me. In the strictly Freudian sense, I was reconstructing the world as I chose through my work; and through fantasy, I was really doing it up right.

"But when I started writing, I never wrote about trolls or mythic kingdoms, but on a very realistic level. It never occurred to me to do anything else. I had this fix on the mundane daily events of life, so that I could never go off into the mists; I could never write—or read—things like Tolkien.

It's totally alien to me. There must be something of the mundane, an element of realism. To me, fantasy is done best in strictly realistic terms."

As early as nine years of age, Matheson saw his stories and poems published in the *Brooklyn Eagle*; but he had no thoughts about a career as a writer.

"There was a practical side, which I still have. I came from a family where there was no such thing as a creative person — it was never done professionally, I mean. So although no one discouraged me, no one said, 'Oh, yes, why don't you become a professional writer?' I always thought, as they did, in more practical terms."

He attended Brooklyn Technical High School and studied structural engineering: "And I was good enough — I did well in mathematics and so forth, but it was not my bag at all. If I did well in any subject, it was always English." But following high school, he enlisted in an Army specialized training programme in engineering and attended Cornell University. The programme folded; it was 1944, and the Second World War was raging: "I ended up being tossed into the infantry and being sent overseas as an eighteen-year-old soldier." His experiences, culminating in a discharge for a combat-related injury, served as the basis for his sole mainstream novel, *The Beardless Warriors* (1960): "The writer's justification for any horrible experience is, if he gets a novel out of it, it's OK."

Was it inevitable that he would become a professional writer?

"Well, I happen to believe in astrology. Not in the sense of reading the newspapers to see what to do that day, but in a much broader sense. I think that people are born, not necessarily to be in an exact profession, but certainly circumscribed within a limited area. And I think that I was, if you want to put it that way, born to be introspective and creative in one manner or another. I could have done other things, but my inclination was just in that direction.

"I wrote music; I still write music. When I got out of the Army, I went to a vocational guidance counsellor because I was torn between concentrating on music or writing. And it became obvious to me that writing was the much more practical choice. To most people, that seemed not only impractical, but insane. They would say to me, 'How long are you going to give it? How many years are you going to try it?' And I would just give them a fish stare because I didn't know what they were talking about. Once I had made up my mind, that was it—for life. And I think that's the way it has to be."

He entered the University of Missouri, majoring in journalism, and graduated in 1949. "I thought in terms of getting a job on a magazine or newspaper. But an editor at *Esquire* told me that if I really wanted to be a writer, I should get a night job, do just anything, and write. And even then, my practical side would not allow me to think in terms of writing as my entire career."

His first story, the classic "Born of Man and Woman", was published in 1950, when he was twenty-three years old. He moved to California, hoping for work in the motion picture industry. Instead, he landed a job as a machine operator at Douglas Aircraft, writing in his spare time. Although his first published novel, *Someone Is Bleeding* (1953), was a mystery, he was drawn inexorably to write fantasy, horror, and science fiction.

"When I started writing, naturally I latched onto Ray Bradbury, as every young writer did in those days. We were all influenced by him, Bradbury clones running all over the place. You wanted to step on them, there were so many. And then those of us who stayed in found our own voices."

The voice of Richard Matheson's horror and dark fantasy fiction speaks profoundly and distinctively of paranoia: "My kids used to call me Mister Paranoia, and people have described my work as being the embodiment of paranoia. A French essayist and editor recently wrote the introduction to a collection of my short stories over there, and the first line of the essay, which depressed me for a long time, was 'The key word is anxiety.' But I realize that's true."

He traces the roots of his anxiety to his childhood.

"For whatever reason—whether it came from my mother, whether it came from the fact that my parents separated, whether it came from the fact that I was overly introspective— there was a great anxiety in me as a child, and probably still is to a large degree, about things outside of myself. Not with what was going on inside, but outside.

"And of course, if you had an imagination, then you could people that inchoate outside world with any kind of monster you could dream up. I think that's what horror writers do to a large extent. They cannot deal with the real horror. That is why people go to see all of these horror pictures; they can't face the horror of what's going on in the world today. But in writing it down, or seeing it on the screen, you can face a substitute horror and it is resolved. Then you can go home and go to bed."

His short stories soon saw publication in many leading magazines, both mainstream and genre-oriented, including *Playboy* and, in its final years, *Weird Tales*. A collection of his science-fiction stories, *Born of Man and Woman*, appeared in 1954; in later years, his tales of terror would be collected in the often-reprinted *Shock!* (1961), *Shock II* (1964), and *Shock III* (1966)—and, more recently, in an omnibus edition, *The Collected Stories of Richard Matheson* (1989).

But those early years were lean ones for the newly married writer: "When we got married, I had only made about $500 from short stories. There were very bad years. One of my anxieties is financial insecurity. My theme in those years was of a man, isolated and alone, and assaulted on all sides by everything you could imagine."

That theme produced three of the best early horror novels of this generation. *I Am Legend* (1954) found a single man battling a world in which all other humans have become vampires; it has been filmed twice—as *The Last Man on Earth* (1963) and *The Omega Man* (1971)—and was the inspiration for George A. Romero's classic *Night of the Living Dead* (1968). In *The Shrinking Man* (1956). Matheson portrayed the plight of a man literally forced to shrink by the social, political, and economic forces surrounding him. A *Stir of Echoes* (1958) depicted a man whose mind, freed of its restrictions by hypnosis, is subjected to relentless psychic attack.

Both *I Am Legend* and *The Shrinking Man* were inspired by films; indeed, Matheson had found his first real fear in the movie theatre.

"My mother took me to see *Werewolf of London*. I don't know how I talked her into it—I guess she didn't know the word 'werewolf'. And when I saw Henry Hull changing into a werewolf, I literally fell out of my seat and crawled up the aisle and wouldn't see the rest of the picture. My mother came for me and we left. I was terrified.

"My sister was a great film-goer, and she took me all the time. I remember going to church and then having lunch somewhere and then going to see a Shirley Temple movie or something. The things that appealed to me most when I was a teenager were Val Lewton's movies. I remember being completely knocked out by *The Cat People*. And there is a perfect example—it was done in realistic terms, done all cerebrally, to the point where you never saw anything.

'I loved films when I was growing up. I always wanted to get into motion pictures. It is the medium of our time; it reaches the most people and has the greatest impact."

His film ambitions were fulfilled when Universal Pictures, anxious to acquire *The Shrinking Man* as the next project for director Jack Arnold, accepted Matheson's condition that he would sell film rights to the book only if he could write the screenplay. The motion picture version, retitled *The Incredible Shrinking Man*, appeared in 1957, and Matheson's screenwriting credit proved an all-important entrée into script work.

In 1959, Matheson and his good friend, fellow writer Charles Beaumont, were invited to a private screening of a half-hour film called "Where Is Everybody?". It was the pilot episode for *The Twilight Zone*. Rod Serling had already adapted two of Matheson's short stories for the proposed series, and Matheson and Beaumont soon began writing both original scripts and adaptations of their published stories. Their work was often among the series' best, partly because Serling's personal commitment to the show demanded that he turn out teleplays at a relentless pace. Fourteen of Matheson's scripts were used on *The Twilight Zone*, in episodes directed by such notables as Richard Donner (*Superman: The Movie*), Norman Z. McLeod, who directed the original *Topper* and the best of the Marx Brothers films; and Jacques Tourneur, director of *I Walked With a Zombie, Curse of the Demon*, and other classic horror films.

The Twilight Zone holds a special place in Matheson's heart, but he wonders aloud at the recent wave of nostalgia for the programme.

"Knowing Rod was a great pleasure. Certainly, my friend Charles Beaumont and I worked together happily on it for five years. And going to the rehearsals and having some interesting scripts done—in that sense, it was very pleasant. But the reverential feeling, certainly from the people involved, must be retrospective rather than something that was actually felt at the time. The programme was struggling for its life all of the time. Every year, they wondered whether they were going to get renewed or not. We had no sense of being involved in a cult phenomenon; that developed over the years.

"It's hard to say what your real feelings are about something that happened that long ago, because you had one feeling when it was going on and you have another feeling now, and you get them sort of mixed up. You don't know which is really which. I have very pleasant memories. I don't recall at the time—or even to this day—being knocked out by what was done with most of my stories. Some of them I was extremely happy with; some weren't done to my satisfaction."

To what does he attribute the series' continued popularity?

"The stories. What fascinates people is that the stories are so interesting. There is a certain primitivism to the production—to the directing, the acting. They were great for their time, but you see it now and it looks primitive. I don't really think it's a good idea to revive these things. You know, they keep talking about *The Show of Shows*, but when you look at it, it's really not that great anymore. At the time, it was wonderful, but it's been by-passed. *The Twilight Zone* has lasted because the ideas and stories are interesting, however they are done. And a lot of them are done very well."

His work on *The Twilight Zone* led to numerous screenwriting assignments for a variety of television programmes, including *Bourbon Street Beat, Have Gun Will Travel, Richard Diamond, Star Trek, Thriller,* and *Wanted: Dead or Alive.* In the early 1970s, he returned to work with Serling, scripting two short episodes of *Night Gallery.*

At almost the same time as he began work with *The Twilight Zone,* Matheson was approached by the legendary low-budget filmmaker Roger Corman to adapt Edgar Allan Poe's "The Fall of the House of Usher" as a motion picture. *House of Usher* (1960), starring Vincent Price, was filmed in fifteen days on a budget of less than $200,000. "I took it really seriously. I was really very impressed with the idea of doing a classic. They were amazed that it not only got good reviews, but it made a lot of money for them. And they hadn't expected that at all—they thought it was a one-shot. And that started the whole cycle of one Poe picture after another." He worked on three additional Poe adaptations for Corman, all with Price as leading man: *The Pit and the Pendulum* (1961), *Tales of Terror* (1962), and the comedic *The Raven* (1963). His other motion picture scripts include *Burn, Witch, Burn* (1962) (an adaptation of Fritz Leiber's *Conjure Wife*, written with Charles Beaumont), and two Hammer films, *Die! Die! My Darling* (1965) and *The Devil's Bride* (1968).

In 1971, he scripted probably the most famous of all made-for-television movies, *Duel*, based on his novelette of the same name. The idea had come to him nearly a decade before:

"It was the day that President Kennedy was killed. I had been playing golf with Jerry Sohl, and when we heard the news, we broke off our game and headed home. As we were driving back through a narrow pass, a truck started tailgating us. This went on for miles and miles. We were depressed and infuriated, and this was just too much—we were screaming with rage at the truck driver until finally we pulled over and let the son of a bitch pass us."

The movie, depicting a road battle between a travelling salesman and a truck whose driver is never seen, played a major role in establishing its young director, Steven Spielberg. Matheson followed *Duel* with scripts for the popular "Kolchak" television movies, *The Night Stalker* (1972) and *The Night Strangler* (1973), and a number of other made-for-TV movies for producer Dan Curtis, including two pilot films, *Trilogy of Terror* (1975) and *Dead of Night* (1977).

But he had effectively withdrawn from horror fiction after writing his first novel in nearly eleven years, *Hell House* (1971), and adapting it for the screen as *The Legend of Hell House* (1973). It is Matheson's most violent and sexually explicit work, chronicling the disintegration of a group of psychic investigators who confront the reputedly haunted Hell House.

"My intention was to write a haunted house novel, and once I had set the premise that this was the most horrible haunted house in existence, I couldn't very well do otherwise than make it as horrific as I could. I had to let out all the stops. To say that this is the most evil house in the world, and then to have leprechauns running around, would have been silly."

The book seemed to drain away his interest in horror fiction. "I no longer wanted to write it, period," he says. "You change through the years. I change all the time. My views change all the time. And it just no longer interested me.

"You have to change. You have to have a built-in mechanism of some sort that adapts as time goes by. That is one reason I am still working; but the main reason is that I am creating things for myself."

The change was soon manifested in *Bid Time Return* (1975), which won the World Fantasy Award for best novel of the year. This story of a writer who wills himself back through time to pursue a hopeless love affair was adapted by Matheson for the screen as *Somewhere in Time* (1980), starring Christopher Reeve and Jane Seymour.

"That was totally different for me. It was a love story. I had reactions from readers and filmgoers that were so totally different. Usually, I received letters from teenage kids who said, 'Hey, I really liked them vampires'—which didn't do much for me as a husband and father of four. But then I was receiving letters from women, from grown ups, who were talking in entirely different terms."

He soon wrote a resolutely mainstream television movie about alcoholism, *The Morning After* (1977); his next novels, *What Dreams May Come* (1978) and *Earthbound* (1984) (the latter published under the pseudonym Logan Swanson), were mild fantasies based in Matheson's long-time interest in theories of reincarnation and afterlife. Although he has recently returned to the field of horror for such projects as the scripts for *Twilight Zone: The Movie* (1983) and the ill-fated *Jaws 3-D* (1984), his enthusiasm has admittedly waned.

"I have never liked horror films. Terror, yes—but as horrible as I care to take it would be *Rosemary's Baby*, which is a wonderful film—the ultimate in 'coffee and cakes' horror. When you feel like averting your face, that's not frightening, that's revolting. It makes you feel like you're going to throw up. But that's literally what I think of most horror films: they don't frighten your mind, they turn your stomach. And I don't really see the point in that.

"A word I use all the time now is 'irrelevant'. What's the point? The way things are going in the world, why bother? Today, almost everything I see on television or in movies, and read in books, is irrelevant."

Is there too much fear in his life?

"Nuclear war is frightening. It's something that could happen, simply by accident. Probably the one thing I'm most fearful about, although I accept that it likely will occur, is what will happen to me and to my family and friends as the earth changes, especially here in this state. I believe that monster earthquakes are due in California; I think, eventually, that it will become unliveable.

"I fear earth changes rather than what mankind might do. And anyway, mankind doesn't start wars; it's always the leaders, that fringe on top that decides that we have to assert ourselves.

"I would just as soon not be around when the earthquakes happen. I don't want to have a mountain fall on my head.

But it's nothing I can alter, and I'm still living here. I feel that this is where I can do my best work, and maybe when I've done a certain amount, then I will take off and forsake the place."

But Richard Matheson is not done with his work. We discuss his latest project, an immense television mini-series proposal based upon his lifelong interest and belief in what he calls the "supernormal". "Not the supernatural," he is quick to add. "I don't think there is any such thing.

"We are more than what we appear to be. The world is more than it appears to be. Mankind, generally speaking, is very limited in its awareness of what's really going on. Parapsychology is an attempt to work at the edges of it, to find out more about what we are.

"I believe that every human being is surrounded by some bioenergy field—what they refer to as the 'aura'—that creates psychic phenomena, that can affect healing and is responsible for telepathy, telekinesis, precognition. This field is connected to the body during this lifetime, disconnects itself at death, and is eternal. Our body is just the vehicle it uses during this particular phase of its existence. And then it comes back and attaches itself to another vehicle—which is, of course, reincarnation.

"There is an overall meaning to everyone's existence, which is this constant cycle of living, dying, coming back. We are headed somewhere—back to where we came from initially, when we were perfect in a very real sense."

Has he had any personal experiences of psychic phenomena?

"Just very minor stuff. And I don't think one would acquire a philosophy by having a paranormal experience.

"I am sure that you and your wife read each other's minds all of the time. This is psychic experience. When people are married a long time, this energy field I speak of, which they both have, becomes so strongly intertwined that, when one of them dies, it's like having a huge living chunk taken out of the other. It's not just grief that survivors are feeling. I think that explains why people who are so close sometimes die within minutes of each other."

How do these beliefs intersect with his religious upbringing?

"I don't have any organized religion today. I stayed with Christian Science through my years in the Army. When I went to college, I used to attend a different church every Sunday and come home and, in my sophomoric way, analyse it. Usually it would be a sly put-down, as one will do at that age. But I tried to see the values of each of them, and I gave up organized religion.

"I don't believe in the necessity for organized religion. I regard myself as much more spiritually oriented now than I ever was when I went to church.

"Evil is not something separate from us. I read an article recently in the *Los Angeles Times* in which these theologians were arguing about belief in God: 'How can God allow a child to be hit by a truck?' I think it is a mass delusion to believe in some bearded patriarch up in the sky saying, 'OK, kill somebody on the freeway.' Each and every one of us is responsible for evil. Anything that's wrong on earth comes from us, and it is up to us to find a way out of this, to solve our own problems. We can, by certain means, elevate ourselves to become in touch with higher energies—not necessarily higher beings—but what is going on down here is our problem. We made it, we have to solve it. And the abysmal bottom of the barrel is the military commander saying, 'With God's help, we will . . .'

"I'm not sure exactly what is out there—there's something, certainly, which is vast. But whether it is just one specific type of thing . . .

"We may well have created God ourselves as a concept. This use of God as someone you turn to, who you blame things on, who you wonder why he lets things happen, is a philosophical, theological cop-out. We made the world what it is. The problems in the world today were created by mankind; God didn't have anything to do with it."

As Matheson and I page through the volumes and volumes

of scripts for his proposed mini-series, he suddenly looks up and says, "This is it, though." He tells me of his plans to devote more and more of his time to the novel form. It has always been his favourite type of writing. "If only for satisfaction as a writer—because it's yours. Writing a best-selling novel is in total opposition to writing a good screenplay and making a good motion picture. A best-selling novel involves a lot of characters, sub-plotting, length and breadth of action. Baseball is the novel of sports—everything else is short stories or films. Only in baseball can you have long periods where nothing happens, but link development and growth with sudden spurts of action."

But it is also clear that he is losing patience with the frustrations of screenwriting.

"You can't beat Hollywood. It's the inertia of the system. The companies are sprinkled with ineptitude all the way through. I remember talking with Steven Spielberg—this was just as *E.T.* was starting to really roll—and he said that he wanted to have a company of his own that could control everything, not just producing and filmmaking, but the advertising and distribution; and I guess that's what he and George Lucas have achieved. They do everything. They have total control. And that is the only way that you can get what you really want out here.

"Ultimately, you come to the realization that the bulk of what you tried to do has not been transferred that well to the screen. I've been fortunate, mostly in television. I feel dissatisfied that, of the tremendous amount of work I've done for close to thirty years now, the amount of satisfaction is very low compared to what it would have been if I had been able to continue to write books all of those years, and just sell the books for films.

"I regret now all of the screenplays I have written. I have written a lot of screenplays—that is the lament of all screenwriters. But I have written a lot of good screenplays that were either ruined when they were made or that were never made at all. If I had taken that time and written novels instead, I would be a lot better off. But as my wife keeps reminding me, we had four children to raise and they paid better for screenplays than for novels."

His efforts with the mini-series proposal have only confirmed his views. "I had completely forgotten what it is like to go to television with an idea—what you have to go through, all the compromises you have to make. So I'll never do that again.

"And I was going to give up novels!" he exclaims. "Now I intend to go back to novels, simply for the satisfaction of being able to get my own things down on paper. Then I'll sell it for film, hopefully. And then if they change it, it won't matter, because I'll still have the book. You can't change the book."

Richard Matheson's legacy extends beyond his fiction and screenwriting: three of his four children have followed in his footsteps as writers. And his oldest son, Richard Christian Matheson (with whom he has collaborated on short stories and scripts, including the adventure-comedy film *Loose Cannons* (1989)), regularly contributes horror stories to major anthologies and magazines, and has recently published a collection of his own, *Scars* (1987).

"He's done wonderfully," Matheson notes with a father's pride. "He has a great regard for craft, which is something that—if I imparted anything to them—would be what I emphasized most. To try to write what you really feel strongly about and to be craftsmanlike about it, and not slough it off. Maybe I overdid it. He's so concerned with getting it exactly right; but there is a lot of competition and I think you have to be that way."

Did he ever imagine his children following in his footsteps?

"I always thought they would see me moaning and groaning, Mister Paranoia lamenting about the life of a writer. Writing was the last thing I expected of them. For a long time, none of them showed any signs of being writers. Richard did not start writing short stories until college. Our daughter Ali only started scriptwriting a few years ago. Our younger son, Chris, has been into scriptwriting only a short while. Yet both are really succeeding with it now. I guess it's from being exposed to it so much.

"Around here," he acknowledges, shaking his head, "you can't get away from it."

William Peter Blatty

"If there were evil spirits, why not good?
Why not a soul? Why not life everlasting?"

On a rainy, unseasonably cold June morning, just after dawn, I walk across the parking lot that borders an Exxon service station on M Street in Georgetown, the perenially fashionable district of Washington, DC. A steep stone stairway leads upward to a house once owned by William Peter Blatty, whose novel *The Exorcist* (1971)—along with Ira Levin's *Rosemary's Baby* (1967) and Thomas Tryon's *The Other* (1971)—set the stage for the horrors that swept this country in the late '70s and early '80s. It was here, on the pavement beneath my feet, that Blatty's exorcist, Father Karras, died; with him fell forever the notion that horror fiction and film had a limited, specialized appeal.

Three days later, I stand with William Peter Blatty, gazing west across the sunlit Pacific Ocean from the deck of his beachside home in Malibu. The sense of distance—two thousand miles from the gloom of Washington to the archetype of sunny southern California—collapses as Blatty talks of moving back to the east. He wears a blue sweatsuit, opened at the chest to reveal a Georgetown University T-shirt. It is difficult to believe that he is in his mid-fifties; he appears at least ten years younger—athletic, handsome, moustached—and I cannot help but draw mental comparisons with his Damien Karras.

He and I both feel it appropriate to set the record straight at the outset. How does he feel about being called a writer of horror fiction?

"I'm neither comfortable nor uncomfortable, but as you know, I'm not primarily a writer of horror fiction. If one looks at nine books and twelve motion picture scripts, only two novels and one script," and that's double-counting *The Exorcist*, "were in the horror genre. All the rest was comedy. So maybe I do feel a little uncomfortable being thought of as a writer of horror fiction. I like the expression 'ghostly' fiction, by the way, because it removes the vast package of excrescence under which we lump *The Texas Chainsaw Massacre* and *Halloween* as 'horror'. 'Ghostly' is a much more accurate description of what I do.

"Actually, my discomfort goes beyond simply the appellation. Most people think that I landed on this planet with the manuscript of *The Exorcist* under my arm."

In fact, Blatty's career as a professional writer began nearly thirty-five years before the publication of *The Exorcist* when, at about age ten, he won five dollars in a twenty-five-words-or-less contest for *Captain Future* comic books. He wrote:

Gentlemen: I like Captain Future Comics because it's about the world of tomorrow, and anything about the world of tomorrow is interesting.

The world of tomorrow could only be interesting to the young William Peter Blatty, for his world of today was a difficult one. He was born on 7 January 1928, on the verge of the Great Depression, the fifth child of immigrant Lebanese parents; his father left home when he was aged six. It was a time of "flexible living": his mother peddled jelly on the streets of New York, and in the space of ten years, the family lived at twenty-eight different addresses. In school, he was an outsider, set upon for his peculiar name and his dark complexion: "I wished that I were Irish so that I could blend. I would have given eighty million dollars for just one crummy freckle."

But Blatty would never wish his childhood away.

"I have an intellectual awareness that I was, in fact, unhappy during those times. And yet it's almost impossible for me to try to recreate the emotional sense of my misery.

I reflect on those times as a blessing. If you can come through any sort of crucible intact, you're going to be steeled — but if you melt, you're sludge, and that's the end of it. I think it was a very beneficial formative period. I was miserable, but I would never undo it if I could. That's the childhood I want to have had."

His religious upbringing was very rigorous and very Roman Catholic. "My mother was a deeply religious woman, very devout. I attended Catholic grammar school, St Stephen's, in New York; Brooklyn Preparatory, a Jesuit High School; and Georgetown University, also a Jesuit school. Pretty strong and structured.

"As Loyola, or one of the early Jesuits, is reputed to have said, 'Give me the boy, and the man will be mine forever.' I think that's true. There's no such thing as a former Catholic. The people who say so are the very people who were scared to death by *The Exorcist*.

"I'm a relaxed Catholic. I think Catholicism is as close to the truth as any organized religion has come, and I look forward to the day when the more daring of the theoretical physicists nudge Catholicism into some sort of amalgamation with the philosophic insights of the Eastern religions."

When did he stop wanting to become a priest?

"Never! I think most of us want to wait until our sex drives wane. Then we'll make the great sacrifice."

Blatty escaped from the harsh realities of his childhood through the fantasies of radio plays such as *The Shadow* and *Captain Midnight*, and through reading comic books and pulp magazines.

"People sometimes ask me where I learned to write. Even though I have an MA in English literature, never once did I take, even in high school, a so-called writing course. I learned from reading.

"I do remember a composition class at Brooklyn Prep which taught imitation. And imitation consisted of being confronted almost daily with a classic paragraph of English prose and then being asked to change the subject matter. If it dealt with birds, you could choose anything else — let's say shoes —

and then you had to construct each sentence in the entire paragraph in the style of the classic you were copying. If you came across a metaphor, you used a metaphor but you made it relevant to your subject. You kept doing that and doing that, and you know, something rubs off. You begin to write that way. If you go to Ireland and stay there for a year, you'll wind up speaking with a little brogue.

"And reading is another form of the imitation approach to learning how to write. If you're reading the very best, something has got to rub off on the unconscious—which, I'm sure you appreciate, does all the work anyway. We do the sweating, but it does the thinking."

His inspiration to write for a living is locked in his memory; it was an early story, "Time Wounds All Heels", by none other than Robert Bloch.

"I remember very distinctly reading a funny ghost or terror story in *Unknown* by Robert Bloch. He started me on my writing career. I just fell apart with laughter, and I would call my friends and read the entire story to them. And I caught fire. I wanted to write something like that. And I started trying comedy, because it was the laughs that got me.

"Some years ago, I was on a talk show with Stephen King, and beforehand, he said to me, 'You know, in a way, you're my father.' Well, if you see Robert Bloch, tell him that he's *my* father."

He continued writing from childhood to his college years, when he made his first serious attempts at being published. "For a time, it was poetry. That's all I wrote. And although there was a market for poetry at the time, not even the *US Dental News* wanted any of *my* poetry."

His break came in 1951, when he joined the Air Force after his graduation from Georgetown. His duty assignment brought him to his parents' homeland, and he found that his Lebanese looks and passing fluency in Arabic gave him entrée to occasional humorous episodes reflecting the clash of American and Middle-Eastern cultures. He placed a series of articles with the *Saturday Evening Post*—one of which involved him posing as the son of King Saud—that would serve as the groundwork for his first book, *Which Way to Mecca, Jack?* (1959).

"It all happened in a very Horatio Alger-ish way. After years of accumulating rejection slips, I cracked through and published a couple of times in the *Saturday Evening Post* and *Coronet*. Then an editor at McGraw-Hill wrote to me and said, 'I've been following your work. Have you ever thought of writing a book?' And I said, 'Oh, yes, I've been thinking about that'—for, my God, since puberty! So I started writing; and when I had completed an outline and perhaps 150 pages of *Which Way to Mecca, Jack?*, I sent them to the editor, but he couldn't get me a $300 advance.

"I was working as the chief publicist at USC, and a man came to me who was starting a new publishing company and was looking for a ghostwriter. He had received many names from various literary agents in New York, and mine being the lowest in alphabetical order, he was seeing me first. It was an advice to the lovelorn sort of book, and I was interviewed by the person I was to write for, and I got the job. At my last meeting with the publisher, I gave him *Which Way to Mecca, Jack?* He said, 'No, we only publish celebrities, but I'll be happy to give you some advice.' A week later, he called and said, 'I want to publish your book.' And he did. One little irony is that the book that I ghosted was a raging bestseller; of course, the one written under my own name was not.

"Then, I somehow got myself on the old Jack Paar show to talk about *Which Way to Mecca, Jack?* I got a fast five minutes and was invited back. The wife of a producer at Columbia Pictures was watching, and she said to her husband, 'You'd better come and look at this boy, he's very funny.' He got my phone contact and interviewed me. Columbia had decided to shelve a treatment for a projected comedy film, and he wanted me to take another crack at it, looking toward writing a script. I did, and they decided to make the movie—*The Man from the Diner's Club*—with Danny Kaye. Since then, I've just stayed one or two steps ahead of the sheriff.'

Blatty quickly became one of Hollywood's leading comedy screenwriters, scripting *Promise Her Anything* (1962); *John Goldfarb, Please Come Home!* (1963), from his 1962 novel of the same name; *What Did You Do in the War, Daddy?* (1965); *The Great Bank Robbery* (1967); and several films with Blake Edwards, including one of the earliest and best "Pink Panther" movies, *A Shot in the Dark* (1964), *Gunn* (1967), and *Darling Lili* (1968). During this time, he also published the novel *I, Billy Shakespeare* (1965), and his first noncomedic work, the psychological suspense novel *Twinkle, Twinkle Killer Kane* (1966).

In early July of 1969, unable to find screenwriting work, he rented a cabin in the woods near Lake Tahoe and began writing *The Exorcist*. His life—and the modern horror novel and film—would be forever changed.

Needless to say, William Peter Blatty will never escape *The Exorcist*. "And let's not knock it," he is quick to add. "Better that than nothing. When I wrote *The Exorcist*, the primary source of my livelihood—screenplay writing—was comedy. And comedy had dried up. I couldn't get a job, and no one would take me seriously as a writer of noncomedic motion pictures or fiction. And I thought that I'd better write the book now, because I wanted to prove that I could write something other than comedy, and get on with my life—and because I had nothing else to do at the moment.

"Now, since *The Exorcist*, I know of one specific instance in which a producer who had once done a couple of my comedies went to Paramount and pitched an idea for a comedy, and when they all agreed that it was a good idea and should be done, he said, 'I've got the perfect writer for that—Bill Blatty.' And they said, 'Blatty? Comedy?' So the wheel came full circle. *The Exorcist* has eclipsed the comedy writing, and before *The Exorcist*, it could only be comedy. This is a preposterous profession!"

The novel had its beginnings during Blatty's junior year at Georgetown University. He had read, in the 20 August 1949 edition of the *Washington Post*, an account of an exorcism by a Catholic priest of a boy allegedly possessed "by the Devil".

It confirmed what Blatty had heard from one of his Jesuit instructors, Father Eugene Gallagher. "Apparently, at least one of the assistants in the exorcism was being housed on the campus at Georgetown, and quite naturally, in the recreation room or wherever, people heard things. People asked questions. And a good deal of it filtered through to us in class. Some of it turned out to have been completely hyperbolic, whereas some of the equally interesting material was never mentioned."

His reaction was not one of fear, but of wonder. "First of all, I believed every word that Father Gallagher reported. And I thought, 'Oh, my God. At last, proof of transcendence, or at least of the reality of spiritual forces.' I mean, intelligent, discarnate entities—demons, devils, whatever. It seemed a validation of what we were being taught as Catholics, and certainly a validation of our hopes for immortality. Because if there were evil spirits, why not good? Why not a soul? Why not life everlasting?

"Well, that excited me. And I thought that it would be wonderful if someone were to investigate the case and write a non-fiction account. But I never connected myself as the one who should write it. I was going to be an English teacher in those days."

As the years passed, he collected information on the phenomenon of possession, but with no specific goal. Early in the '60s, he proposed writing a book about the case, but neither his agent nor his publisher favoured the idea. At a New Year's Eve dinner in 1967, a conversation with the editorial director of Bantam Books provoked Blatty to write the book. Although he was biased from the outset by his religious training in favour of belief in genuine possession, he was "very sceptical" of the accounts that he had read: "They were far removed in time, for the most part; or, if not removed in time—like the case in Earling, Iowa, in 1928— the account seemed to have been written by an overly credulous and pious nun, although it was written by a religious brother. I was just extremely sceptical. I was like Thomas— I needed to put my own fingers in the wounds. So I started digging, trying to find the exorcist in the 1949 case; and Father Gallagher gave me the name—Father William Bowdern—and told me where he might be.

"I wrote to him, but he wrote back and said that he had promised the family of the victim that there would never be any publicity and that there would be complete secrecy. This piqued my interest, because the usual nut case is dying for publicity. And he said, 'The only thing I can tell you is that the case I was involved in was the real thing. I had no doubt about it then, and I have no doubt about it now.'

"I felt the blood prickling up my back as I read those words. And, of course, I wrote him a very impassioned letter as to why the greatest thing for the Catholics would be to have a book of this kind written. I proposed that perhaps he should write it—again, I was still thinking it should be non-fiction.

"He reiterated that he would simply have nothing to do with it. And then he begged me to write nothing that would connect the victim to the case, because it would be deeply traumatic to the boy and to his family. That's why, when I wrote the book, I changed the boy to a girl. I changed the location; it did not happen in Washington, DC, it was . . . elsewhere.

"But somehow, after the book was published, *Newsweek* showed up at Father Bowdern's door. His first quoted words were 'I have been dreading this day for ten years.' Of course, he would tell them nothing. He said that I had never spoken to him—and that's true, we never spoke; we corresponded, and he told me nothing.'

After *The Exorcist* was written, records of the exorcism were found in the library of the archdiocese of Washington, DC.

"It was a daily diary, a record of events kept every day for over three months during the course of the exorcism and signed by each and every witness who attended. And it was absolutely electrifying. There were clearly exterior, paranormal phenomena going on. The old bromides about mind over matter and things we don't understand about electromagnetic forces aside, these were of that category that when we say,

'Well, show me a miracle,' this is what we have in mind. Only later do we think to ask for natural explanations.

"The diary merely verified the sense of the authentic that I got in that very first letter from Father Bowdern."

The Exorcist, published in 1971, promptly sky-rocketed to the top of the bestseller lists; and its 1973 motion picture adaptation, scripted by Blatty and directed by William Friedkin, stunned the nation. The spectacle of a young girl's possession, rendered in the first unleashing of graphic special effects (presided over by Dick Smith) in a big-budget film, set the media abuzz with debates about exorcism, horror, and morality. Movie-goers ran shrieking from theatres, with occasional claims that demonic possession had occurred to viewers watching the film. The Reverend Billy Graham pronounced: "There is a power in the film that is beyond the film."

To this day, Blatty remains honestly bemused by the reaction to *The Exorcist*—and disappointed that its horrific elements overpowered his spiritual message.

"I've never understood. It's probably a confession of failure on my part. Oh yes, I wanted it to be spooky, eerie, intriguing—making you turn page after page—but I have no idea of what was going on with all the hysteria.

"With the film, the people were just getting the rollercoaster ride. Let's face it—the message was adroitly snipped out of the film. It wasn't there.

"On the most basic level, the film argues for some kind of transcendence: if there are demons, why not angels? Why not God? And one religion, the Catholic Church—if not others as well—seems to have power to command the evil spirit, which seems a validation of religious belief. But the real point of the book is nowhere to be found in the film.

"About three or four months after the release of the motion picture, I had dinner at the home of a Warner Brothers executive. And I recounted at dinner how annoyed I was that a number of people who had seen the film didn't seem to understand that it was not a triumph of evil over good; it's quite the opposite. 'People actually think,' I said, 'that the demon got possession of Father Karras and triumphed by throwing him out the window.'

"And the executive said, after a pause, and God bless his honesty, 'That's what *I* thought happens.' He had no idea. He'd seen the film countless times; and he had read the novel—I guess that's part of the reason why I think people who speed-read are in desperate need of a firing squad.

"I mean, what's the point? What, by God, is the point of possessing this little girl? I had written a very brief scene for the film in which Father Merrin explains to Father Karras what all these horrors we've been seeing are about; he says, 'The little girl is not the target. It's you and me, people in this house.' And the subtext of what Merrin tells him is that 'It's you, Damien. It's your faith. Your salvation. This is the crucible of your faith. The demon's aim is to make us despair of our own humanity, to make us feel that we are bestial and vile, so that even if there were a God, He could not possibly love us.'

"What a terrible idea it was, even commercially, to leave out that moral centre. Because I'm sure you've noticed that a lot of people who were thrilled while they were watching *The Exorcist* despised themselves later for liking it.

"I know what happened. When Billy Friedkin came on the scene, the novel was a phenomenal success. I gave him a screenplay that departed from the novel, and it terrified him. It's the usual movie mentality—when you do not have a positive and active understanding of why something will please a reader or a motion picture audience, then you rely on what worked the last time. Since he didn't understand why this particular novel was so popular, he felt that he'd better not change any little element of it.

"On the other hand, one can't argue with success. The film of *The Exorcist* will always remain a phenomenon, but it will never be a classic. It's just a roller-coaster ride—as elegant a roller-coaster ride as you can find, but that's all it is."

He shakes his head. "Having the girl's head turn around

360 degrees! You asked me why the audience found that movie frightening. I ask you, how could they *believe* that?"

In both book and film, *The Exorcist* brought a new legitimacy to the field of horror: in publishing and film-making parlance, horror was now profitable. It did not make writers like Stephen King and Peter Straub possible, for they were well on their own way to success; but it made the publishing and film industries much more receptive to the tale of terror as a marketable commodity, and certainly helped assure the early financial success of some of horror fiction's leading writers.

"I don't take any particular responsibility for that," says Blatty. "The usual thing said is that *The Exorcist* rode a wave of popularity caused by the public's sudden interest in the occult. But where was this wave when *Rosemary's Baby* was around? Where was all this interest when countless occult novels were published? It was the same place it was when *Frankenstein* appeared. This 'sudden' wave of 'inexplicable' interest in the occult has been with us since men sat around camp-fires.

"I also don't think about it much. It's difficult for me to connect myself with the person who wrote *The Exorcist*, and it's all the more difficult these days—I can't get any studio to make *Legion*, which is the sequel to *The Exorcist*."

The problem would not have arisen if Blatty had chosen to write his sequel close on the heels of *The Exorcist*. Instead, he delivered *I'll Tell Them I Remember You* (1973), a non-fiction memorial to his mother.

"My publisher took it because I wanted to do it, and they were looking ahead to my next novel. They did as well as they could for it—I mean, they really tried. But the bookstores were really hostile; they were my new advisers: 'A terrible mistake,' they said. 'You should immediately do another horror novel, if not a sequel to *The Exorcist*.' Then Warner Brothers offered me a lot of money if I would agree to write the sequel to *The Exorcist*. I didn't. But frankly speaking, I wish I'd done it now. Then at least we would never have had *The Heretic* . . . "

Blatty is quick to divorce himself from *Exorcist II: The Heretic* (1977), a disastrous exercise in cynical film-making.

"They asked me to write the screenplay, I didn't want to do it. A friend of mine pirated a copy of the script, and after my initial astonishment, I thought, 'This is some kind of sly send-up. They're trying to torment me; this is a joke. They're not really going to do this.' I called the producer of the film at Warner Brothers, and he said, 'Well, everybody here thinks it's a masterpiece.'

"The first time at least somebody over there started thinking that they might have trouble came when one of the 'adapters' of the script—and apparently without asking anybody whether it was a good idea—wrote a novel called *Exorcist II: The Heretic*. The studio wanted my permission, and I said, 'Those characters are *my* characters. Nobody else can use them in a novel. It's extraordinarily bad judgement.'

"They came back and offered me $100,000 against half the royalties of the book. I didn't have to do anything, just say, 'Yes, you can publish this.' And I said, 'No.' The first Warner Brothers response was that turning down a free $100,000 was 'not the act of a rational man'. But the next response was to think, 'He really thinks it's that bad?'

"The only suggestion I made was after I saw *The Heretic*. I was living in Georgetown, and I went with a paying audience on opening night. And just at the point where I had predicted it would happen when I read the script—where Louise Fletcher put the helmet on Linda Blair's head—we went up and we never came back down. Oh, what a night that was! I called the producer and suggested that they retitle it *Son of Exorcist*, that they give me the film and allow me to write some additional funny dialogue and dub it in and well, you know, go with it. Make them think we intended it should be camp.

"He hung up the phone on me."

Blatty finally wrote his sequel, *Legion*, but more than ten years after *The Exorcist*. Those years were marked by two marriages and two children, but very little writing. After *I'll Tell Them I Remember You*, he revised *Twinkle, Twinkle Killer Kane* under the title *The Ninth Configuration* (1978), then scripted and directed a motion picture version that won the Golden Globe Award for best screenplay in 1981; but that was the extent of his writing work. What happened?

"Well, why don't I tell the truth? Mario Puzo was sitting right where you are, about a week ago. And he said, 'Is it getting harder for you to write as you get older?' I said, 'Of course it's getting harder.' And Mario said, 'God, who would want to write if you could find something better to do?' And then he said, 'But there's nothing else to do!' I feel much the same, at least with respect to dramatic fiction.

"Writing comedy is quite a joy for me. There's an instant reward. If I've written a really funny line, then, for a moment, I become the audience and I laugh, I enjoy it, I know it works. I don't have to wait for opening night. But with anything other than comedy—not just spook fiction, anything—I just don't know. Sure, there was a period when I was about two-thirds of the way through *The Exorcist* that I started telling everybody in my family, 'This is going to be the number one bestseller.' But a few weeks after that, I was back into an uncertain apathy about whether it was good or not good. I didn't know. I had to wait . . . to wait.

"Certainly for me, there isn't as much blood, sweat, and tears in writing comedy. Writing anything else is more akin to mental manual labour. Comedy is not; it's exhilarating."

When we met, Blatty was half-way through a new musical comedy; but he talked of a new novel, a suspense thriller with a theological theme. "I keep looking for things to distract me from it, frankly, because I'm very obsessive-compulsive when I work. And a play or a comic novel is one thing— you're talking a maximum of ten weeks, twelve weeks; but remembering *The Exorcist* and *Legion*—and this one is much bigger in scope and size than either of those—I just don't relish a year inside the cave, not seeing sunlight, writing every day. It'll take over my entire life, and this just isn't the time for me to do that.

"When I was younger and consumed with ambition, it was one thing; but at this point, I find that virtually everything is going to have to be an entertainment from now on, because

I've said all I have to say about anything that is of any importance to me. Besides questions of who am I, and where am I going, and what is my ultimate destiny, writing books and movies about the evils of television and the like is just ponderous irrelevance."

Legion, published in 1983, climaxed a trilogy designed by Blatty to confront these "qu stions": *The Exorcist* posed the problem of evil; *The Ninth Configuration* countered by posing a greater mystery, the problem of good—if there is no God, how does one explain good and the power of self-sacrifice; and *Legion* offered Blatty's solution.

"Even the novel of *The Exorcist*, though it poses the problem of evil and glancingly suggests a few rather tired old answers, does not give an answer that is satisfying or intellectually convincing. It wasn't until the point at which I determined to write *Legion* that I finally had the answer—a really satisfactory answer to the problem of evil. That is to say, if you grant its assumptions, there is not a loophole or a flaw to be found in it. Or an unsatisfactory element—by which I mean, for example, Rabbi Kushner's book *When Bad Things Happen to Good People*. His solution to the problem of evil—which is supposed to be very satisfying, but which I personally find unsettling—is that yes, God is there and He's good, but not all-powerful. Well, imagining myself a child, that is not the father who I want to protect me. That entity is not the father upon whose judgements I would rely.

"I agree with Kinderman's theory in *Legion*. This world is interpenetrated by another, and the Fall of Man is really the fall of some immensely powerful and luminescent being—for whom the name Lucifer is as good as any other—and somehow we are incorporated in that being. We're part of the body of that being, regrouping, finding our way back toward God.

"The theory is only that much removed from the orthodox religious recital of Original Sin in the Garden of Eden. I find it satisfying. It's quite startling, but I would think that someday very orthodox religious thinkers and theologians might come to embrace it, because it makes a great sense out of some nonsense that orthodoxy has to try to explain, and they usually have to start explaining it to children in the second grade of Catholic school—that's when we begin thinking about these questions and these paradoxes. 'Do you mean to tell me, Sister Evangeline, that because one person did a bad thing, every child who is ever to be born on earth is going to be psychically crippled and bear the so-called 'stain' of Original Sin? Every child is going to be vulnerable to being born with cancer? Have to endure not only illness but earthquakes and the thousand other natural calamities that the human body is subject to in this savage world?'

"But if Adam and Eve—metaphorically you and I, everyone—are parts, individual parts, of one luminous personality, and that personality, for whatever mysterious purpose, chose to undergo what we now call 'suffering', that's perfectly plausible. That's understandable. Now I know why I might get cancer, even though innocent."

But again, recalling his dissatisfaction with the reaction to *The Exorcist*, he is concerned that his intent in writing *Legion* has been misunderstood. He discusses the reviews of the book.

"They don't discount my attempts, and they don't fail to take me seriously. Something else happens. They become annoyed, if not hostile, because the work before them is to be taken seriously. That's not what they normally go to the spook novel for.

"A case in point is the review of *Legion* in the *New York Times* by John Jay Osborne, who wrote *The Paper Chase*. He said that the story worked, the characters worked, the philosophy worked, all that—and then he said, 'But why doesn't it scare the hell out of me, which is the main object of this kind of book?'

"Well, that was a presumption on his part, because that was not *my* object. But what is popularly thought to be the object, even by the reviewer, is superimposed on the work. And when it doesn't fit the presupposition, they get annoyed. I'm sure that many of the people who ran out and bought *Legion*, and who had been weaned on the more current crop of so-called horror novels, were probably bitterly disappointed that they had to start thinking on page two—that one of the characters had *ideas*."

He talks of the juxtaposition of fear and hope at the heart of both *The Exorcist* and *Legion*.

"In *Legion*, a character is preoccupied with communicating with something—some intelligence, he thinks—via the use of a tape recorder. I've done similar experimentation myself, and occasionally, I will take a friend to my office and play the tapes. When they hear what sounds like a voice, sometimes speaking their name, their reaction is invariably one of fear.

"Now I don't understand that. Mine is one of the tremendous elation. If there really is something manifesting on that tape—and God knows whether there is or not—then that is one more piece of evidence for the continuity of our lives, for survival after bodily death. What is frightening about that?"

He asks if I would be interested in listening to the tapes. The prospect is enticing, but I am hesitant; I would find fear, I tell him. It is the fear, perhaps, of those who were taught that faith, not acts, was at the centre of religion.

"Faith is fine," he replies. "But I'm a lot like the centurion in the New Testament who wants Christ to come to his house to heal his servant. Christ tells him, 'Why don't you go back to your house, your servant is fine.' And the centurion says, 'I believe, but my faith is weak. Help me.'

"So for some of us, faith is not enough—because one can have faith that, say, Martians and UFOs are going to save us from the final cataclysm. One can have faith in all sorts of misguided opinions and conclusions. Faith is more closely associated with our emotions than with our reason and our observations. Christ Himself seems to have given those around Him miracles enough to buttress whatever they believed; he certainly gave them some reasons to have faith that were more closely related to the mind and observation.

"Now if we want to talk about drawing pentacles and trying to invoke demons and spirits or whatever, include me out, as Sam Goldwyn used to say. Fiddling around with Ouija boards is dangerous—not because some genie is going to pop out of a bottle and do terrible things to us, but because *something* moves or gives us the sensation that the planchette is moving by itself; powerful unconscious forces are at work. If you really get into fiddling with a Ouija board and you start thinking you're getting messages—or you're *getting* them— you're tapping into the unconscious, and there is the danger that you're accomplishing something akin to five years of psychoanalysis in a ten-minute session. And a lot of garbage comes up from the unconscious that is really terrifying.

"But you know," he points back toward his house with a smile, "I certainly have no objection to an apparition appearing on the top of my house and saying, 'Listen, everything's going to be great. Trust me.' "

[William Peter Blatty persisted in his quest to film *Legion*, and ultimately wrote and directed his sequel, *The Exorcist: 1990*.]

Dennis Etchison

"I want to know what happened when you walked down to the corner 7-Eleven. What happened? What scared you?"

He is one of the leading writers of horror fiction, but in this era of "brand names" spawned by best-selling novels and big-budget motion pictures, he is a virtual unknown outside of the field. His fiction has been published professionally for almost twenty-five years, yet he is often heralded as a "new discovery" or one of horror fiction's "bright new stars". Not until 1982 did he have a book entirely his own, and then only through the auspices of a maverick small press publisher.

His name is Dennis Etchison, and his fate is of his own choosing: he writes short stories. And he is, very simply, America's premier writer of the horror short story.

We meet at his house in Beverly Glen, a wooded ravine in west Los Angeles near the UCLA campus. His directions suggest a road map of disaster—"Yeah, turn there," he says. "That's the intersection where Ernie Kovacs died." The words haunt me as I drive out Santa Monica Boulevard, past Century City, and into Beverly Hills; it is rush hour California-style, a hurry-up-and-wait nightmare that begins in a maze of health spas and used-car lots, and ends in a tree-lined canyon, with one detour as police clear the debris of a collision. When I bring the car to a stop across the road from Dennis Etchison's rented house, he stands calmly for a full five minutes before traffic clears, allowing him to join me.

He apologizes for not inviting me into his home: "I'm finishing a book, and you don't want to see the mess." He is concerned with appearances; as we drive up into the hills for Chinese food, he apologizes again, this time for a panel we were on a year before that climaxed when Etchison cried out "Do you want to see something *really* scary?," pulled on a "Mr X" wrestling mask, and began ranting about the uncanny resemblance between fellow horror writer Karl Edward Wagner and professional wrestler Big John Studd.

"God, that was embarrassing," he says, but he can't resist a smile. He enjoys his paradoxes—the portrait of the artist as a pro wrestling fan—but constantly berates himself for indulging in them before his readers. "I want them to know my stories," he says. "Not me."

After dinner, we settle in at a friend's home in Benedict Canyon. Her eleven-year-old daughter sits at Etchison's feet, looking up at him with a mixture of pride and adulation. But the relaxed tone of our conversation changes once the tape recorder is on the table. We move from a sitting room to an open-air porch; we talk about mutual friends, recent books, recent movies—about anything but Dennis Etchison. He is clearly uncomfortable, and I ask him why.

"I have a great ambivalence about interviews. I believe writers should be read and not heard from. There are certain writers whose personalities are more responsible for their reputation than their writing. And who use their personalities to make their works popular. I resent that, because they get far more attention than their work merits. And other writers who are really much better, but who are quiet and invisible souls, are not noticed at all.

"Part of me wants to be totally anonymous. The writer who I really admire most for his image is B. Traven, who wrote *The Treasure of the Sierra Madre*; he was totally unidentified in his lifetime. I admire that."

He speaks reflectively, concerned with the impression that he will make even as he disparages himself for doing so. And despite his misgivings, he does want to talk.

"Look," he says, tugging at the cigarettes he will chain-smoke throughout the interview. "You know what I want to say. So let's get it out of the way.

"I have never thought of myself as a horror writer. Someone said that there are two kinds of writers, those who find out what the market is and write to fill it, and those who write and then find a market that will take their work. And I think I'm the latter kind of writer. I've always tried to write whatever I wanted most to write and then send it out, usually starting with the top-paying markets and working my way down. And if the story ended up in a girlie magazine or a science fiction magazine, that was essentially accidental. I never had much of an interest in horror fiction, although I loved horror movies. I don't come from a background of heavy reading in the field, and although I can remember reading a number of people years ago who were very good, I don't really come out of a tradition."

Over the years since his first professional story was published in 1961, Etchison's fiction has appeared in magazines as disparate as *Fantastic*, *Rogue*, and *The Oneota Review*. His identification with the horror field began in the early '70s, when he was asked to contribute to the anthology *Frights*; its editor, Kirby McCauley—now Etchison's literary agent—had admired an Etchison story in the horror fiction magazine *Whispers* ("Which I had sent in," Etchison notes, "simply because it was listed in *Writer's Market*".). The *Frights* story, "It Only Comes Out at Night", produced a response unlike anything he had previously experienced. "All of a sudden, people—Stephen King being one of them—came up to me and introduced themselves and said, 'God, that was a good story!' And the story was a breakthrough for me. I found myself sending more things to that sort of market, and they began to be published more and more in that field.

"All of a sudden, after a couple of years of selling several things in a row to the same market, for a very limited audience, people noticed the name being repeated. So for the first time in my life, I had some recognition value. I felt no particular loyalty to the horror field. Before, science fiction constituted about a third of my work, mainstream was about a third, and a kind of weird fantasy was the other third. I would try to change from story to story. If I did a science fiction story, I would consciously try something else the next time, so that I wouldn't type myself, wouldn't start censoring my ideas and focusing them all in one direction.

"I wanted to try to preserve the honesty of my creative impulses, so I purposely tried to avoid categorization. But only as you become known do you command anything above the absolute rock-bottom price for your work. And if your goal is to support yourself from your writing, so that you don't have to work other jobs, then you are going to have to be paid more than the minimum. I was never in it to make money; I was never in it to try to get rich. On the other hand, I knew all along that what I was getting paid for these stories was not enough to live on. I always had to work other jobs."

He talks of those other jobs, which he has drawn upon extensively in his fiction, with a sense of comic relief.

"I was a shake-and-fillet man at McDonald's for six months; I was the best shake man in the McDonald's system—I could run ten different milkshakes with different flavours at the same time. The company didn't want people to drive by and see a bunch of idle employees, so they would give you just busywork. You would take the screws out and wash the screw heads and put them back in, things like that. I got to the point where I was beginning to flip out—I could wipe every drop of water out of my milkshake area and fold the towel a certain way and have zero drops of water on the stainless steel and have everything arranged perfectly. I would start talking to myself; I called my milkshake machine 'Immaculata'."

He washed dishes, sold shoes and jewellery, and even sold newspaper subscriptions over the telephone. "The best job I ever had was for three-and-a-half years at the Jiffy Gas station in Malibu on the Pacific Coast Highway—the gas station of the stars. It was a self-serve station, and I worked there on my shifts totally alone. People would pump their own gas and come up and pay me. I kept an extra typewriter there, and I would sit there and write stories." One of his customers, he notes, was William Peter Blatty. "They finally closed the Jiffy Gas station on five days' notice. That was the best thing that ever happened to me. I never worked at another job after that.

"My support has been a hundred per cent from my writing since 1976. But curiously enough, it wouldn't have happened if I hadn't begun to publish my things in the horror field.

"The interesting thing is that I don't think my work changed. The stories of mine that were mainstream continued to sell in the horror field. My science fiction sold in the horror field. 'The Dark Country', a story that was resolutely mainstream, was submitted first to *The New Yorker*, *Playboy*, *Penthouse*, *Paris Review*, and *Atlantic Monthly*, and was rejected by all of those places. It then sold to *Fantasy Book* here and to *Fantasy Tales* in England, even though it had zero fantasy element whatsoever. Not only that, it won the British Fantasy Award and the World Fantasy Award. That proved to me that I had been right all along—that a writer should not worry about questions of genre. That is something for editors and critics to worry about."

The success of his short fiction in the horror field has given him only a semblance of security.

"Now, when I write a story, I don't have to start going down the list in *Writer's Market* to find a place to sell it, because I already have five letters sitting at home asking if I have stories for anthologies. I have more requests than I have stories to fill them with. So selling a short story is no problem.

"I can now get, I guess, the best rate that they can afford to pay, but it's still not enough. If I sold a story a week, would I be able to get by—even at ten cents per word, which is a very good rate today? With the inflation factor, I am actually making less in real money than when I sold my first story in 1961. As you know, magazines were paying three to five cents a word for stories then; today, they are still paying less than five cents per word unless you are a top name."

Etchison soon learned the striking indifference of major book publishers to the short story. Anthologies of original horror fiction are rare commodities in mass-market publishing, and collections of the work of a single author are seemingly anathema. Traditionally, horror writers have seen their stories collected in book form only after publishing a succession of highly commercial novels, or in small print runs from speciality publishers. The writer whose first published book is a short story collection is indeed the rarest of breeds.

Unable to sell a collection of his stories, Etchison turned to the novel form in order to survive; working under contract with a major New York publisher, he spent more than two years in the late '70s writing *The Shudder*, only to see it, after numerous rewrites, rejected by its editor. He then produced four novelizations of horror films: *The Fog* (1980), *Halloween II* (1981), *Halloween III* (1982), and *Videodrome* (1982), the latter three under the pseudonym Jack Martin, the protagonist of several Etchison short stories. He winces at their mention: "They were compromises," he says, "though I did the best job I possibly could with them; I had to eat." The books made more sense of their subject matter, however, than the films on which they were based.

In 1982, an enterprising Californian named Jeff Conner founded Scream/Press, a small press devoted exclusively to horror fiction, and determined that his first priority would be to publish a hardcover collection of Etchison's stories. *The Dark Country* (1982) was an unmitigated success, receiving highly favourable reviews everywhere and quickly selling out four printings; a second collection, *Red Dreams*, was published in 1984. That year, Berkley brought Etchison's "real" work to the mass market for the first time with a paperback edition of *The Dark Country*.

Darkside, his first original novel (discounting two pseudonymous books in the '60s), appeared in paperback from Berkley in 1986; but the short story remains Etchison's preferred mode of writing, and Scream/Press published his third collection, *The Blood Kiss*, in 1988. He doubts that he will return, at least in the immediate future, to the novel form.

"I am interested in shorter forms; I'm a natural for short stories and screenplays, not novels. I write haiku, not epic poems.

"The stories are essentially pure. There's not enough money involved in a short story sale to think of anything other than the artistic—unless you are going to be a prolific hack and turn out a hundred short stories a year and try to live on them. But I don't, I work slowly. So every short story has been exactly what I wanted to write most.

"Of course it's dangerous to say 'never', but I find writing novels so extraordinarily difficult that it's not worth the suffering I go through. In the last six months of writing *Darkside*, I was saying that I was not going to write another novel for at least five years. It's just so difficult for me, because I have trained myself as a short story writer for twenty-five years. To start working with that same degree of precision for 350 pages instead of 20 is excruciating—all life stops for six months. One could go through a list of physical and mental ailments that arise from doing it.

"Anyway, I think the novel is an outdated form. It was a moribund form that was created in centuries past for people who had no other entertainment during long winter nights than to sit by the fire with these huge thick books. In our time, the novel is a curiosity. Occasionally someone will do something brilliant with the form, but the idea that we should all have to write stories that run 350 pages is as absurd as saying that all films should run between 90 and 120 minutes. Sometimes the best length for a film is 45 minutes, but film-makers don't do it, do they? Because you can't exhibit a 45-minute film, and consequently, they pad it to twice the length for the marketplace, and you have a film where everybody says, 'Boy, the last half-hour I was really falling asleep.'

"I wish that we could all write books that went for however long they needed to be and then stopped. We would have 78-page novels, 122-page novels, and 10,000-page novels or however long it took. But if it's too short or too long, it won't be bought and published. What I am saying is that it's because we live in a capitalist culture. We are victims of the dictates of the marketplace."

In recent years, Etchison has turned to editing short fiction, with the two-volume *Masters of Darkness* (1986, 1988), *The Cutting Edge* (1987), and *Lord John Ten* (1987). How does he assess the present state of the American short story?

"It seems to me to be essentially dead except in the genres. I know I am doing a disservice to the occasional writer like John Updike and Donald Barthelme, but it was said years ago that science fiction had kept the short story alive for twenty-five years. That was largely true, because as the slick short story markets dried up, the science fiction magazines flourished. In 1954, there were forty different monthly science fiction magazines on the newsstands—there was a far bigger market than there were writers to fill it. As a result, new talent was pouring into writing short stories. Since then, I find very little of interest in literary magazines or mainstream magazines.

"The work that science fiction was doing in the '50s and '60s to keep short stories alive is being done now in the horror field and in the avant-garde, the cutting edge of the fantasy field.

"Science fiction seems to be regressing to the worst elements of space opera and escapist medieval romance. I have an interest in contemporary science fiction that approaches absolute zero, which is very sad, because it was important to me for many years. The real excitement in short stories is going on in the horror field right now—Clive Barker and Ramsey Campbell, for example. Some of Ramsey's stories are more innovative, more technically daring, than anything else that is going on. I have learned more from studying an individual paragraph of Ramsey Campbell than I have learned from reading anybody else in the last twenty years.'

He sees, in what he calls the "regression" of science fiction, a warning for the future of the horror story.

"I've been concerned about it in the last couple of years. I find it basically a silly, juvenile, dull field.

"Very little fiction that you read feels like it cuts very deeply. It's all a sort of description of events that happen for no particular reason. How many writers can you think of who have a consistent thematic unity in their work? Writers who are obviously writing very sincerely with passion about something, particularly horror? The This, The That—you know, *The Regurgitation*, whatever, all those endless novels. I mean, really—they are all about possessed children or they are about the ghosts of dead Indians or they are about haunted houses. And that's *all* they're about! Who else cares about another possessed child, haunted house, or ghosts of dead Indians book? And it's a shame, because some of my friends write that stuff.

"I mean, who gives a shit anymore about the man who is confined in the attic or the haunted house with the cobwebs in the cellar? I can't read the stuff, so why would I expect anyone else to read it if I write it? I want to read about what really frightens me, what really frightens the person who is doing the writing. I mean, come on. I don't really believe in vampire stories. I don't really, in my gut, believe in ghosts. I want to know what happened when you walked down to the corner 7-Eleven. What happened? What scared you?"

Dennis Etchison was born in Stockton, California, on 30 March 1943; when he was six years old, his family moved to the greater Los Angeles area, and he has lived there ever since.

"I can think of nothing in my childhood that was in any way out of the ordinary. I don't remember any tragedy befalling my family. I can remember no great fear, no great unhappiness, certainly no family break-ups or family problems of any kind. I had, I think, a very ordinary childhood. I was an only child, so there was a subtle, unconscious pressure on me to be good, to be perfect. I don't think my mother was aware that she was putting that trip on me. And I was a perfectly well-behaved boy, never did anything bad, and went on to become sixth-grade president and student-body president in junior high and class president in high school, essentially because I was trying to be the 'good boy'.

"And about half-way through tenth grade I dropped out of all that, reading Kerouac's *On the Road*, realizing that I had been on a treadmill all of my life trying to live up to others' expectations, all of a sudden letting my hair grow long—which was very unfashionable in the '50s. And dropping out of everything, becoming the resident beatnik of the school."

His religious upbringing was virtually nonexistent.

"I am not formally religious. When I was a small child, I went a few times to the Lutheran church and a few times to the Presbyterian church, because those were the religions of my parents. They told me that I was free to go or not to go to Sunday school, as I chose, which I feel is a proper attitude to take. I chose not to go and did not have much formal religious upbringing. I am not theologically inclined.

"The only time that my religious views ever became clear was when, in the '60s, I chose to be a conscientious objector during the Vietnam war and resisted the draft. I was required, as part of that process, to define the nature of the universe and describe my religious views. They gave me a few blank lines on a form. I ended up taking many pages, and I spent a couple of weeks writing it. That was the most difficult thing I have ever written. I tried to be completely honest. And I had never really formalized my thinking until then. I decided that I believed that there was a force in all living things that strove to perfect itself. I had no particularly original thoughts, except that I was really deeply committed to the idea of the struggle of life versus death in the universe."

His interest in writing was spawned when a sixth-grade classmate gave him two science fiction magazines as a Christmas present.

"At that point, I launched immediately into reading adult fiction. Bradbury hit me very, very hard—*The Golden Apples of the Sun, The Martian Chronicles*. That opened me up to the possibility of language and feeling that had never occurred to me before. The most significant event in my life—probably not just as a writer, but as a thinking and feeling person—was to read the works of Ray Bradbury at that age; they had an electrifying intensity and a sensuality unlike any other writing I had seen. To understand that words could have taste and colour, all the senses to them, and that they could correspond directly to emotions. That you could make a word or line sing from the heart.

"Then, of course, I wanted to *be* Ray Bradbury for a few years. I had to work for years to try to throw off the influence of Bradbury on my style. I haven't ever completely succeeded."

He immediately began writing stories.

"In the sixth grade, we used to sit down and write pastiches of the science fiction stories and books that we had been reading and turn those in as compositions. And that taught me some fluency, to turn in something that had 'The End' on the last page every week. It taught me that I could write a story, even though most of the stories were steals from other writers."

When he was twelve years old, he won $250 at the local Elk's Lodge for an essay called "What America Means to Me". At age thirteen, he began placing original stories with school literary magazines.

"In junior high, I became editor of the school paper and won some competitions in journalism, and then moved on to journalism in high school. My journalistic training was extremely important, because it taught me how to say things in the fewest possible words. It taught me about clarity and brevity. After a certain point, though, journalism becomes destructive, because it teaches you to channel your content to fit the format.

"Schoolwork was always the great burden, because I never had time to write. I really wanted to write. Came the end of the eleventh grade, I had been waiting all year to write something. And at the party for the journalism staff on the last day of school—a swimming party at a girl's house—everybody was off in the pool, but I asked the girl if she had a typewriter. And she brought an old upright typewriter outside.

"I sat there and started typing the first few lines of a story. I did what Ray Bradbury said to do, which was to take the first two or three words that come into your mind, put them on paper, and then go from there—let the story write itself. So I put down the first three or four words that occurred to me and started typing, and when I got home, I worked for six nights on the kitchen table until I had finished the story:

'Odd Boy Out'. It went through two drafts. I mailed it off to five or six science fiction magazines, all of which turned it down.

"Then I remembered something else that Bradbury said, which was never try to anticipate an editor's needs; always submit to the least likely market you can think of. So I looked through *Writer's Market* and found a girlie magazine at the top of the list called *Escapade*. I thought that that was very unlikely since the story had no sex in it—it was a science-fantasy story about teenagers. I sent it off to them, and they sent me a check for $125 back in the mail. The high school paper had a picture of me on the front page with a caption that said 'Etchison Launches Career on $125'. And that's how it started."

His initial exposure to horror, however, did not come through fiction, but at the movies.

"My first horror is not an unusual memory—I am sure that a lot of people share it. I remember seeing *The Wizard of Oz* and having to be taken out into the lobby, hysterical, when the witch had Dorothy in the tower—the flying monkeys and all that. I thought, being little and inexperienced, that they really were going to kill Dorothy."

The cinematic experience thrilled Etchison; it has become the most vital element of his life. He is an inveterate movie-goer, talks constantly about film, and would really rather be a motion picture director.

"When I was ten, I saw *Shane* and decided that I wanted to be a movie director. I have never changed my opinion. I went to UCLA film school in the '60s, started writing screen-plays commercially in 1968, but no one is ever going to give me the chance to direct a movie unless I have enough money to make my own, as John Sayles did with *Return of the Secaucus Seven;* or unless I have some success as a screenwriter, so that someone will say, 'All right, on your fourth low-budget picture you can direct.'

The film influence on his fiction, not surprisingly, is pervasive: "I am a child of the movies, so I am extremely visual in my imagination. Some people think that my work is too cinematic, too much like movie scripts. But on the other hand, the art of movies is visual selectivity. A director will zero in on a specific detail of a scene to reveal the character's emotions or to further the plot. If you can do that in fiction—describe a tiny physical detail that somehow summarizes the whole scene—you are going to make a strong, vivid impression."

In pursuit of a film career, Etchison has written screenplay adaptations of his own stories, as well as of works by Ray Bradbury, Stephen King, and Colin Wilson, but none has been produced. Although he talks of pending screenwriting projects for John Carpenter and his work for the HBO cable television series *The Hitchhiker*, it is with an undeniable sense of frustration.

"Screenwriting is absolutely unsatisfying. It is an ersatz kind of writing. It's a blueprint for someone else to make a movie. They are never going to film it the way you wrote it. When you first start screen-writing, you put in all of the camera directions, all of the cuts, all of the angles, all of the details in the shot, as if you are directing a paper movie in your head. After a few years, you find out no one ever follows that. The director is going to shoot it his own way. The cutter is going to cut it his way. If they can't find a way to shoot what you have described, then they are going to shoot something else. So it's not written for publication—it has no literary value. The only thing that would satisfy me would be to try to direct my own movies—some low-budget horror films—but I'll probably never get the chance."

If given the chance to change to any career he wished, would he become a film director?

"I would rather be a musician than a writer. A jazz musician. I played the clarinet when I was in junior high and high school, but I'm not any good. So writing is my third or fourth choice in life, below photography. And I don't begrudge it—I'm not talking down writing—it's just that there are other things in life I would rather be doing.

"I know writers who were born writers; it was just one of three or four things that I was interested in. But it was the only thing that people patted me on the head for when I was twelve and wrote that essay. So maybe one could view the story of the development of a person's life as being the path of least resistance. The thing that you get some strokes for. Maybe there are all kinds of people out there who are more talented than we are, but who are not writers because they never have gotten any pats on the head for it. Maybe that's all it would take, a pat on the head at the right time."

He clearly feels that his "path of least resistance" has been that of writing horror fiction. He repeats, to emphasize his concern: "I don't think of myself as a writer of horror fiction. The people who are really good at it transcend it. I have nothing against the horror field; there is some very exciting work being done in it. There seems to be a renaissance in the field. There is some experimental work being done in short stories in this field that's not being done anywhere else.

"I would like to make a conscious effort in the next five years to write outside of the field, because I am in danger of falling into the trap of censoring myself. The problem is that if you manage to break some new ground and you manage to do it well, all heads turn to you—and your natural inclination is to go on doing the same thing. But people lose interest because you are competing with yourself. You have established a new standard and you are competing with it, and it takes someone like Clive Barker to come along and suddenly give you something new. You've got to purposely push yourself off into new areas. In music, I think of Cat Stevens—everybody was turned on by the first Cat Stevens album, but after that, no one bothered to listen to him.

"For one thing, I don't have much more to say in the realm of horror. I can continue to concoct and contrive interesting and amusing variations on those things; but if we are talking about writing from a serious level, from a deep level, that which is in your heart of hearts, I really don't have anything more to say for the moment. If I were to continue to do that, I would trivialize myself as a writer and I would become simply another old fart in the field. And I would rather not do that.

"If I want to maintain my own growth as a person, which is another way of saying as an artist, and if I want to maintain the interest of an audience, I am going to have to drop this thing and go off into completely new territory, something that I'm uncertain about, chin myself. And I don't know quite what that will be. I am sure that I will continue to come back. Maybe what I think is entirely different will still read like the same old Etchison horror story to everybody else. I don't know.

"The question is whether a writer identifies himself with a genre or not. And I don't identify myself with a genre. I have always tried to write the best story I could and sell it to whoever would buy it."

Then why do his stories tend to be dark?

"If I had a normal childhood, as I say, and if I'm just a regular Joe as I try to present myself, then whence comes all this morbidity?

"I don't know. Maybe I have a great concern with death, with mortality, maybe that's what I am trying to question. But murder and death and dying and decomposition in horror stories may just be symbols for larger issues. Just as science fiction stories are popular science, then horror stories are popular existentialism. When we read Bradbury's *The Martian Chronicles*, we don't believe that it is really about spaceships going off to Mars. But when you get to horror fiction or film, it's assumed that nothing is a symbol. That, in fact, if we have a woman being beaten up, it is literally because we have a great animosity toward women. And I find it a great disappointment that people can't look beyond that."

He selects, as an example, one of his finest stories, "The Late Shift" (1980): "If I were really talking about dead people working at the 7-Eleven, I would write an essay about it. But if I am writing fiction about dead people at the 7-Eleven, obviously I am more concerned with the meaning of it than the possibility of the event itself. So I don't really think that there were dead people at the 7-Eleven on Pico and Twenty-sixth in Santa Monica. But I do think that it is a way of getting at questions of exploitation under capitalism, which is what that story was really about. Now I wasn't consciously making those decisions when I wrote the story—it comes out of you if you listen to your inner voice. All I know is that there is a boiling white heat when you know what you are going to write next. What it's about only emerges later."

Does he like to be scared?

"Yes, I really do. The world is always being divided into two camps. People are always saying there are people who like sushi and people who don't. Well, I think there are people who like to be scared and people who don't. Most of the people I know as personal friends are not at all interested in horror—they don't want to be anywhere near it. I find it just delightful. I would like nothing better than to go to an all-night marathon of sleazy films.

"Maybe it goes back to early experiences. Some people, at some point in their childhood, learn to associate pleasure with being frightened, while other people don't. Consequently, some little kids like scary rides like the roller-coaster and some can't stand them. Now I was always really scared by the roller-coaster; but I loved it, because when you got off you knew you were alive—you had survived. And there is never a moment that you feel more alive than when you get off of the scariest ride in the world. You have just survived. And *now* I'm ready to do it again, and now I *know* I can do it."

Etchison clearly values his ability to bring the experience of fear to his readers: "I respect artistic achievement. I don't mean to be arrogant to think it superior to other existences, but the artist has the chance that most people don't have, which is to be integrated psychologically. Most people have occupations which do not involve their souls. They have occupations in which they perform activities to earn a living—which is certainly not to be sneezed at. But the artist is attempting to heal the rift between himself and the rest of the universe. He's exploring his place in the universe, his relationship with the world, with other people, what the meaning of it all is. And I don't know that other professions have that. Doctors certainly must have that feeling. Theologians, perhaps.

"The artist is attempting to heal himself—and, by example, to help other people. That seems to me to be worth doing, it really does.

"Of course, one could take a really cynical view, and say that people in the arts are just people who can't make it in the real world, who are so egotistical that they just want to do nothing but talk about themselves and what they are thinking for the rest of their lives. And they want people to pay them while they do that. But it seems to me that Homer was a noble person. Shakespeare wasn't just fucking around. Steve King is the Dickens of our day, a great popular artist who is speaking to a great many people about true human concerns; and I respect him for that."

It is late; the children have gone to bed, Etchison renewing his promise to take them to the movies tomorrow. I cannot help but note that there is often a great difference between a writer's work and his personality. He agrees: "I think that I am a fairly social and fun-loving sort of person; but if you were to read my writing and if you had never met me, you would think that I am some sort of incredibly serious, lonely person. Here I am, playing with the kids tonight, and I will take them to the movies tomorrow, and . . . I mean, the writing doesn't have anything to do with my real life. Maybe the reason writers are so different in person is because they are getting rid of the animus, the dark side; the shadow self is being worked out in the writing.

"Still, if the work is good enough and clear enough and strong enough it should stand by itself; it should contain the expression of whatever it is you have say."

And there should be no interest in the writer as a person other than as expressed in his writing?

"I don't see that it's the writer's job to foster that, because then his personality is getting in the way. If you become successful and you have a great personality, you may be successful because of your personality.

"But here I am contradicting myself by sitting and talking

into a tape recorder. It's just ultimately irresistible to get together with people who are like-minded and discuss something that is interesting to me.

"My ideal," he repeats, as the circle turns fully, "is to be an anonymous writer. But the reality is that we have a certain amount of egotism. Writers need that more than most people, because this is one of the few professions where you work a hundred per cent alone and you don't get any immediate reward. In any other job, you get paid every week or every month; but writers may not get paid for years after they do the work. Your friends, by and large, don't read that sort of thing and would never notice. If I show it to them, they say, 'Oh, that's nice.' But it doesn't have any particular value for them. You have the impression that no one out there is noticing at all. I mean, you cash the cheque; the money is gone.

"The only feedback you get is when you are on a panel and a bunch of people are there and they are interested and they are asking questions and they come up for your autograph or to ask questions about your work. And you suddenly realize that they actually dug down into their jeans and spent their own money for the book, $2.95 per copy.

"And they come up and say, 'Would you sign this book for me? I really liked it.' And you look into that person's eyes and see that this is someone who actually read it and liked it. Maybe you helped them in some way; maybe you changed their life a little bit.

"Otherwise, you are talking in the dark. You really are talking in the dark, talking to yourself, talking to a closed room . . . talking and talking."

Ramsey Campbell

"The deeper you dig into a horror writer, the more likely you are to find that he writes that way, or she writes that way, because they have gone out on the edge somewhere."

What makes a writer of horror fiction?

Ramsey Campbell has an answer—not *the* answer, he is quick to observe, but one that he believes is the explanation for why his writing career, with ten major novels and more than two hundred published short stories, has been devoted almost exclusively to the tale of terror.

We meet in his home town of Liverpool. Liverpool is known as the capital of comedians, soccer teams, and rock-and-roll bands from the Beatles to Frankie Goes To Hollywood. It is a grey industrial port with its share of urban blight, but it is not the gloomy purgatory that a reader of Campbell's fiction would come to expect.

Nor is Ramsey Campbell a gloomy or brooding presence; he has the appearance of a displaced child, with a wide, smiling, boyish face that belies his forty-plus years of age. His eyes, perennially twinkling with mischief, seem confirmation of a happiness wholly at odds with the fact that he is a writer of horror fiction. But when I ask him why so many horror writers seem so genial, his face pales and grows mock-serious.

"It's a façade," he says with a dramatic whisper. But then, taking a deep breath, he explains that he is indeed serious—that it *is* a façade.

"I've been too concerned in interviews with presenting

myself as a genial, everyday guy who just happens to write horror stories. I don't believe there's any such animal.

"The deeper you dig into a horror writer, the more likely you are to find that he writes that way, or she writes that way, because they have gone out on the edge somewhere. It's like the question I'm often asked: 'Does writing this kind of thing have any psychological effect on you? Does it actually tend to disturb you in any way?'

"The answer is that the psychological effect and the disturbance *precede* the writing. In fact, far from disturbing me to write it, it tends to be a way of dredging up things that I've more or less—and probably rather unhealthily—tucked away."

In 1983, Campbell introduced the American edition of his novel *The Face That Must Die* with an autobiographical essay that is probably the most disturbing piece of non-fiction that I have ever read. "I think it reads coldly," he says. Its conclusion: Ramsey Campbell was born to write horror. If there were such a thing as a Petri dish for the breeding of horror writers, then his childhood would be the model.

An only child, born in Liverpool on 4 January 1946, when his mother was thirty-six years old, Campbell grew up in a house divided. His father, a policeman, became so alienated from his mother that, when Campbell was about three years old, his parents began living in separate parts of the house.

"I didn't see my father face to face for nearly twenty years, and that was when he was dying," Campbell says. "His unseen presence was infinitely more powerful than anything I might be told about him. I used to hear his footsteps on the stairs as I lay in bed, terrified that he would come into my room. Sometimes I heard arguments downstairs as my mother waylaid him when he came home, her voice shrill and clear, his blurred and totally incomprehensible, hardly a voice, which filled me with a terror I couldn't define . . . In my teens I sometimes came home, from work or from the cinema, at the same time as my father, who would hold the front door closed from inside to make sure we never came face to face."

His mother tried to make up for his father's absence, "though perhaps she never realized that his presence was the problem". She encouraged Campbell to read and to write, and they often attended films together—she particularly enjoyed horror movies. During his adolescence, his grandmother moved into the house, and until she died there, when he was fifteen years old, he had to share his room—and his bed—with his mother.

"It must have been soon after the funeral that we began to have our differences. I was the only one left there in whom she had invested her affection, and I suppose it seemed a betrayal when I turned into a drinking, cursing adolescent . . . I became involved in science fiction and fantasy fandom, which she viewed with deep suspicion: half the writers were probably homosexual and lying in wait for me."

His mother's mind began to fail. "I tried to persuade her that things weren't always as they seemed to her: that Liverpool wasn't full of people conspiring against her, that radio programmes weren't about her under an imperfectly disguised name. My denials seemed like betrayals to her, and she tried to find reasons why I was changing: I'd turned gay, I was taking drugs (which I wasn't and hadn't been), my friends were turning me against her. Sometimes I tried to argue her out of her paranoia, but it was fruitless: she would accuse me of trying to drive her into a hospital or a home, and make me swear never to have her put away."

Shortly after his marriage in 1969 to Jenny Chandler—the daughter of Australian science-fiction writer A. Bertram Chandler—Campbell's father died, and his mother's mental condition only worsened. "I felt helpless and increasingly desperate whenever I thought of her. Usually on my visits I had to try and disentangle the truth from her account of something that had happened, or that she claimed had happened, since my last visit; often we had violent arguments over nothing at all—sometimes we came to blows.

"My mother kept calling to say that heads were looking at her out of vases or to plead with me to take her home from the house someone had left her in. She slept downstairs on the couch, because people came into her bedroom and pushed her out of bed. By now I left the phone off the hook when I went to bed, but more than once I woke in the dead of night convinced I'd heard it ringing."

Only after his mother died in 1982 did Campbell begin to realize that the horror fiction he had been writing for two decades was laced with strong autobiographical elements.

"It seems I had to write about my deepest nightmares before I could remember what they were. The process of overcoming my fears as best I could, which I take to have been the process of gaining confidence as a writer and performer, somehow involved forgetting them while acquiring whatever was necessary—technique, distance, trusting to imaginative instinct—to write about them. It has often been disconcerting to realize that I could have forgotten, or at any rate filed away in the dustiest rooms of my mind, so much."

Was he concerned to learn that he had been exposing so much of his life for others to read about?

"It didn't bother me. Neither did writing the introduction for *The Face That Must Die*. Not on that level. It was very painful to write, for reasons that I am sure you can imagine, but not in the sense of thinking, 'Oh, my God, shall I really do this, really tell people about it?' My belief is simply that you have got to be honest in this business, or there's no point in doing it at all."

He is certain that his writing has contributed to his psychological health: "It is certainly difficult to know how it could have done anything else." He finds a similar cathartic impact in viewing horror films—"because of their more visceral quality"—but not in reading the fiction of other horror writers: "I don't see how one can really read things like the best of Algernon Blackwood or M. R. James and have that sense at all. They were much more concerned with a sense of awe—the attempt to suggest something larger than the story ever shows, which, to my mind, is the best kind of terror in fiction."

Despite his new awareness of the autobiographical underpinnings of his writing, Campbell found, during work on his novel *Incarnate* (1983), that his childhood experiences continued to emerge unconsciously as he wrote.

"It came on with a curious revelatory quality after I had finished *Incarnate* and delivered it to Macmillan. It was all done up—I think I had just read the proofs—and I went out for a little bit of a rest, drove into the countryside and had a walk. And it occurred to me then, although it wasn't particularly apparent to me while I was writing, that this was about a child being terrified that her mother was going to go mad—and, more to the point, that the mother in the dark in the room with no windows, the mother as the monster, is clearly a projection of the child's fear about her actual mother. I didn't know I was writing that. To my mind, not being precisely aware of what your feelings are is very fruitful in this field.

"Normally, when I do take on a theme in a straightforward manner, when I am too aware of it, then it tends to get awfully pretentious. It's more important that I get on with telling the story. Then the themes seem to surface of their own accord. They suggest themselves in the working out of the plots, simply as elements to achieve certain things in terms of the structure, rather than my saying that now I am going to put this bit of lived experience in here."

Writing about his fears and experiences was not, however, such a natural and immediate process as it might seem. He began writing in his youth by imitating favourite writers— "the kind of story that just grabbed favourite bits from everywhere and tried to put them into some kind of borrowed structure". Soon, like many other beginning horror writers, he fell under the spell of H. P. Lovecraft.

"What appealed to me about Lovecraft was that sense of enormous, cosmic awe; his early stuff seemed to work extremely well in terms of building things up very gradually, almost musically. It certainly worked for me then—not so much now, I am afraid, although I still do like Lovecraft; I find him fascinating for various reasons."

By the age of sixteen, he had written a collection of Lovecraft pastiches, *The Inhabitant of the Lake & Less Welcome*

Tenants, that was published in 1964 by Arkham House, the small press established in the 1930s to preserve Lovecraft's fiction in book form. His Lovecraftian fiction has been collected more recently in *Cold Print* (1985). "I was attempting, very clumsily, to get at that sense of awe. But at the same time, it was also very much a means of not dealing with my own fears. It was actually a means of writing about quite different things, and probably rather comforting in some way, being able to achieve something that had nothing directly, personally, psychologically, to do with me. Then I could actually say, 'Yes, I've done it.'

"Only when I became impatient with the Lovecraftian structure, and began to write about the sort of awkward adolescent figure that I was until my mid-twenties, did I begin to get on to dealing with things that were a good deal more personal.

"Lovecraft is the most widely imitated American horror writer; M. R. James is the most imitated British writer; Hitchcock is the most imitated director. The reason is precisely that their technique is part of their surface—you can actually see their technique. It is in the foreground of their stories, to the extent that you can actually see it working and take it as a model.

"So Lovecraft was very much about the style being literally appropriate to the material, but I felt that there were other ways of doing it. When I was seventeen or so, I picked up Vladimir Nabokov's *Lolita* in paperback. And it became apparent to me that you could do all sorts of things with style without essentially obscuring what you wanted the reader to experience directly. That style actually could be used in all sorts of ironic and counterpointed ways that would nevertheless convey the essence of the experience to the reader."

Leaving school in 1962, Campbell worked first for the Inland Revenue and then as a librarian; he became a full-time writer and film reviewer in 1973. Over some twenty-five years, he would produce an impressive array of short stories, the best of which have been collected in *Demons by Daylight* (1973), *The Height of the Scream* (1976), *Dark*

Companions (1982), *Dark Feasts* (1987), and *Scared Stiff* (1988). These books, marked by stylistic sophistication and an intensely subjective vision, established Campbell as Britain's leading writer of horror stories.

Particularly notable in Campbell's stories is the manner in which he bent the traditional English ghost story, with its settings of upper-class elegance and sentimentalized wildernesses, to the modern urban landscape of the middle and lower classes. That landscape is essential to Campbell's fiction, in which settings are often depicted as extensions of supernatural and psychological elements. His vivid, disturbing portraits of urban life are drawn directly from experience.

"Shortly after encountering Lovecraft, I began to go to the movies to a considerable extent, catching up on all of the horror movies because I could then pass for sixteen, which was how old you had to be to get in. I had never been more than a couple of miles from home without my mother, and when I started going to the movies, figuring out bus routes for myself, I was going into areas of Liverpool where I had never been before, and it was quite an adventure. I was going through these derelict streets, heavily hit in the Blitz in the Second World War. And I used these settings in my writing with a kind of perverse lyricism; there is a direct use of them as terrible and depressing places—which they are, obviously—but my feeling toward them is also much more romantic."

During my visit, we take a tour of Ramsey Campbell's Liverpool—from his childhood home and an eccentric pub called Meacham's Baltic Fleet (the setting of his "Watch the Birdie") to such genuinely haunting landscapes as a shadowed underpass ("The Man in the Underpass"), a deserted oceanside funfair ("The Companion"), and the ravaged housing projects at Cantril Farm, site of *The Face That Must Die*. One setting—the concrete park shelter of his award-winning story "Mackintosh Willy"—has been obliterated by a public works project; and at Cantril Farm, we learn, to Campbell's shocked disbelief, that the broken-windowed, graffiti-covered projects will soon be converted into condominiums. "I'd best keep writing," he jokes, "in the interests of urban redevelopment."

Although Campbell has chosen to remain in metropolitan Liverpool, he moved in 1981, with his wife and two children, across the Mersey to the suburb of Wallasey. There are no horrors there.

"Here it's a different thing. This is like Sunday every day. It's very strange. Wallasey is like the '60s, basically. When the spring comes, you'll see several admittedly rather gloomy-looking men in their late thirties, early forties, sitting around in the park rolling joints. So this is where the '60s ended up."

Despite his initial focus on the short story, Campbell has more recently embraced the novel form. In 1976, his first novel saw print: *The Doll Who Ate His Mother*, in which supernatural forces animate a man's seemingly insane behaviour; it was followed by three novelizations of classic horror films, written under the pseudonym Carl Dreadstone: *The Bride of Frankenstein*, *Dracula's Daughter*, and *The Wolfman* (all 1977).

His next novel, the intense psychological thriller *The Face That Must Die* (1979), was told primarily from the perspective of a serial murderer; it confronted rather explicitly Campbell's first-hand experience with schizophrenia. It was edited significantly in Britain and published in America only in 1983, by horror speciality publisher Scream/Press. Campbell comments on the book's limited appeal.

"You don't start a novel of this kind by setting up the fact that your viewpoint character is extremely unpleasant and deranged. And editors, particularly, would say to me, 'I don't want to spend the length of a book with this guy'—and clearly felt that the reader would not want to do that, either. Obviously, it was not a commercial novel. But with an edition specifically directed to the horror readership, it is going to reach the people who tend to be able to take it. What I mean by 'take it', I don't know; I suppose, in a sense, I quite hope that people can only *just* take it. But I don't know what I ought to have done with that material to make it more palatable or acceptable. I am not at all certain that making it more palatable or acceptable would be justified in any way."

With *To Wake the Dead* (1980), published in America as *The Parasite*, his novels began to find the commercial audience that had, to that point, escaped him; it was succeeded by a haunting inquiry into cults and random violence, *The Nameless* (1981); a master blurring of the lines between dreams and reality, *Incarnate* (1983); a pseudonymous novel (by "Jay Ramsay") of cannibalism and revenge, *Claw* (1983); published here as *Night of the Claw;* and an ambiguous novel of the Faustian dilemma, *Obsession* (1985). His more recent books—*The Hungry Moon* (1987), *The Influence* (1988) and *Ancient Images* (1989)—embrace more extroverted landscapes and themes, confirming Campbell's ever-growing ambition.

He now greatly prefers the novel format.

"Basically, I think a novel is much more fun to write. It gains its own momentum, and pretty soon begins to surprise me with what I didn't know was there. Basically, the pleasure that I get from the act of writing is in coming up with something I didn't know I was going to do. And the novel is infinitely more capable of doing that for me than the short story."

He pauses, then adds: "It's good that it should have something to do with commercial reality as well. On the other hand, when I do get a good short story idea, one that makes me feel like I should do it again, between novels, I will write it."

He discusses the difficulties of sustaining himself over the long periods necessary to write a novel.

"There are tricks to writing full-time—to relaxing into it, basically. My trick now is to say to myself, 'OK, do one paragraph this morning.' Then I'm done with it. I never actually am done with it, unless I have a particularly appalling hangover and fall back into bed again. Once I have done that one paragraph, I think, 'Well, I can do another one, and the rest of this page, maybe, and then we can go over to the next page for a while . . .'

"Writing is a compulsion. I actually get extremely edgy if

I am not writing for any length of time. When I take a holiday, even then I tend to be working in some way on what I am going to write next. It's very much like an addiction, really. You take it away, and I become difficult to get along with—even more difficult than usual. Just ask Jenny."

Campbell's novels and stories are best described as humanist tales of terror, linking the element of the supernatural to the psychology of his characters. "Psychology," he says, "is a way of preparing for the supernatural in a story. Generally speaking, it is impossible to separate the two, one from the other, in my fiction." Typically, a childhood fear or trauma that has been repressed re-emerges in adulthood in a more deeply terrifying form. Campbell's characters are thus, for the most part, victims; but they are not passive.

"The stories aren't really about the struggle between good and evil, but about a struggle with something within the character. My characters are not so much victims as people coming to terms with themselves. The horror field is better equipped to deal with this kind of thing than any other popular genre. And if the conventions aren't equipped to contain it, then clearly, one pushes back the conventions."

His fiction eschews explanation; the stories have a form of self-discovery, and their inward-looking style has garnered Campbell a reputation—particularly in novels—as a writer who is demanding of his readers. The reality he depicts is likely to shift within a page, a paragraph, a sentence.

"I have always been interested in shifts of consciousness. I had the odd experience, when I was in my teens, of seeing the pattern on a seat opposite me in a railway car suddenly become lines of characters in an unknown symbolism. I actually looked at it and thought, 'Oh, this is quite interesting'—I mean, it was possible to run one's eyes down it, then look up at the top again, and the whole thing hadn't moved, it stayed quite constant. I think the important part is that I actually found this rather intriguing and wasn't bothered by it.

"When I was younger and had a fever, I experienced something that people might call astral projection—though I would not. I remember suddenly thinking, 'Hey, this is OK. I'm up here, and there I am down there. Here I am, up under the ceiling, and it's rather pleasant, and I wish it could go on.' But it didn't; in fact, I didn't go floating off anywhere. I'm quite happy to take that as being some kind of different consciousness.

"Certainly I have always been interested in appearances that turn into other appearances, or appearances which are not the real thing. Reviewers of *Demons by Daylight* suggested that the whole thing was based upon psychedelic experiences, but in fact, I hadn't then got into that at all. To a certain extent, the experiences that I later had under LSD and so forth were things I had already done verbally in my fiction; in writing those stories, I had seen them as a way of playing with words, sort of pleasant tricks with words, such as a totem pole which turns out to be a child on its father's shoulders. But it wasn't something I had actually seen, it was something that I was doing verbally.

"But there's no doubt that that sort of ambiguity of image does relate to one's experience of reality."

Not surprisingly, the real fear in Campbell's life is of insanity: "It is a fairly common fear, but possibly I know more about what it's like. But at the same time, I actually like extending consciousness as far as one reasonably can. If a bit of fear is involved, that's not too bad, so long as one can come back from it.

"I don't know. I say I am afraid of going mad, but I suppose I would be more aware, at least, of the kinds of options that are involved. And therefore I might be able to do something about it.

"Perhaps this is only to say that the things I am really afraid of are those I haven't dredged up yet, and I am not yet aware of them."

Campbell was born Catholic and educated at a Christian Brothers school. His only comment: "This is a pretty good way of turning one against religion for life."

What are his feelings about the existence of the super-natural?

"I don't have any strong feelings at all. I assume that there are things beyond our immediate perception which, on occasion, one becomes aware of. Whether this is the supernatural, I don't know. I suppose that 'supernatural' is as good a word as any for what it might be. Whether one could conceive of it as some kind of sentient entity, I don't know, really. I wish that, as a writer, I could have that kind of glimpse more often.

"When we moved to Wallasey, Robert Aickman wrote to us very gravely, saying that crossing water was one of the momentous decisions in one's life. I find it perfectly strange that people say such things. My mother's doctor once said to me, after observing that a cat of my mother's had disappeared, that cats will never come back when you have broken a mirror. Which proved to be true. My mother had broken a mirror, you see, and the cat had gone.

"I am becoming more and more convinced that, in Aickman's terms, the supernatural is everywhere. He always thought that the supernatural is simply an extension of everyday life—a heightened dimension of which we should be aware."

Campbell's fiction is noted, among other things, for a rather unremitting gloominess. "There was a stage in my fiction," he laughs, "where you knew perfectly well that the worst that could happen to the characters was going to happen."

Does that bleakness reflect a grim world view?

"I suppose so. Without religion, perhaps I am just expressing a lack of knowledge about where the whole thing leads, apart from a dark at the end of the tunnel. And looking around at the enormous number of lives that are cut short around the world every minute that we are talking, I would have thought so. I mean, Nabokov tossed a cheery one up by saying that you came out of that darkness in the first place, so OK, you are just going back to the same place at the end. But somehow I can't actually feel that—although I appreciate that it's true. The whole idea of cutting off consciousness completely is a terror which I have never dealt with as a writer, not yet."

If he were not a writer of horror fiction, he has no doubt what his chosen occupation would be: "A stand-up comedian. Assuming I'm not already and just don't know it.

"Part of the reason, I suspect, is that if I had to be holed up somewhere with only a few movies, there would be quite a lot of Laurel and Hardy in there.

"I certainly don't see it as a preferred alternative. I do like to put jokes in my stories. There is a kind of dreadful deadpan approach to some horror fiction, and there is also some horror which refuses to accept that there is an absurd side to it. But the absurdity is one of the crucial aspects of horror.

"Part of the business of writing horror fiction, I suppose, is to have the courage to risk the absurd. Humour and horror tend to meet in the grotesque—a thin dividing line where the writer hopes to control the reader's emotions.

"I very much like reading my stories to audiences. What's particularly interesting, although sometimes somewhat disconcerting, is that the reaction can vary from audience to audience, so that you will get an audience that is going to laugh at all the gags—and even some that you didn't know were there, but which you are quite happy to spot once somebody puts you onto them. This tends to happen particularly in America; in England, they tend to be a much more reserved audience, so that you wonder what the hell is happening out there until pretty late in the story. So in a sense, it's a similar experience to that of a stand-up comedian."

As we discuss the differences between horror fiction in Britain and the United States, it is clear that the critical reception given contemporary horror in England particularly troubles Campbell.

"It's virtually nonexistent. America seems considerably better about reviewing it. Part of the reason may be that, as far as I can see, it's generally reviewed there by people with a fair knowledge of the field. Over here, if it is reviewed at all, it tends to be reviewed by someone who saw *The Exorcist* on video, and that's the extent of their qualifications.

"Particularly here, when it is described as the English ghost story or something like that, it is given a certain respectability, so that it tends to be talked about rather sympathetically—as something that is now safe. Generally speaking, British reviewing tends only to talk about something when it's safe in some way—and, of course, that's certainly one reason for all this hysteria recently in Britain about horror on video. The extraordinary sort of persecution of horror films here clearly seems to me to indicate that some of these films have a lot of power. The same sorts of questions were being asked in Parliament and in the newspapers thirty years ago about the Hammer films. I am convinced that the whole thing is cyclical. The objections remain the same—and equally interesting, the stuff that is objected to later becomes accepted and therefore safe."

Although it is traditional to think only of the subtle, delicate English ghost story, a second convention of English horror is the *conte cruel;* indeed, an entire publishing category now exists in England for a type of horror novel called "Nasties". Campbell wrinkles his nose at the phrase: "It is a publishing ploy. I object to the term whenever it is used."

The polarity, according to Campbell, lies "in the British blood".

"The notion of English horror stories being oblique and suggestive has always been half the story. You could look back to 'Selwinism', the fine British tradition of voyeuristic sadism—going to public executions, that sort of thing. Presumably, this sort of thing appeals to something in the British. Of course, so does corporal punishment."

Campbell is concerned that extreme violence in horror fiction and film will lead to a coarsening of the field.

"It bothers me that one sees good writers or film-makers being forced to produce coarse material. To my mind, the single most dismaying example has got to be John Carpenter, who, after making *Halloween*, which I think is very restrained in terms of its graphic violence, then feels it so necessary to compete with the imitators of *Halloween* that he shoots extra gory details for *Halloween II*, a film that he didn't himself direct. Certainly that does bother me.

"On the other hand, I don't think one would ever have seen old Robert Aickman being forced to go in that direction if he didn't want to. I think that the writers who have a commitment to subtlety and so forth are not going to be forced in another direction.

"It's a difficult issue. It depends on where one draws the line between coarsening and the development of the field. David Case, an extremely intelligent and skilful writer, none the less has written one of the most graphic scenes of violence I have ever read, where a chap must sever his own foot— 'Among the Wolves'. But the difference is that he is writing in such graphic detail in order to confront you with what it would feel like if you had to do it yourself. And that seems to me to be utterly legitimate, whereas others who write in that fashion are doing it simply to exploit the maximum amount of graphic detail. And there is no emotional correlative whatsoever, apart from what one assumes is a kind of pornography that won't own up to what it is."

Incarnate and *Obsession* were written, to some extent, as a reaction to the trend of increased violence. "All my novels up to that point depended to some extent on at least the threat of physical violence as one of the major elements— which not many of my short stories do. So I actually wanted to write a novel where the threat of physical violence was virtually nonexistent. It is there, actually, in *Incarnate*, but for long, long stretches it isn't present, and the terror of the book comes through an entirely different thing. I was quite happy to be able to carry that through. And in *Obsession*, I don't think there is anything of the kind."

The true irony about the "disreputable" status of horror fiction, Campbell concludes, is that "one of the worst problems is the people in the field. It seems peculiar to this field that a number of practitioners, particularly when they stop writing it themselves, decide that nothing else worthwhile is being written. So we have Roald Dahl complaining that ninety-nine per cent of all ghost stories are rubbish, which presumably means virtually all of M. R. James, Algernon Blackwood, Sheridan Le Fanu—which is a load of pernicious nonsense in my view. One does wonder that they are so bothered by the competition that they feel bound to denigrate it in that way.

"At the same time, it's probably true that horror is always going to be disreputable, simply because it takes on taboos as part of what it does. I mean, horror fiction—certainly quite a lot of good horror fiction—is fundamentally in the business of going too far. And to that extent, people are going to say, 'Well, this is not quite nice, or this is too much, or this is not literature'—anything but actually try to face what is there. I suspect that it's a means of trying to dismiss it as quickly as possible so that it will go away and not bother them anymore.

"It is clear that, Roald Dahl aside, not many people are going to say this about M. R. James and Lovecraft and the other early twentieth-century masters, who are generally accepted now. Another thirty years, and perhaps Steve King and I will be looked upon as the kind of grey-haired old masters who have become acceptable. We will become sort of nice old gents who get wheeled around in wheelchairs, and just occasionally spew green bile when we are in a bad mood."

David Morrell

"Let's face it, I'm incapable of eliminating
the grotesque from what I do."

Iowa City, Iowa: a writer's town. Hidden in mid-west farm-
land, site of the University of Iowa and its Writers Workshop,
Iowa City is the place where Kurt Vonnegut started *Slaughter-
house Five*, where John Irving began *The World According to
Garp*, where so many of America's writers—Vance Bourjaily,
T. Coraghessan Boyle, Raymond Carver, John Cheever, Gail
Godwin, Nicholas Meyer, Flannery O'Connor, Philip Roth,
Walter Tevis, and Tennessee Williams, to name but a very
few—have walked and talked, taught and been taught.

It is also the home of David Morrell—former professor of
American literature, best-selling thriller novelist, sometime
horror writer—and, as he readily acknowledges, the man who
brought violence to modern fiction.

At the outskirts of town, away from the hilly campus and
the strips of fast-food restaurants and motels that have
scarred this once-charming landscape, David Morrell lives,
with his wife and daughter, in a quiet, tree-lined neighbourhood. He waits for me on the porch, beer in hand—compact,
moustached, engagingly energetic; he is, I soon learn, a dedicated jogger and non-stop talker. And when he talks of
horror—as when he writes it—he grins with a mixture of
delight and dread.

David Morrell was born on 24 April 1943, in Kitchener,
Ontario, where his father had been stationed with the Royal
Air Force during the Second World War. He never met his
father, who was killed in the war.

"I had a terrible childhood. I was raised, from my earliest memory, in an orphanage. My mother had to give me up temporarily in order to work—it was a basic practical choice.

"I don't blame her at all; she couldn't pay the rent, and she had to work. When she remarried, when I was about five, I was transported from the orphanage into a family with a father I didn't know, and he didn't care about knowing me. As a kid, I ran around with street gangs to get the attention I couldn't get at home.

"When I learned about my real father, and what had happened to him, I couldn't stand to see any kind of violence. I would go to the theatre, and I couldn't see a war movie. I couldn't go to westerns. I couldn't watch the news on television; I couldn't even watch the weather, for fear they would announce that war had broken out.

"There was this great tension inside me; it was bound to work out of me in some way. It sounds too simple, and it probably is, but it really wasn't until I found this kind of fiction that I write that there was a resolution. It could be that I'm grinning so much when I write these violent scenes because I'm getting the crap out of me from when I was a kid."

He began to write in the late 1950s, after he first saw the television programme "Route 66", and attempted to write scripts of imaginary episodes for pleasure. He was inspired to send a letter to Stirling Silliphant, who was then the principal screenwriter for that programme. To his delight, Silliphant responded, and the two began a correspondence that prompted Morrell to study and write fiction.

After attending St Jerome's College in Kitchener's twin city, Waterloo, he came to the United States in 1966, entering Pennsylvania State University to study American literature, and receiving a Master's degree in 1967 and his Ph.D. in 1970. There, he met and fell under the influence of Professor Philip Klass (better known within the science fiction community by his pseudonym, William Tenn).

"Klass convinced me that generic writing could be approached seriously," recalls Morrell. "He showed me everything he had written as Tenn. I was very naive about generic fiction. I had been reading only so-called serious literature—Hawthorne, Melville, people like that. My fiction, as a consequence, had the staleness of the back room; it was old-fashioned. Klass saw certain situations in my writing that were generic—that what I was doing unconsciously was working in a 'thriller' format.

"I had never read a 'thriller'. Klass introduced me to the novels of Geoffrey Household, which really proved an influence on all of my writing. He also introduced me to books by John D. MacDonald and encouraged me to read detective fiction. I grew very fond of that tough, violent way of writing. And he told me, quite simply, 'Write what you like to read.' I decided that I would like to write books that anyone who was interested in the genre would pick up and enjoy, but also that would push the idea of the genre so far that, in effect, it toppled over into mainstream."

The result was *First Blood* (1972), which thrust Morrell into an uneasy limelight; it was powerful, chilling fiction, written too seriously and skilfully to be discounted as exploitation, and yet extremely visceral and violent, and thus controversial. Morrell's assessment of its terror is precise: "a realistic novel in which people are pushed into such extreme action that it becomes a horror novel".

Rambo, a long-haired, bearded hitch-hiker, has been rousted and sent packing in town after town as he crosses the country. When he reaches Madison, Kentucky, he refuses to be shoved again; and he is not what he seems to be—a former Green Beret and Medal of Honor winner, survivor of captivity and torture in Vietnam, whose expertise in killing has not waned. And the Madison sheriff becomes the last man to push Rambo. Their confrontation sets the Kentucky countryside ablaze as Rambo literally "brings the war back home".

First Blood is perhaps the quintessential manhunt novel, and its breathless action was perfect for motion picture adaptation—a relatively tame film version starring Sylvester Stallone reached blockbuster status in 1983 and spawned the

1985 sequel, *Rambo: First Blood II* (for which Morrell wrote the novelization, published in 1985)—and, with seeming inevitability, *Rambo III* (1988). Morrell's penchant for horror is obvious in the original novel's claustrophobic cave sequence, which simply could not be translated to film.

"I wrote that in one sitting. The logic was that I knew that the two main characters were experiencing almost surreal senses of their environment. Rambo was hiding in the cave, while the sheriff was outside leading the search. I am very conscious of motifs in literature, and there are certain situations in which things must proceed to logical conclusions in terms of our expectations of stories, or else undertake dramatic inversions. Once you have people in a cave, you must push them farther and farther into the cave, until they reach what, for them, is the ultimate horror—something so awful that, if they survive, there is some doubt whether they would remain sane. If you do not follow that motif, the reader will be disappointed. So I asked myself what was really horrifying and yet told us something about the character. And I thought that I would send Rambo into a bat cave; and with that in mind, when I sat down, that fairly long section came spontaneously, in one day, without any revision. It is easily the scene that everybody who reads *First Blood* talks about."

Did it scare Morrell when he wrote it?

"Not at all. No, I was having lots of fun."

The intensity of Morrell's books, particularly in their graphic depiction of violence, has not escaped criticism. When *First Blood* was published in 1972, *Time* devoted its lead book review to accusing Morrell of inventing a new form of fiction—"carnography", the violent equivalent of pornography. The reviewer's alternative definition was "the meat novel".

"Despite the reviewer's disapproving tone—he compared my book to the My Lai massacre—I felt briefly flattered. After all, good or bad, I'd been called an original writer.

"But I soon had to admit that the reviewer was wrong. In film, *Bonnie and Clyde* and *The Wild Bunch* had already thrust far beyond the limits of conventional violence. In fiction, I'd been anticipated by Hubert Selby's *Last Exit to Brooklyn*. Nonetheless, I knew what the reviewer meant. Hemingway, often accused of being too violent, depicted his subject in a muted, romantic way. Even Faulkner, a more violent writer than Hemingway, seldom lingered on his carnographic scenes: castration, beheading, rape by means of a corncob. I certainly don't compare myself with these classic American writers, but I can understand why *First Blood* seemed new.

"Remember the year: 1972. Vietnam was ending. You could turn on the evening news and watch the streets of America burning down. Violence was on our minds. By depicting it, I responded to new conditions. As a consequence, I seemed new."

Soon, the graphic depiction of violence became a common feature of popular fiction, with its most pervasive impact in the field of horror.

"People forget that, along with *Last Exit to Brooklyn*, this book let violence out of the closet in mainstream literature. And sometimes I feel a little bitter, because it made quite a difference in publishing trends but isn't given credit for having done so. People reading the book for the first time today will not find the violence in *First Blood* to be innocuous, but they also will not find its violence unique anymore. It is an extremely forceful book in terms of violence, but was done for serious reasons, fulfilling certain aesthetic intentions. Yet in truth, when I write such violent scenes, I don't think of the violence as being strong."

Morrell is interested in thrilling the reader, he says, and his depiction of violence, although extreme, is directed toward that goal.

"I thought that *Friday the 13th* was merely gross, appalling, almost insulting gore. It scared me, but it didn't make me happy. I am more interested in a story where the suspense is such that you feel you are having a good time even as you are frightened. There is a fine line between thrill and shock, and *Friday the 13th* certainly crossed that line."

The responses of readers and critics to *First Blood* prompted him to consider that line between thrill and shock, as well as the point where the act of reading—and writing—moves from thrill to pathology.

"My fan mail was scary. Mental patients. Felons in maximum security prisons. If *Time* thought I'd been too extreme, my enthusiastic readers thought I hadn't gone far enough. Because *First Blood* had to do with contemporary warriors, I'd been forced to dramatize action graphically, almost attractively, to account for its fascination. But I'd never expected anyone actually to find it attractive."

We talk about the limits of violence, and the dangerous spectre of censorship that has recently arisen: "The problem relates to individual taste. Some liberals don't like John Wayne movies; some conservatives don't like Jane Fonda movies. In the same way, some people enjoy strong action in movies; others don't. So what?

"There's nothing inherently good or bad about any subject matter. For me, the test is whether or not the subject matter is handled intelligently, with style and skill. Is the story compelling? Are the characters interesting? By those criteria, most 'splatter' movies fail. Maybe that's why we call them 'splatter' movies in the first place—because their only purpose seems to be their close-ups of spraying blood. In its predictability, *Prom Night* was boring. On the other hand, *The Howling* seemed unexpectedly witty. Who's to judge? Intelligence, style, wit—these terms themselves are relative.

"The market place controls itself. Audiences are fickle. What seems fresh becomes stale if a lot of writers approach it in a familiar way. The dwindling box-office receipts on recent 'splatter' films suggest that the genre has exhausted itself and its audience.

"There is no need to talk about censorship. In an acceptable way, the best kind of censorship has already happened. Now that the shock has worn off, no one's going to pay money to read another of these books or see another of these movies unless it transcends its genre and becomes distinctive. Maybe that's another way of describing art."

True to these perceptions, Morrell wrote his second novel,

Testament (1975), in answer to the reaction to *First Blood*, considering violence from a reverse perspective.

"When I wrote *Testament*, my conscious model was horror of a believable and ever-increasing sort, particularly as depicted in the wonderful motion picture *Cape Fear*. There is no supernatural element in that film, which makes it all the more frightening. Robert Mitchum's hounding of Gregory Peck really reaches the point of a horrific haunting—it is, without doubt, a horror movie. And it was this insistence that I sought to create."

Morrell performed true to his goal: from the book's opening pages, where a baby is poisoned to death, *Testament* is, in a single word, relentless. A free-lance writer's exposé of a paramilitary organization ignites the wrath of its ruthless, enigmatic leader. As one by one, the writer's wife and children are killed, he is stripped of his civilization, fleeing from the city into a primordial wilderness, from which he then emerges to exact his revenge.

This descent into the wilderness plays a significant role in Morrell's fiction; again and again, his characters are drawn to the state of nature, with violence the inevitable result. Yet Morrell does not believe nature to be a negative force.

"I like being in nature. But I reject Rousseau's notion that man in the state of nature is essentially innocent. My research for *Testament* made it necessary to take survival training. I went to the National Outdoor Leadership School, which operates out of Lander, Wyoming. It was designed by Paul Petzoldt, who was, among other things, an Army instructor in mountain evacuation techniques, and one of the primary developers of current back-packing and camping techniques. The course took us into the wilderness for thirty-five days, where we had to live by our wits—only on occasion were caches of food available. The graduation exercise was a three-day trek over 150 miles—and that was as the crow flies—in the Continental Divide. We were left in groups of about five, without guides or food, just a map and a compass. The effect of this experience was that, on the one hand, I had a tremendous sense of the awesomeness and wonderful beauty of the wilderness. But I also learned that Rousseau was wrong. Man in the state of nature has to pay attention, has to live on the edge; he is constantly in danger. People die on these courses. The effect on me shows in my writing: whenever my characters move into the wilderness, they tend to be uplifted and more sensually aware than they are in civilization; but the further they are taken back into a primitive condition, the more they realize that they are getting to the source of everything, which is the need to stay alive, to survive. And that, in turn, produces the intensely violent things that happen in my books."

The "uplifting" effect of wild nature is seemingly transmuted into an intensity of experience that borders on, and indeed often explicitly evokes, the mystical.

"Perhaps I've read too much transcendentalism over the years," he suggests, "or maybe it's the interest in Zen Buddhism that began in college, but I am fascinated by states of mind—usually intense ones involving desperate action—in which a person's mind operates on a more pure, immediate, intuitive way than we normally do in civilization. One of the attractions for all my characters is that if the action becomes more intense, granted they are afraid, but at the same time their psyches are jacked up—it's like being on speed."

The nearly mystical perception attained by Morrell's characters creates a doubling effect that occurs too often not to be conscious. In *First Blood*, the sheriff actually sees what Rambo, his quarry, sees, in a manner that a traditional horror novel would view as a psychic phenomenon. In this and other books, the perception is a fundamental aspect of the reversal of the roles of hunter and hunted. "I can't get away from the doubling—it's instinctive. I am fascinated by the phenomenon of *déjà vu*—not simply the haunting feeling of having been here before, but also the fact that you become intensely aware of your surroundings, immediately involved, terribly conscious, reaching the kind of supreme perception we rarely attain. I use that feeling in different ways in the novels, not only depicting *déjà vu*, but also by having characters discover that they must face the same situation they have faced before.

They experience the definite, real recollection that it has happened before and now must unbearably happen again. And again, the repeated horror accelerates their sense of consciousness and awareness and heightened reality."

Although he talks about how rarely his writing frightens him, he admits terror at the central scene of *Testament*, where the journalist finds an apparent haven for his wife and daughter in a surreal ghost town. They meet an old man there, and one night the journalist listens in shock as the old man tells his daughter a story about an Indian woman who was sliced in half and then raped.

"The purpose of the book was to develop at its very centre an ultimate evil that would tip the balance—such a horrifying ugly thing that would be so stunning and revolting that it would tip a realistic novel into fantasy, where in a sense you had taken the last step, and now fall over into another world. At the same time, the protagonist is horrified that the old man would tell the story, yet the protagonist's occupation is a writer—a story-teller—and he slowly realizes that all of the horror has been brought down upon his family because of a story that he wrote. There are thus layers upon layers, and the reader, hopefully, realizes that, in turn, I am aware of the difficult moral position that I occupy as a novelist, in the way that I fool with people's minds, just as the old man and the protagonist fooled with people's minds. Yet try as I could, that point could not be made explicit. The plot was too strong for that sort of amplification, and every time I tried to write it in, it died.

"The trouble, then, is that you have a 'message' book, and however satisfying it might be philosophically, it might not be very exciting to read. And for me, the problem has always been how to tell an exciting story, while at the same time including ideas which I consider to be important enough that I wanted to write a book about them."

At the close of *Testament*, the journalist is transformed from hunted to hunter; but as he focuses his gunsight on the killer of his family, he finds himself incapable of pulling the trigger. Morrell refused to change the ending, despite considerable pressure from his editor, and his adamance may have detracted from the book's commercial and critical success.

"The formula, and the expectation of the reader, seemingly dictated a climactic bloodbath. And it was exactly that formula, and that expectation, that I wanted to question.

"Here, too, I hoped I was responding to national preoccupations. The year was now 1975. It seemed to me that we wanted to turn our backs on the nightmares we'd lived through, to rest and heal our souls. I found I was wrong. My fan mail scared me even more. Readers delighted in the graphic murders and criticized me for my hero's refusal to get his revenge.

"I'd written what I intended to be a moral book. Instead, I'd disappointed my audience. A complicated issue."

The western elements of *Testament* interested Morrell in writing another book, "an attempt at a new kind of western, one that was approached with a sense of experimentation, of distinctly developing the form". That book, *Last Reveille* (1977), is the most stylistically ambitious, yet least well known, of Morrell's novels. It blends fact and fiction, using as background Pancho Villa's 1916 raid on the New Mexico border and his pursuit by American troops under "Black Jack" Pershing.

The visual imagery of *Last Reveille*—and, indeed, of all of Morrell's books—is remarkable; one scene from Villa's raid is actually replayed from different perspectives. Film influence is obvious, and Morrell credits Sam Peckinpah: "*The Wild Bunch* is the movie that has most influenced me. Like *Citizen Kane*, it is a perfect example of what film can be about. I have been heavily influenced by all of Peckinpah's work, although he tends to indulge in surly brutality on occasion; even if his images are beautiful, sometimes you are a little disgusted. Those disgusting moments appear in my books, but he steps further across the line. I have learned an immense amount from Peckinpah—what a genuine artist he was."

With the elements of horror so pervasive in his novels, it

was inevitable that Morrell would turn to write a more traditional horror novel. After completing *Last Reveille*, he fell under the influence of Stephen King and *'Salem's Lot* "Steve had demonstrated that an original vampire novel still could be written. My thought was to use my tendency toward compression and research to write something truly different about vampires and werewolves."

The Totem (1979), one of the outstanding horror novels of the '70s, was the result. Research took Morrell to an anthropology text that theorized that vampire and werewolf legends sprang from rabies scares in the Middle Ages. "The theory has convincing elements. Wolves and bats are excellent vectors for rabies; the abhorrence of water, including the vampire's supposed aversion to holy water and to crossing running water, is typical of rabies victims, as is the aversion to light—and think of the appalling effect of the full moon, the brightest light of night, on the werewolf. The rabies motif of *The Totem* is practical, and not the essentially metaphysical and symbolic form used in David Cronenberg's *Rabid*."

The Totem is imbued with the terror of a community descending into chaos; it is the dark side of David Morrell's clear obsession with control.

"Once you've lost control, God knows what will happen. What civilization can exist without control? You would know this as a lawyer: the whole reason for law, whether it is good or bad law, is control. Certainly I don't mean to confuse legality with morality—what I refer to is the structure. I believe with Freud. *Heart of Darkness* is a terrifically important book for that reason, because only when you are 'out there' will you learn exactly what kind of person you are—and you never know, you might turn out to be a devil. The single element that separates you from the animals and makes society work is control. Repeatedly in my books, when things really start to go wild, the protagonist says, 'Wait a minute. Stop. Get a hold of yourself. Get *control*. A job must be done; therefore you must do it.' With stern motivation and character, you *can* do it.

"At least in our society, people have been making choices

that demonstrate a lack of control, in their lives and in their character. Ultimately, lack of control leads to a greater lack of control. This is the dark side. I understand the school of thought that says you must take risks, and that if things lose control, then go with the flow and see what happens; but the risks are incredible, and not for many of us."

Most of Morrell's major characters are professionals, and their business is violence or violent arts. Again, the question is one of control.

"Somewhere along the line, I began to divide the world into amateurs and professionals. Most people really are not in control of their lives. If you think of living as a business, most people are going bankrupt because they lack good business skills. But every once in a while, you meet someone really in control of his life, who knows what he's doing and goes ahead and does it—he is a thorough professional in the business of living. I find that kind of person impressive, and my novels stretch that idea. The ultimate professional in the business of living is the person whose occupation is such that if he screws up he'll actually get killed. So over the years, I've become fascinated with depicting people who have a violent occupation. Every aspect of their life has to be treated in relation to that occupation, so that they become a thorough professional in everything they do, because sometimes something so insignificant as taking a drink of water can cost them their lives.

"Beyond that, I am fascinated with the conflict I see in Zen Buddhism, which is essentially a contemplative philosophy, which aims toward perfection in the spiritual sense, but whose greatest hero is the Zen Archer. This is the man whose life is based upon contemplation, but who is also aware that he lives in a physical world and that he must sometimes be prepared for the kind of violence that happens in that world. This Zen Archer is then a master of military arts, and his contemplation occurs as he draws the Zen bow, which is extremely hard to draw, and requires a kind of spiritual concentration in order even to pull it back. Then he zeroes in on the target and lets the arrow loose, and in doing so is not only existing in a physical world and protecting himself against those things which would interrupt his contemplation, but at the same time, in the act of drawing the bow, is contemplating. It's a peculiar blend of the physical and the spiritual, and I've tried in most of my books to have what I call a Zen moment, that is to say, a moment when the heroes, in practising their violent profession, become so involved in the physical plane of defending themselves, of existing violently, that paradoxically the physical activity becomes a spiritual one. It is, I know, a paradox—how can violence be spiritual?"

Morrell can offer no answer. His own religion, he says, is nil: "I was a Roman Catholic. So I believed in guilt, and absolutely that there was a Heaven and Hell, that that if you did bad things, you would go to Hell. So I felt guilty all the time. I was an altar boy; I used to know the Mass, by heart, in Latin.

"Now I'm lapsed. I suppose I'm an agnostic, if not an atheist. In large part, it had to do with the shift away from the traditional mass and conservative attitudes to things like guitars in church and the debasement of other traditions."

After *The Totem*, Morrell spent a year writing original screenplays. "We had nibbles; in one case, we closed a deal only to have the producer renege. And after a year of writing, I had nothing to show but original scripts that nobody would buy. Mind you, I learned a lot about writing and about story construction in that year; but in a sense, I just threw away a year. So I came back, somewhat desperate, and wrote an espionage novel which did not get published. So I put it on the shelf, and then wrote the book which I think was the great missed opportunity of my career. It's the one I feel best about. It was called *Intruder*, and it was going to be a really horrific pursuit novel. I wrote a third of it, and showed it to several publishers, but nobody wanted it. They said it was too violent, its subject too grim. I was crushed, because I was sure that I was on the money. I thought about completing it, but then realized that I was in the same situation as writing all those screenplays. You can't throw good time after bad.

So I put it on the shelf. When I got to know Steve King through *The Totem*, I sent the thing to him and he went nuts over it; he said, just as I felt, that it was the best thing I'd ever done, and that it should be published. I continue to work on it, off and on. So far I've written over 400 pages. Maybe some day."

He then turned to a project originally titled *Stronghold*, which proved a major turning point in his career. "That I would use the espionage form should be no surprise, after my work with other thriller formulas; but the element of romance is something different. I tend to divide literature into two groups: classical and romantic. I associate classical literature with intellectual literature; it is extremely controlled, with few emotions, and form is of importance in a self-conscious way. Alexander Pope and Horace are premier examples of classical literature. Editors no longer want classical books; they want romantic books, with an intense amount of emotion and high reliance on the exotic. That trend is really incompatible with my way of thinking, but it is a technical problem and that always intrigues me. So I attempted to provide a solution. The age of the anti-hero is dead; all right, let me get a hero, and indeed, a romance. And that was the breakthrough, when I realized that romantic novels generate from romances, not in the pejorative 'boy meets girl' sense, but as the term originated in the Middle Ages, with Arthurian fantasies about knights in shining armour venturing about on quests. The dictionary tells us that romance is, from the Middle Ages, knights doing heroic things. A romance is a highly emotional story dealing with marvellous adventures in remote time and space. A romance is a love story. And I said to myself, I am going to write a book which has all of these things, but is set in today's world."

The result, *Blood Oath* (1982), set the stage for Morrell's best-selling successes in the espionage genre, *The Brotherhood of the Rose* (1984), *The Fraternity of the Stone* (1985) and *The League of Night and Fog* (1987). These books twist the conventions of the espionage novel into mystical and medieval romances, filled with Gothic undertones. And, as Morrell adds, "You will also find a sense of brooding horror throughout the books—let's fact it, I'm incapable of eliminating the grotesque from what I do."

Despite his recent success in the espionage form, Morrell continues to work in the horror field: a darkly sentimental fantasy novella, *The Hundred Year Christmas*, was published by Donald M. Grant late in 1983, and an increasing number of his short stories have appeared in such anthologies as *Shadows* and in publications from *Ellery Queen's Mystery Magazine* to *Twilight Zone Magazine* and *Whispers*.

Given his publishing record, what was David Morrell doing as professor of American literature at the University of Iowa?

"I taught primarily American literature, mostly courses in the novel. On occasion I taught courses in specific American authors: Henry James, Ernest Hemingway, William Faulkner. I also occasionally taught a course in modern fiction which included both American and European writers, such as Sartre, Camus, and Beckett. I taught no writing courses.

"My goal from the beginning, though, was to write novels—novels that would appeal to as wide an audience as possible, yet also would appeal to that sophisticated reader we normally call the academic. Anyone who wants a good read can go to the supermarket, pick up *The Totem*, and say that he got his money's worth; on the other hand, the academic kind of reader—who seems determined *not* to have any pleasure in the visceral qualities of prose—would at least have some intellectual satisfaction by recognizing that I am aware of the conventions and traditions, and I am playing with them, producing a quasi-anthology of horror literature as well as something new."

He resigned his professorship in 1986, recognizing that, at bottom, intentions and aspirations aside, David Morrell is a story-teller—and not by choice, but by compulsion.

"Writing is an unnatural activity. It is not natural for people to sit down day after day after day and bat away at a typewriter, making things up out of their head—particularly when these are fantasies. Most writers are writers not because they want to be, but because they have no choice: there is a compulsion in them that forces them toward that typewriter in preference to all other things. If I don't get several hours at a typewriter each day, I begin to break out in hives. The writers I know—people like Stephen King—write because there's something about them that is compelling them to sit down and do the work. It's something that I think would-be writers should think very hard about. There are a lot of people who are interested in being writers but who don't like the work. And there are other writers who have no choice— every day they type almost reflexively. And those are the writers who tend to be published, as opposed to the people who like the idea of being a writer but find the idea of sitting down to do the work very painful."

Has he ever felt the urge to write what his former colleagues at the university might view as serious literature?

"No, never. I'm not sure that I'm capable of writing scenes in which the action is slowed down for the sake of philosophic exposition, which is the principal goal of what I would call the academic novel. I believe so much in energy—that if you're writing a book, by God, let's move that sucker along. Try to do as much as you can in a limited space, but if all else fails, just keep that narrative moving. You can't do that and still do the kind of novel that academics most admire."

How was he viewed by fellow faculty members?

"Except for a few people, my colleagues perceived me as an enigma. They didn't know what to make of me. They seemed to think of me as this strange person who writes these odd popular books. They treated me seriously as a teacher but not as a writer, though they recognized that I brought some weird notoriety to the school."

David Morrell leans back with a smile; he clearly enjoyed that "weird notoriety" and the duality of his career, both with the glee of a successful schoolboy prank and with a more serious sense of accomplishment. We reach for the tabs on another round of beer and head downstairs. In his book-lined study, the manuscript of his newest book is stacked neatly upon his desk, in the process of revision. We settle comfortably into easy chairs as Morrell turns on the television, engaging one of his favourite videotapes, *The Creature from the Black Lagoon*. Outside, the sun is setting on Iowa City, and one senses a resolution to the paradoxes that are David Morrell—that here, on the outskirts of this shadowed university town, in a small study surrounded by the standards of American literature and of suspense and horror fiction, lit with the image of a stalking, eldritch creature, David Morrell is in his element. And a final question produces an apt confirmation. How does John Barth—about whom Morrell has written the academic study, *John Barth: An Introduction* (1976)—fit into all of this?

"John Barth is the other half. I wrote my dissertation on Barth because I respected him immensely—and frankly, because not much had been written about him at that time. His writing is quite unlike mine, but I honestly feel a kinship with it. I think that my book on Barth illustrates my comments about straddling the fences of so-called high-brow and popular literature. I can have a whole lot of fun watching *The Creature from the Black Lagoon*, and yet on the other hand, I have a study of John Barth on the shelf. When all is said and done, I suppose that what I have been trying to do with my writing is to find out what would happen if John Barth wrote *The Creature from the Black Lagoon*."

[Following our interview, David Morrell's teenage son, Matt, died suddenly and tragically, a victim of cancer. Morrell was shattered, and for a long time could write nothing. As a form of exorcism, he produced *Fireflies* (1988), a fantasia on his experience whose proceeds were donated to children's cancer research. He returned slowly but triumphantly to the writing of fiction, first with the award-winning "Orange is for Anguish, Blue for Insanity" (*Prime Evil*, 1988), and then with a novel, *The Fifth Profession* (1990).]

James Herbert

"You can forgive virtually anything—any perversion,
any nastiness—if it's really done with style."

James Herbert was born on 8 April 1943, in the East End
of London, the third son of street traders. His family lived at
the back of Petticoat Lane in Whitechapel—once the stalking
ground of Jack the Ripper—in a house that had been con-
demned as part of a slum clearance scheme. Bombs had
ravaged half of the street during World War Two, and only
gutted shells of houses were left standing. The ruins were
alive with rats.

My train ride south from London into the heart of the
Sussex countryside is uneventful but telling. The greys of
the urban centre soon transmute to the greens of forests and
rolling hills, and for miles, the railroad is the only vestige
of human life in an otherwise unspoiled landscape. James
Herbert's surroundings have changed since his youth; but he
has never escaped the rats that once besieged his home. They
have helped make him Britain's best-selling writer of horror
fiction—and also one of the most maligned and least understood horror writers working today. From his first novel, *The
Rats*, to his most recent one, *Haunted*, Herbert's fiction has
been identified so closely with violence that he is often
accused of writing solely for the sake of violence.

At Hassocks station, Herbert waits behind the wheel of a
shining black Jaguar XJS. He stalks forward to greet me, in
jeans and leather jacket, moving with the graceful wariness
of a bantamweight boxer sizing up his opponent. With a thick
East End accent, he doesn't hesitate to say what he "finks"

"I don't give interviews much anymore," he tells me. "But this is different. You're not one of these newspaper types down to do a job on me." We repair to the nearest pub for a pint of bitter, then travel across winding roads to his isolated country home.

There, we talk of his youth, drinking vodka and lime in an enormous living room that is a study in restrained elegance. He gestures self-consciously to the *objets d'art* that surround him as he evokes his East End upbringing.

"It's very hard to tell about my background without getting very clichéd. It was very poor. Very poor. My old man was an old pisspot—a gambler and a brawler—and he still is at seventy. He had a stall in a market called Brick Lane, and another at Bethnal Green. A stall is like a glorified barrow, with its own walls and a roof. And he sold fruit and vegetables.

"What we lived in was a slum. It was a very narrow street, cobble-stoned, only gas lighting in those days. Two doors from our house was a little alleyway where Jack the Ripper cut up one of his victims. Behind us were stables where they used to keep their fruit and veg, and it was alive with rats. We had two monster cats to keep the rats down.

"We moved into this slum because it was due for clearance, and we thought we would get a nice council flat. Well, they didn't knock it down until fourteen years later. So I spent fourteen years in that place."

But he is quick to dismiss any sympathy for the poverty of his youth. "Look, as a kid you don't notice such things. Everyone around you is living under the same conditions, and many are far worse off. It was great. I loved it then; I love it now, on reflection."

His first reading experience—and his first exposure to horror fiction—came through comic books.

"My oldest brother used to come home with these horror comics from American army bases. Now in England you didn't have colour comics in those days; they were just black and white. He used to get these terrific colour comics—*Tales from the Crypt, Frankenstein*. And he used to hide them under the floorboards just outside his bedroom. He would to take me to see all these old horror films, Bela Lugosi, and we used to sneak in the back way and sit under the seats and watch them. So it was kind of ingrained in me, all this horror stuff.

"I used to draw, because that was what I wanted to be—an artist. So I would spend most of my time just drawing and painting—and reading, of course. I used to draw comics—like *Frankenstein* and cowboy comics—and I would charge the kids at school to read them. My great hero was a cowboy called Casey Ruggles, in a comic by a brilliant American artist named Warren Tufts. It was violent, it was sexy—the hero in it even married his own sister by mistake. And it was very advanced for its time and beautifully drawn. I learned more about drawing by copying hands and feet and heads from this guy than I did in four years of art school. And what I was also picking up at the same time, though I didn't know it, was writing, because he used to write very succinctly and amusingly—very dry humour, this guy had. And I really did not learn just about art and writing, but a kind of attitude toward life, so that was one of my biggest, earliest influences. H. G. Wells was also a big influence on me. Edgar Rice Burroughs. Then, when I started really getting into horror and science fiction, it was Richard Matheson and Robert Heinlein.

"What I used to do was to tell the other kids stories. Just sit in the playground and tell them stories. And, in fact, they used to pay me to do that, too."

He shrugs and laughs. "I guess this is where it comes from."

We talk about the seemingly relentless need to explain the genesis of a horror writer, as if that will explain away his writing.

"I think people have to theorize about somebody who is in a category, whether a comic or ballet dancer or horror writer. They have all had this shock as a kid. I had none at all; I had a very good childhood.

"The house we lived in was creepy though. I was left alone

a lot as a kid. My brothers would be out, my parents would be in a pub, and so I would be there alone, sitting and painting. It was a very narrow, tall house, three floors with a cellar where the coal was kept—and we had a meter down there for the electricity, a shilling meter.

"At times I would be sitting there and the house would creak around me. It was very old; I mean, it was collapsing into itself. It would creak, which is scary enough if you are a kid. You're there on your own, and you're on a sinister street anyway, and you know there's rats at the top of the street, old stables behind you, and then, the lights would go out. And I would have to get a shilling, if I had a shilling, and go down to the basement, into the cellar, grope around in the dark and put the shilling in and twist the thing till the lights came on. There were no lights down there, anyway. So when the lights came on, nothing happened down there. And there were all sorts of things in this cellar. You know, a lot of rats. I mean, it must have had my imagination rioting—it was all getting ingrained down there, it must have been.

"Our toilet was out in the backyard. The yard was cone-shaped, with half a corrugated roof and a toilet at the far corner, next to this eight-foot-high wall. And it was so scary, no lights. There was this heavy back door down a flight of stairs to the open basement area. And when I was alone, I used to creep down there, just open that door, and pee out of it. I wasn't going out there in that yard. I mean, it was scary.

"But it was not an unhappy childhood. We had our rough times. My father, he was kind of rough to live with, although he was never bad to us as kids. He was a good man. Never bad—though he did take an axe to my mother once."

Herbert chuckles and assures me that we could spend the day with stories of his youth. "If you start from the bottom, you can go through all these things and live them and experience them and that way you actually know them. If you start at the top, there is no way you can go down and find out what it's really all about. You can only go up. So for me, as a writer, it's been great."

Leaving me in wonder about his mother and the axe, he launches into his schooling. After attending a local Catholic school, he passed a scholarship examination, allowing him to attend St Aloysius College in Highgate, "a rather plush grammar school run with strict discipline by priests. At that time they were taking pity on the East End kids—you know, 'We've got to get these kids out of that environment, and get them into these grammar schools.'"

At sixteen, he went on to Hornsey College of Art, studying graphic design, print, and photography; it was there that he became interested in advertising as a career. "Seems I was always in trouble there, but after the harsh regime of a Catholic grammar school, I guess I had to run a little wild. The good thing was that I was moving through a broad spectrum of people, still living among East Enders but mixing with old college friends and the art school crowd. It opened up my eyes and mind.

"I sang in a band in art school; I was the poor man's Ricky Nelson. I played a gig there, at the art school dances. I sang all these nice rock-and-roll numbers—Chuck Berry's things—and then a week after me, this unknown band called the Rolling Stones played. They made me look pretty sick."

After graduation, Herbert had a difficult time finding work; eventually, using the name and resumé of a friend who had job experience, he found employment in a small advertising studio "as a paste-up artist, paint-pot washer, and general dogsbody. It was a crazy place, just four of us in a loft area around the corner from the main agency. I learned more in six months about advertising than I did in four years at art college."

Two years later, he joined a leading London advertising agency as a typographer. "I did tell them my real name this time—and it was great, I never looked back. From typographer, they made me into art director. And then, at twenty-six, they made me a Group Head. I was handling about five million quid's worth of business in those days, flying all around the world. I loved it. But after a few years, I found the challenge had gone. I wanted to do something to expand whatever I've got inside me."

It was then, at age twenty-eight, that he decided to write a novel.

"When I started writing, I didn't tell anybody. Because I thought, well, it's never going to be published, and I'm going to look like a jerk, like all these other people in the office look, talking about books they are doing and not actually getting them published. So I never said anything to anybody in that year that I was doing the book. But once it got accepted, I really rubbed it in. I walked into the office and said to the copywriters, 'Morning, Hacks.' "

He worked then, as he works now, entirely in longhand, writing in a series of notebooks. "I can type a little bit, but I always think of myself as a drawer and painter, and therefore, that I am actually drawing words on paper. The connection from the brain down the arm onto the page is a good connection for me.

"I don't do drafts. I write through without ever looking back. Every book I have done, I've always wished I had the time just to sit down and write the whole thing again, because you can always improve. But I don't. When it's done, the baby is born and that's it. I read through it all once—the term I use is 'crossing out'. I make it flow a bit more, cut out the countless repetitions, and then it's done. The only thing I go on when I am writing is whether it feels good.

"When I'm writing, I'm not sure what's going to happen. Once I've done it and I am reading through, I know exactly what's going to happen and it's a bloody bore. So that's the painful part."

His novel was a pilgrimage to his childhood, and a confrontation of its paramount image: rats.

"As I told you, the street I lived in was over-run by rats. Big ones—monster rats. I mean, my cat actually came home bald once; he had been in a fight with a rat. And I used to watch them out the window. We always had a window open in the summer, and one day, the cat jumped in with a big rat in its mouth, so that obviously stuck with me.

"I came back from a Friday night drinking session, and I switched on the TV and *Dracula* with Bela Lugosi was on—where the madman, the one who eats spiders, said he had had this dream, this vision of a thousand rats looking up at him, staring at him, with red eyes. And for me, as an art director, that was very visual. I could see myself looking out the window, and a thousand rats staring up at me. And it all clicked."

The Rats, published by New English Library in 1974, depicted London under siege by monstrous, flesh-eating rats, their origin unknown, but their meaning clear: they were a personification of neglect, and indeed, of the political and economic system that allowed the slum of his childhood to exist.

"The whole idea was a kind of allegory of one man against a system, and this is what I do with nearly all my books. It is one man against the system. Now it's a system that we all know, that we have all come up against, whether it's political or the tax man or your boss. It's a system that's eternal and you are up against it all the time. I've always been up against it and I've quite enjoyed the fight. The rats represented that big system, which is not necessarily evil—but to me, it is, because it's invulnerable, we can't actually beat it. And that's why *The Rats* was open-ended: the hero won his individual battle, but the system still marched on. It still won. He didn't get rid of it. It still went on."

With one book under his belt, the notion of a writing career was far from Herbert's mind. "The senior editor at New English Library took me to lunch and tried to get me drunk, hoping I'd sign my life away. Luckily, I'm a handy drinker. At the end of our session, he was under the table, not me. I wasn't going to be pressured—I had no idea whether I could write another book. I said I'd have a go first, and if I came up with something they liked, then we could talk business."

One day, in the midst of a heated business meeting at the

advertising agency, a co-worker walked to the window. "And I thought, 'What would happen if you jumped out?'

"And then I thought, 'What if everyone, all over London, started jumping out of windows for no accountable reason?'"'

Working nights and weekends, he wrote *The Fog*, chronicling the effects of the escape of an insanity-inducing nerve weapon; it was one of the most powerful horror novels of the '70s, brilliant in its dark ironies and its breathless depiction of random violence.

The Fog was published by New English Library in 1975, and Herbert began to think of writing full-time. "Naturally, they wanted another book, then another . . ." After completing *The Survivor* (1976) and *Fluke* (1977), he left his advertising position, then moved his family to Sussex in 1978. Novels like *The Spear* (1978), *The Dark* (1980), and *The Jonah* (1981) established Herbert's reputation as a rough-and-tumble stylist whose novels delivered hard-hitting and bloody confrontations between good and evil; his readers adored him as passionately as certain critics, typically those who had read little of his fiction, reviled him. With the publication of his eleventh novel, *Moon*, in 1985, his worldwide sales totalled nearly twenty million copies; by the close of the decade, with *The Magic Cottage* (1986), *Sepulchre* (1987), and *Haunted* (1988), and an increasing American readership, he had doubled that amount. But that immense popularity has been shadowed by the extreme violence that admirers and critics alike have found in his work.

That link with violence began even before his first novel was published, when New English Library deemed *The Rats* as a "Nasty" horror novel, thereby creating an entirely new marketing category in England.

"Publishing was so tame in those days. Fifteen years ago, it was all James Bond, and the next spy novel, and another spy novel after that. But no gutsy stuff.

"*The Rats* was gory—it was doing things that had not been done before in the publishing scene over here. And Bob Turner, being a very shrewd and commercial man, said, 'How can we categorize this?' Soon every other publisher in

London jumped on that bandwagon and brought out all these other 'Nasty' horror novels. For Bob, it was a shrewd move; for me, it was something I have had to live with ever since. I didn't even know he was doing it—if I had known at the time, I would have taken the book away, even though I knew that *The Rats* was nasty. There was nasty stuff going on—the same is true with *The Fog*—but there was a lot more going on as well."

By the 1980s, the term "Nasties" had become pejorative in England, and the focus of a raging controversy about the censorship of films and video—and, some are concerned, books—in that country. Herbert roundly denies that his books exploit violence; he simply tells the truth.

"I think if you are going to describe an atmosphere, or a house, or a person, why fall short of the violence? Why don't you explain what happens if somebody hits you with a meat cleaver? Why shouldn't you explain exactly what happens and how nasty it is?

"It's the old cliché of Tom and Jerry: which is more harmful, the kind of violence that's in cartoons and John Wayne movies, or the violence that is explicit? To me, I think the Tom-and-Jerry syndrome teaches people that it doesn't hurt to hit somebody over the head with a mallet. You know, when John Wayne hits someone on the head with a rifle butt, there's no pain, they can be up in five minutes, drinking at the bar again. I think you've got to show that it bloody well hurts and there's no getting up from it."

He wrote two of his best-crafted books, *Shrine* (1983) and *The Magic Cottage* (1986), in response to his critics.

"When I wrote *Shrine*, I included nursery rhymes at the beginning of each chapter. We have all been brought up with these mini-horror stories from nursery rhymes and the Brothers Grimm—so what I am doing is nothing different. In a way, I was trying to explain why I write violence, why I write horror, saying I am not doing anything different, anything new.

"It's just more graphic these days. We have come to this period of our evolution where we need the reality to come to any truths. You can't fob people off with things like those shoddy old novels that used to get to the sex scene and cut away. And this is the interesting thing about the supernatural novel—that's why I think it's popular. Because the kids are thirsty for that knowledge. And if somebody comes along who tries to see beyond this life, to explain in some way what happens after you are dead, then they are interested—they want to know. *I* want to know. That's why I explore the possibilities. And the kids want the truth; they are grabbing for it."

Can the depiction of violence be too graphic? Are there limits that should be observed?

"I saw *Friday the 13th*, and it scared the hell out of me. I was really frightened—I had never seen anything quite like it. I liked it because it did scare me, on reflection. It was one of the first of the really nasty movies. And I was of two minds: is that film really bad, shall I just be disdainful of it; or should I be honest and say that it did grip me? But again, like the books, you get everybody jumping on the bandwagon and doing it badly. And that's the thing you can't forgive.

"You can forgive virtually anything—any perversion, any nastiness—if it's really done with style. And so many of these films have no style. So I don't like most 'Video Nasties'; I don't like films that can't involve the viewer—if only to the extent of having sympathy for the characters. I don't believe in showing blood just for the brilliance of the technique.

"It's an intangible thing with me, like looking at modern art: I like what I like. If a thing grips me, if I am involved, then I can appreciate it. For example, I think David Cronenberg works from the heart. He does some terribly gory things, but I think he believes in what he is doing, the same way that I believe in what I am doing."

The Rats has remained Herbert's best-known work; he has written two sequels, *Lair* (1979) and *Domain* (1984), but he has also stimulated a menagerie of emulators and imitators, from the occasionally entertaining—such as the "Crab" novels of Guy N. Smith—to the increasingly ridiculous, including such titles as *Killer Flies* and *Slugs*. His reaction?

"I quite enjoy it, although I don't actually read them. I mean, there's enough room for all of us as writers. It worries me only when other writers are not as good. People will pick up a book that says, 'In the tradition of *The Rats*,' and they will say, 'Oh, *The Rats* is the same kind of book as this?' Now that is not true, and it does denigrate my work, if you like, and that worries me.

"In terms of sales, and being successful, I shouldn't have to worry about anything; but I do, you know, because I write seriously. I joke about it. When not writing—that's when I am on holiday—I like to joke about things. But when I am doing it, I am so intense, and so wrapped up in the whole thing, it hurts when somebody criticizes, and you know that they are just judging you on the whole mess of 'Nasties'.

"My editor said the other week, 'You're an institution, so you've gotta take the knocks because you are there to be knocked.' I don't think I am. I am just this guy who sits in my study and writes all day. I don't believe the letters I get or the articles—that's some other guy."

Much of his success, as well as the wide-ranging imitation of his work, arises from the fact that his fiction has a unique voice.

"That's what makes me James Herbert—the books are written by James Herbert, nobody else. I am not influenced too much by film—not consciously. Books? My favourite book of all time—it influenced me first—is *The History of Mr Polly* by H. G. Wells. Current day: William Peter Blatty for *The Exorcist*. William Goldman. David Morrell's *First Blood* was a great influence on me because of its pace.

"Stephen King's words are golden to me. He doesn't influence me, because we have totally different styles, but I just admire his stuff so much. And I don't just admire it, I enjoy it. I get the same feeling from his books as when I used to go around Petticoat Lane searching out those Casey Ruggles comics. You know, there was a little bit of sunshine in my life when I got one of those comics. And it's the same when I get Steve's books."

Does he have an audience in mind when he writes?

"Only me. I can't think of other people when I write. I say to one person, 'Come on, I want to tell you a story'—this is it, very intimate. That's why strangers who have read the books feel they know you so well, because it's a very intimate thing. You are sharing a lot of inner feelings with that person. And it's always a bit awkward, because they feel that you should know them as well as they seem to know you."

The prospect of being typecast as a horror writer has never disturbed him: "Over here, you see, horror is not quite respectable. It's not respectable and it's not respected. But I don't mind being called a horror writer, because that's what I do. That's what I enjoy doing. When I want to do something different, then I'll do something different."

After his early successes, Herbert indeed attempted something different: *Fluke*, a fantasy about reincarnation. It remains his favourite novel, albeit his least successful commercially; it was also a lesson in typecasting.

"My publishers nearly fell off their seats when they saw the script. This nice, easy, humorous book—no horror, very little violence in it, I mean, it's killing the golden goose. But I can only work that way. And I said, 'If you don't want to publish it, don't do it.'

"The editor took me to lunch one day, and he had my manuscript. He started going from page one and right away I was getting mad, and then he got to page two and I was nearly overshouting that poor guy. And on page three, he had to go to the toilet. And I grabbed the manuscript and looked through it—they were crossing out and writing all over it, trying to make it into a horror novel."

We discuss what the critics and the gorehounds have overlooked about his books: the humanity of his characters, the strikingly ironic sense of humour, the instinct for pacing and structure. There is also a thematic pattern to his work.

"But it's not something that I talk about too much. Because I know it's there—and it's for the reader to realize. Some readers are just going to like the gory bits or the exciting bits, and that's fair enough. It's their entertainment. They pay their money, they get what they want from their books.

But lots of others have got the underlying message. I think the books are very moralistic.

"I had a discussion the other day with a local priest, who said, 'I'm a bit worried about your responsibility to the people who read your books. And we know a lot of young people read them, because they are into horror, the young.'

"I said to him, 'I bet if we were in a room with a group of teenagers, I could influence them toward goodness far more easily than you ever could, because they see me as an individual who is not too good, but he's not too bad—someone who seems to understand life.' They would listen to a priest, but there comes that turn-off point where they know that he's just there for goodness and goodness alone. He's not a man of the world.

"Now in my books, there's a strong moral tone. It is good against evil. But the heroes are not too good. The hero in *Shrine* is my favourite hero, actually, because he's a bit of a shit. My heroes are people you can identify with—they don't pontificate, they are not goody-goody, they're not wet, they are a little bit rough-and-tumble, but they do stand for the overall good. And they are the individual fighting for what is right. Whether it's against monster rats, a fog that drives people mad, anything, it is the individual fighting for his own peace of mind, if you like. Which is the right.

"What I did for a long time—I don't do it now—was never describe what the hero looked like. And that was always conscious, because I wanted the reader to be the hero, whether it was a man or a woman, I wanted them to be that hero. I didn't want to give the hero an image.

"It's right against wrong. I mean, it sounds very simplistic, but it's a bit more subtle than that, because my heroes are not goody-goody. And I do cry, I do get scared, and I do get hurt. So, yes, that's what I am doing, that's what I believe I am doing. And when people don't judge my books that way, that kind of gets to me—that annoys me."

He finds that horror fiction focuses too often on absolute notions of good and evil.

"In my books, some things are absolute, like the rats. They

are absolutely vicious, nasty, horrible; but there are greys in between—nothing, ultimately, is that bad. A lot of horror writers don't realize that. With the trash horror writers, it's just either good or bad—mostly whatever is bad.

"There was an old dosser who used to take me to the pictures when I was very tiny, about five or six. He worked for my father. He used to sleep in my father's stable, where my father had a horse and cart. Now, to me, he was a really nice man, kind of crazy, but he used to take my hand, take me to the cinema—my old man used to give him the money just to get rid of me for the afternoon—and then bring me home. This guy was put in prison for life: he's one of the last guys to get the cat o' nine tails, and he was put in prison because he chopped a man up with an axe. I think it showed to me that even in the worst sort of evil there is still some grain of goodness. It makes you realize that nothing is absolute. Even Hitler loved his dogs."

In *Shrine*, Herbert explicitly tackled the theme of religious doubt that had been implicit in his earlier novels, examining the effects of an apparent visitation of the Virgin Mary upon a small English village. Is he still a practising Catholic?

"I *am* a Catholic," he replies. "And I am—in a funny way— very, very religious. But I don't go to church, because I can't stand it—it drives me mad.

"There is something higher than all of us. There is a God, there is an Immaculate Conception, there is a Virgin Mary. It's good to have that faith, because it actually works, and overall, it is true. It's not quite the way we understand it, because we will never understand it, but it's not bad, there's nothing evil about it. Being a Catholic introduces you to the mystique at a very early age. Almost from birth, you are taught about miracles and this man who came from the sky. You are taught about the supernatural. And one of the things I can't understand is why the Church is so much against the supernatural, when the whole religion is *built* on the supernatural.

"You could preface every one of my books with 'What if?' In *Fluke*, what if when you died, you came back as a dog? In

The Dark, what if this thing that they talk about in the Bible, this darkness that befell the land, was a real physical entity? What if? That's all I do in my books. It doesn't mean that I believe in these things, although I do believe in life after death.

"After all," he repeats. "I'm a Catholic.

"The whole point about my books, the same as the religious bit in *Shrine*, is that it's all nonsense. The moment we, as men, think we can conceive what is actually happening out there, that's when we've got to be wrong, because it's too big for us. We don't understand it. We can't understand it. And I say that over and over again in the supernatural parts of my books.

"I believe there's something else going on and we are a very small part of it. I think we are going to go on to better things—I hope so. It's just a total conviction."

He pauses. "Well, yeah, we all have doubts. I mean, I believe in God. But, you know, I don't believe that this guy with a grey beard is watching every move we make and putting it down in his book and saying you're going to get your come-uppance. I don't believe in that. But I do believe we are all striving for something.

"I don't believe in the Church and what it teaches. I don't believe in the dogma of the Church. So you have got the two things: this great sort of naivety of believing, of having faith, but the cynicism of not believing in what man actually tells you it's all about. And I think that kind of parallel feeling comes through in the books."

As evening draws near, we walk outside, preparing to leave for dinner in Brighton. He gestures back toward the house, into the dark beyond the trees.

"We've got a big garden out there, which I don't get out to work on much, but I have gardeners who come in and do it. The only thing I do there, I've got a little tractor and I mow the lawn—and there's about three acres out there. And I hate mowing the lawn; it's very boring, so unproductive.

"But I sit there on the tractor, and I think about my old garden. It was about this size." His hands indicate a cone shape of roughly one hundred square feet, the size of a small bedroom. "That was my garden, all concrete. And I get some kind of satisfaction from just sitting there and thinking, This is great.

"But how come? Even to this day I don't understand it."

He talks regretfully about the time spent away from his beautiful home when the onerous British revenue system, which at one time took eighty-three per cent of his income in taxes, forced him into a year's exile in the Channel Islands. As he reflects on the price of his popularity, he remains honestly bemused about the reasons for his success.

"I write for myself, for my own pleasure—what I want to read. And luckily for me, people feel like buying it. Somebody said to me, years ago, 'How did you tune into the public?' It wasn't that way. The public tuned into me, just as they tuned into Steve King, just as they tuned into the Beatles and the Rolling Stones when they came along. And that's timing, lucky breaks, whatever you want to call it.

"The day I consciously sit down and say that I'm going to do this for money is the day I don't think I would be any good. That's what I worried about so often when I went into tax exile; I had to do a book that year. I was paid a hell of a lot of money to do that book. And I worried about how that would affect me.

"I am very insecure about being a writer. I don't understand why I am so successful. And the longer I stay that way, the better it's going to be, because that keeps me on edge, striving if you like. There are so many writers around who have made it, and they sit back and figure they can do it like clockwork, and the books become less good. They're not scared of it anymore. And I'm totally scared of the whole business. You asked what horrifies me—I should have mentioned sitting down and writing a book!"

The turf has changed—from a slum to the seclusion of leisured wealth—but for James Herbert, the rats that haunted his youth, and the system that they represent, have never relented.

"I am out of the rat race," he says, pausing to savour the

pun. "I am out of working for others, out of advertising, I am just doing what I do and nobody can touch it. Then the old system comes along, and it infringes on your territory. That's what I mean. It's always there, the system. You can win your own individual battles. But no matter how safe you feel you are, it still comes around.

"Which is why I keep doing it, I suppose."

Charles L. Grant

"I'm not the new Stephen King;
I'm the old Charlie Grant."

Charles L. Grant and I are sitting in the Manhattan Playboy
Club, trading stories over Bloody Marys. Outside, the July
heat has turned New York City into a walking locker room;
but here, in this curious male fantasyland of chrome and
cushions, art and artifice, all seems right with the world.
Charlie Grant has just struck a major deal with Pocket Books;
though he winces at their wish to call him "The New Stephen
King", he seems poised for the popular success that has
eluded him in more than ten years of professional writing.

On the table between us, next to my tape recorder, sit
copics of Grant's most recent books—a novel and two
anthologies—as well as a copy of David Morrell's *Last
Reveille*, which I've just loaned to him. Throughout the afternoon, the cotton-tailed waitress has restrained herself from
commenting on the obvious fact that an interview is taking
place; but as we ask for the check, she relents.

"Did you write these?" she asks, picking up Grant's *The
Grave*. "I just *love* horror novels . . ."

Her eyes scan the cover, but there is no spark of recognition.

"Are you . . ." She reads the cover again. "Charles L.
Grant?"

Charlie Grant's face brightens; he offers all three books
to her, and she smiles with delight.

"But you've got to *sign* them," she says.

"Sure," he replies, glancing at her strategically placed

name-tag. He borrows my pen and rapidly inscribes the books.

As she takes them back, she naturally looks inside. Her face drains of colour—my God, I think, what did he write in there?

Then she says, with clear disappointment: "Oh, that's my bunny name. I'm Bunny Melissa, see, but that's not my *real* name. Only you signed it to Melissa."

Charlie Grant shrugs—what can he say? But her disappointment promptly disappears as she spies *Last Reveille* on the tabletop.

"Did you write that, too?" she asks hopefully.

Charlie Grant looks to me, and for a moment, his eyes positively glimmer with deviltry . . .

Ironically, it was David Morrell who best summed up Charlie Grant. "Stephen King and Peter Straub are like the luxury liners of the horror field," he once told me. "They're always visible on the horizon when you look out over these deep, dark waters. But Charlie Grant—he's the unseen power, like the great white shark, just below the surface."

In little more than a decade, Grant has published sixteen novels and scores of stories of what he likes to call "dark fantasy". His fiction has captured the readership and praise of fantasy and science-fiction fandom, and he is perennially a nominee for, and winner of, the World Fantasy Awards. With his *Shadows* series, now in its twelfth annual hardcover instalment, and other anthologies—including *Nightmares* (1979), *Horrors* (1981), *Terrors* (1982), *Fears* (1983), *The Dodd Mead Gallery of Horror* (1983), *Midnight* (1985), *Greystone Bay* (1985), and *Doom City* (1987)—he is the premier anthologist of the modern horror story, nurturing and guiding the careers of countless new writers.

But like our disappointed waitress, Charlie Grant has a name that seems to work only for a place: in his case, the clubby and limited world of the hard-core fan. He has never had a major bestseller; his work has rarely been connected with film or television. In fact, his greatest popular—and financial—success has come under a different name, writing historical romance novels such as *Riverrun* (1979), *Mountain-witch* (1980), and *The Silver Huntress* (1984) as Felicia Andrews. Yet he is one of the best writing talents ever to grace the field of horror.

With his wife, Kathy—herself a leading romance novelist, and an entry into the horror field (as Kathryn Ptacek) with such novels as *Shadoweyes* (1983) and *Blood Autumn* (1984)—Grant lives in a century-old house in the rural north-western New Jersey town of Newton. He believes that the house is haunted.

The first of two sons of an Episcopalian priest, he was born on 12 September 1942, and raised in a series of small New Jersey towns. His formative years were spent in Kearny: "An immigrant town—Scots, English, Irish, Italian, and Polish. The Italians and the Poles were rich and lived in the north part of town; the rest of us weren't, and we lived in the south part. My father didn't have the stereotypical Episcopalian parish—he ministered to the middle and lower classes.

"As the son of a minister, I was expected to be good and wonderful, which I tried to be. Everybody knew my parents—my father was very influential in our part of town, and the teachers knew him, the principals knew him. You couldn't do anything without someone knowing about it. Once I went out on a date with a girl, driving the car with one hand, holding one arm around her; when I got home, my father asked where I had been. When I told him that I was on a date, he said, 'Next time keep both hands on the wheel.' Someone had seen me driving, and called to tell him!

"My folks were very strict. They were Old World‚Scots-British—it was that kind of upbringing. We were encouraged to read, but we weren't allowed to watch television, hardly at all.

"It wasn't an unhappy childhood, but it wasn't filled with ease and wonderfulness. We didn't have money. Because my father was a minister, people were coming in and out of the house all the time, so we had an image to maintain, and that was really hard. I wouldn't get included in things like parties, because I was Reverend Grant's kid. I don't think I swore until I was a sophomore in college—I was too scared."

Reading—and later, attending Saturday movie matinées— was his escape from the strictures of home.

"I wasn't like other kids—I couldn't just go out of the house and have fun. I used to read anything I could get my hands on. I never made a distinction—I read everything. By the time I was in the sixth grade, I had read almost everything that the local library would let me read. It's funny, but now, the only specific titles I remember reading are *Mary Poppins* and *Bob, Son of Battle*. Sooner or later, I settled on mysteries—Ellery Queen, Josephine Tey, and John Dickson Carr especially. I read tons of mysteries.

"My interest in horror really stems from the movies that I watched. In those days, Saturday afternoon was the time when your parents said, 'Here's a quarter, go to the movies.' The first nightmare that I can remember came after watching my first double feature—*House of Frankenstein* and *House of Dracula*, with Boris Karloff, John Carradine, Lon Chaney, Jr., all those neat people. I had such a nightmare. My father gave me phenobarbital—I didn't know what it was at the time, but every time I had a nightmare, I would get this shot glass full of red stuff. And I loved those movies; I went to them all the time."

He wrote from an early age, and completed his first horror novel while in high school.

"I was trying to impress Helen Dewar. Needless to say, she was a Scot. We were in history class together. I had this notebook, and I would write a chapter every few days and read it to her before class. It was about these hairy creatures, like mastodons, that came out of the swamp and stomped on people.

"She was terribly impressed; but she would never go out with me, though . . ."

Despite his interest in writing, Grant planned to follow in his father's footsteps as an Episcopal priest; in 1960, he entered Trinity College in Hartford, Connecticut.

"At the end of my sophomore year in college, I had taken three years of Greek in two years, Bible study, all of that. I had the catalogue from the seminary that I was going to attend. And I was in the bathroom, and I looked at myself in the mirror and said, 'Do you really want to be a priest?'

"I had always done everything that my Dad would like. I joined the track team in high school because he had been a track star. But I knew, then, that I didn't want to be a priest."

He shifted his major to history, and after his graduation in 1964, returned to New Jersey as a high school teacher. He began his first serious attempts at writing fiction in 1966, when he was invited to attend the meetings of a small writers' club. Like many contemporary writers of horror fiction, Grant began by selling stories to science fiction magazines.

"When I decided that I was going to try to write to sell, the biggest market was science fiction. I had learned from these various would-be writers in my town that I should study the market. I looked around: *Collier's* was long dead, *Saturday Evening Post* was dying, *Saturday Review* wasn't publishing fiction anymore, and *The New Yorker* and *Esquire* were cutting down. And I didn't want to write 'straight' stuff, anyway; it just didn't appeal to me. I was reading a lot of science fiction at that time, mostly contemporary authors like Harlan Ellison, Ray Bradbury, and Theodore Sturgeon, and I figured that I would have to write it; otherwise, I wouldn't sell. So—it's funny—I started to write science fiction, yet the first story I ever sold was a fantasy.

"One afternoon after teaching, I was reading a *Tarzan* novel—the one in which, at the end, Tarzan swings through the trees of West Virginia to save Jane from a forest fire. And I thought it was so funny that I went into my study and wrote a pastiche of Edgar Rice Burroughs, throwing in the most godawful puns I could think of and choosing the most trite title, 'The House of Evil'. I sent it off in April of 1968, after trying to sell stories for two years, and the first editor to see it bought it. Later that month, I was drafted."

He spent two years serving in the Military Police in Qui Nhon, Vietnam—an experience recorded in two of his short stories, but which he otherwise refuses to discuss. When he returned to New Jersey and teaching, his stories became a regular fixture of science-fiction and fantasy magazines, winning the Nebula Award from the Science Fiction Writers of America twice. His first novel, *The Shadow of Alpha* (1976), as well as four later books, were also science fiction. But he soon shifted his attention to horror: "I flunked chemistry in college, and barely made it through physics, so I didn't have much of a background in science. I was more interested in social issues, anyway, and when I ran out of ideas, I stopped writing science fiction, as simple as that. Because I was still watching horror movies, I decided that I would rather write horror. There was no one particular turning point; my science fiction writing just sort of faded away."

His attraction to horror fiction also arose from a fundamental sense of reality that he found missing from science fiction.

"You can't get much more divorced from reality than the supernatural. Yet the supernatural is a reality in itself—it's an added facet of the reality you think you know.

"I have never denied the existence of the supernatural. I don't believe in it, but I don't deny its existence, either. I don't know if there are such things as vampires or ghosts. I doubt it very seriously, but I will never bet my life on it. I would have to see one to believe it as much as I believe that there is a lot of traffic out there on the street.

"The best horror fiction deals with reality, period. The best horror fiction deals with real people in real situations that have another dimension tacked onto them. *Conan the Barbarian* is not real; that is why I have this terrible block against heroic fantasy, because its characters are not real people. They are not bigger than life, they are just not life.

"What you have to deal with is real fear, and all I do is translate real fears into the supernatural. I just give them a little shove off of the ledge."

After a forgettable first horror novel, *The Curse* (1977), he swiftly made his mark in the horror field with his novels and short stories of Oxrun Station, a fictitious Connecticut village whose peaceful seclusion is a locus for the dark, seductive promise of evil. Noteworthy for its strong female characters and atmospheric terrors, the series includes the novels *The Hour of the Oxrun Dead* (1977), *The Sound of Midnight* (1978), *The Last Call of Mourning* (1979), *The Grave* (1981), *The Bloodwind* (1982), and *The Soft Whisper of the Dead* (1983), as well as three collections of novelettes, *Nightmare Seasons* (1982), *The Orchard* (1985), and *Dialing the Wind* (1989). Several of the Oxrun Station stories, as well as other short fiction, were collected in *A Glow of Candles* (1981) and *Tales from the Nightside* (1981). Although critically acclaimed, none of these books was a major commercial success; Grant supported himself in his early years by writing romances as Felicia Andrews.

Through the Oxrun Station series and his editorship of the *Shadows* anthologies, Grant became the leading exponent of "dark fantasy", setting forth his manifesto in his introduction to the first volume of *Shadows* (1978): "What really frightens us, for the most part, is not all that we do not completely understand, but all that we do not *see* even though we know it is there." His "dark fantasy" is the gentle tale of terror—of "quiet" horror—"without the reliance on blood and gore, mayhem, ghosts, and the usual stable of monsters, both mythological and psychological".

He explains: "Stereotypical constructs don't frighten me. When I write about what frightens me, I figure that if it scares me, it must frighten somebody. I was thinking about this the other day, when I made a note in one of my idea notebooks. All it said was 'the power of love'. That's where much of my horror is based.

"Monsters have been killed by television, because they have become the known, rather than the unknown. The saddest thing I can think of is what television has done to the Frankenstein monster and Dracula and the Wolfman and the Mummy. That's really sad; those are great old monsters, but it's really hard to watch the original films, and really get nervous or tense or even a little bit chilled, because you've always got in the back of your mind those commercials and cartoons that have used the monsters—and *Abbott and Costello*

Meet Frankenstein, which, by the way, is one of my favourite movies."

What frightens him, then?

"Everything I write about frightens me. I don't send anything out unless I'm scared at the end—unless I get a chill and say, 'Ha! I loved that last line.'

"Everything frightens me—love frightens me, hate frightens me, loneliness frightens me. What frightens me most frightens everybody, and that's relationships between human beings; and that is, I guess, what all my stories are about—relationships. Those that fall apart or that never quite get started, or that get started and then are not what the protagonist thought they would be. That is very scary, because when all is said and done, that is what life is all about—human relationships."

In his advocacy of "quiet" horror, Grant has spoken out often against the trend toward violence and gore in recent horror films and novels.

"Violence," he says, "has the same role in horror fiction as it has in any other kind of fiction. Where it is necessary, you use it, and where it's not, you don't—it's as simple as that.

"Gratuitous violence is much more vile than gratuitous sex, probably because sex can be impersonal, but there's no such thing as impersonal violence—people get hurt, they get maimed, they die.

"In my books, I don't kill anyone who doesn't need to be killed. In the shock movies and the shock novels, people die to provide the shocks. There is no definite reason for the violence. *Friday the 13th* is just as loathsome as *The Texas Chainsaw Massacre* in that respect. The only reason for the existence of *Friday the 13th* is to show how many different ways the special effects guy can spill blood and gross out the audience. Well, I don't need to get grossed out. I can get grossed out by seeing a dead deer alongside the highway; I don't need to go to the movies."

"In the *Friday the 13th* films, by the time the fourth person dies, big deal. *Psycho* was so great—and only two people get killed in it. You think it's a bloodbath, but only Janet Leigh and Martin Balsam get zapped—that's it. Class is the difference between *Psycho* and *Halloween* on the one hand, and *Friday the 13th* and *Maniac* on the other. The first films have class and respect for the audience, and the second group doesn't care—they don't care about the people in the film, they don't care about the people who are watching the film. All they want is the bucks.

"The first group wants the bucks, too, but John Carpenter and David Cronenberg and John Sayles respect the audience, and they respect themselves. I really wonder if the people who made *Friday the 13th* have any respect for themselves; if they do, it's awfully shallow. I don't think I'd want to meet them. They are not my kind of people."

While condemning violence, he is equally outspoken against those who would censor violence, particularly on grounds of sexism.

"Anti-sexism is the current popular bandwagon, and I refuse to get on it, which is not to say that I'm sexist.

"I hate buzzwords: 'Chauvinism'. 'Male chauvinist pig'. Bullshit. Somebody calls me a male chauvinist pig, and I reply that I'm not patriotic at all.

"It has been a time-honoured tradition in literature and film that you have a weak or helpless heroine—and, from what I can tell of modern films, this attitude continues even now in this so-called enlightened age where both sexes are equal. What a crock. I mean, we're sitting here in the Manhattan Playboy Club. I can hear people saying, 'Oh my God, that goddamn Grant, he's going in there to look at the pictures of naked women on the walls.' Well, sure I am, what do you think I am—blind? Look at the beautiful waitresses—sure I am, and why not? That has nothing to do with sexism.

"My affinity for the women's movement begins with the idea that it just makes perfect common sense that if a woman and I write the same kind of book for the same publisher, we should be paid the same money. I do find it shocking and totally illogical that women are paid less than men for the same jobs. But I find it equally repulsive to have to face a fanatical feminist and watch every word that I utter for fear of offending her with a 'sexist' remark. Well, shit on that—a broad is a broad. Not every woman is a broad, but there is a connotation to the word, and some women are broads, just as some women are ladies with a capital L.

"I understand the inequities and I deplore them, and where I can, I try to alleviate them in whatever way possible—but I'll be goddamned if I'm going to say 'salesperson' when the word is 'saleswoman' or 'salesman'. No ideology has ever succeeded through an attempt to change the language, and this one isn't going to, either.

"So, having said all that, I don't see the sexism in horror films as much as the rabid feminists apparently do—I also see guys getting chopped up pretty damned good. Jamie Lee Curtis in *Halloween* was anything but a helpless female. And it's only human reaction when you're dealing with horror, whether it's supernatural or psychotic, to run screaming out of the room. But if the screamer happens to be a woman, people scream 'Sexist!'

"It's an overreaction, like McCarthyism. Constant cries of 'Sexism!', this bullshit of the Moral Majority—which frightens me more than anything else, even more than threats of nuclear war—it's a conglomeration of buzzwords and media hype, people's insecurities about themselves, and the fact that they haven't got the guts to stand up for what they believe in.

"It took me a long time to be unashamed to cry, and I do cry. I was brought up Old World Scots-British: 'Be a man, don't cry'—even if it hurts, don't cry. When I got back from Vietnam, a lot of things changed, and one of them was that attitude. If I feel moved by something, I'm going to cry—I don't give a shit what anybody thinks. In the Alastair Sim film of *A Christmas Carol*, when Tiny Tim dies, that is it—I'm wiped out. That one shot of the crutch all by itself at the fireplace, that wipes me out every time. I'm a softy—I think all horror writers are softies at heart."

For Grant, it is this sentimental element that accounts for the continuing popularity of horror fiction. Horror writers, he says, represent "the dark side of Romanticism", digging at the veneer of civilization to remind us of our indefinable but innate fear of the unknown.

"There are things out there that we call the supernatural now because we think that will explain it away. The more civilized and sophisticated we get, the more explanations we offer.

"But we're not as civilized as we think. I really believe that there is no such thing as a truly sophisticated human being. What we call 'sophistication' is all pseudo-sophistication; we are building defences around ourselves with those things that we don't understand, and we replace true knowledge with fast living and shallow study, which allows us to be very glib and to use facile quotes from Bettelheim and all those fellows, and to make it sound profound, when we really don't know what the hell we are talking about.

"It's like whistling past the graveyard. It doesn't explain why, in our house, we hear children laughing at three in the morning.

"A really good horror writer consciously or unconsciously understands that we're not as sophisticated as we pretend to be. It's one thing to walk down a dark street in the middle of New York City at night, because you know the dangers—there are muggers out there. Only an idiot would walk in Central Park at 3:30 in the morning all by himself, but there are also very few people who can walk down a deserted country road in October with the wind blowing and the moon up, and not get a little nervous. They know there are no muggers out there, but that there are *things* out there that you don't know about, and the best writers tap into that, consciously or not."

His religious views have changed somewhat over the years since his decision not to pursue a minister's life.

"I'm rather like Emily Dickinson—you know, the poem about finding God in the garden. If there's a God—and there probably is—you don't need to go to church to find Him. It even says so in the New Testament. So I believe in God, but

I'm not sure what He is. I mean, why did He let Reggie Jackson leave the New York Yankees?

"I'll tell you this. Sometimes I really believe that He sits up there with a two-by-four, and if things get really good and you get cocky, He hits you with it and says, 'Remember me?'

"I can never understand how people can believe in good but not believe in evil. If there's God, there's got to be a Devil—not necessarily the horny-headed type—because life balances. I think there's an opposing force."

When I ask what makes him a horror writer, he is unequivocal:

"Like I said, everybody is afraid of human relationships. People who appear to be the most open and the most vulnerable don't want to be intimate with anybody else. I don't mean that in a physical sense. They don't want to bare their souls because it makes them vulnerable, and it's vulnerability in every emotion and in every human contact that is the most frightening. Some people are more open than others, but nobody is totally open. This is what kills me about this California crap of pseudoreligions and pop psychology—'I'm OK, you're OK'—that's a crock. I'm OK and I don't give a shit about you; or, as Mark Twain said, 'Everybody is a little bit crazy except thee and me, and sometimes I'm not so sure about thee.'

"In the final analysis, nobody is ever totally open with anybody else, no matter how much you insist you are being that way, because you are afraid to be—you don't want to lay yourself open for a killing blow. I suspect that this is one reason why I have my most important relationships in my writing. My relationships with normal people don't always work, and I've been accused of letting out all my energy in my writing—emotional, sexual, and otherwise—and that may very well be true. If someone wants to know me, they'd better read my stuff, because they aren't going to know me otherwise.

"It's a cliché that writers are either loners or brawlers. I wonder if writers are emotional cripples—if they have never really been taught how to handle relationships with real people. What they do is work out relationships on paper, and they either idealize them or make them overly cynical; and maybe writing horror fiction does both, idealizing them on one hand and taking care of them very cynically on the other. I think that is probably close to an unpleasant and painful truth. One of my goals for whatever I have left of my life is to try to translate some of what I can do in my work to real people outside pen and page."

I ask him to assess his horror fiction.

"I've never reread anything I've written all the way through, not even short stores; because that's past history. I don't know that my novels are distinctive. My weakness is that I can't plot worth a shit. My strengths, I guess, are atmosphere and characterization. I can say without false modesty that because I sell, I must be good. I guess I am not great, because I don't make a lot of money.

"All I know is that if I'm not better each time out than I was before, then I'm in big trouble. And it doesn't have to be a major improvement—every story and every novel doesn't have to be a major breakthrough, but I've got to be better at something. If there is a distinctive Charlie Grant story, I would hope that it would be one that is not the same."

If he had free rein to write—and to publish—whatever he wished, would he write horror?

"In my secret heart of hearts, really deep down inside, I want to write a comic novel. But I'm not funny in print—I'm not funny in person, either. I tend to lay a bludgeon about; it's probably because of the kind of comedy I like—Abbott and Costello, the Marx Brothers, Laurel and Hardy. I would love to be able to do a Peter De Vries kind of novel, but since I can't—and I've tried—I just want to write the best horror novel that I can. I want to scare as many people as I possibly can—that includes myself—enough to make them want to read it a second time.

"One of the biggest problems with most horror novels today is that you can't read them more than once. I have read 'Salem's Lot seven times now, and each time there is something different that I missed before, and it is just as effective as the major scares that I had when I read it the first time.

"The best thing about the best horror fiction is that there is always more to the horror than the horror. There are levels to the good horror stories—many of them, deliberate or not—and that's what makes them good. From Poe and Hawthorne to Peter Straub and Michael McDowell and Jack Cady, there are levels aside from just excellent writing. Levels make books worthwhile, and I would hope that my books involve more than just plunking down $3.50 for a quick read on the subway."

But, he is quick to add, this is the very reason that his fiction is not likely to achieve bestseller status.

"My books aren't fast reads. I don't want my books to be subway books or beach books—they're meant for the winter night in front of the fire.

"They move slowly, because that's the kind of book that I like. Atmosphere takes words. I use a lot of imagery—too much, according to some critics. Nothing happens in my books, really; not a lot. But most bestsellers move right along.

"Horror fiction *is* the subway read. People are tuned to that by the likes of John Saul, and it is obvious from the fact that Peter Straub doesn't sell as well as Stephen King, and he should—he tells beautiful stories, but in a less colloquial manner than Steve does. Steve does what he does, the way he does it, better than anybody else—this colloquial, 'Let's sit down on the back porch and pop beer and scare the hell out of each other' style. Straub scares you just as well, but because he is more literary, people won't take the time for him. That is probably the schools' fault—not teaching people to appreciate literature, to appreciate reading more. It's probably the publishers' fault for not being more demanding of their authors. And it's the fault of the people who have bought up the publishers—Gulf & Western and the like—because all they care about is making money and whether an author sells a lot of books."

His assessment of the current market for horror fiction is

a pessimistic one. As an established editor, he sees more and more short fiction each year, and he is dismayed both by its quality and the lack of publishing outlets.

"I really like doing it, but I do read a lot of garbage. I get anywhere from 250 to 300 submissions per volume, out of which I pick anywhere from twelve to fifteen for publication. That's a lot of reading. There's a lot of bad writing out there, even from the professionals, who seem to think that either it doesn't take much to write a horror story—in which case they have no idea what they're talking about—or that I'm a pushover as an editor.

"The market for short stories is lousy, and it will probably stay lousy. Most of the newsstand magazines publishing horror stories have gone out of business. It's so chancy— they're buried with all those cycle magazines and surfing magazines and golf magazines and archery magazines. I don't see the short-story market getting substantially better in the Nineties."

His predictions for the novel market are equally dire: "I see it diminishing—it already has. It's not the bust that science fiction has experienced, but it's the normal shake-up after Stephen King and Peter Straub exploded on the scene and made it respectable, in the commercial sense, to buy horror novels. Publishers bought every horror novel they could get their hands on, and then realized that not every horror novel was going to sell. There will be less garbage novels now than decent ones. And that's probably the way it's going to be through the Nineties—there will be less horror novels, but they will sell well enough not to discourage the new writer. But the major publishers—the ones that will push the books—are going to be more careful about the kinds of books that they buy, not from a literary standpoint, but a commercial standpoint. And the ones they do buy will probably sell pretty well."

Charlie Grant has survived the shake-up; Pocket Books published his recent horror novels *The Nestling* (1982), *Night Songs* (1984), and *The Tea Party* (1985) in successively larger paperback editions. But he was quick to resist that publisher's plan to bill him, on the cover of *The Nestling*, as "The New Stephen King".

"I'm not the new Stephen King; I'm the old Charlie Grant. Not only is that ridiculous hype, it does a disservice to both of us; it deceives the public.

"Publishers are like TV executives. They think they know what the public wants, but they never really go out and ask. They are looking for a bestseller, and they ain't gonna get it from me. I'm not Stephen King. I don't write the way that he does; neither does anybody else. But publishers don't understand that no one else writes like Stephen King. They don't know why Stephen King is a bestseller. They're really confused as to why Peter Straub sells a lot of books but still isn't as big as Stephen King.

"I don't have the answer, either. Then again, I do: all writers are different. It's a fool's game for the publishers."

So Charlie Grant simply carries on, being Charlie Grant—a name growing in recognition such that today, when he turns to other projects that interest him, including experiments in writing comedy, he is cloaked by pseudonyms: as Geoffrey Marsh, he has written the occult adventure novels *King of Satan's Eyes* (1984), *The Tail of the Arabian Knight* (1986), and *The Patch of the Odin Soldier* (1986); and as Lionel Fenn, he authored the "Quest of the White Duck" trilogy of humorous fantasies, *Blood River Down* (1985), *Web of Defeat* (1986), *Agnes Day* (1986). With his newest horror novels, *The Pet* (1986), *For Fear of the Night* (1988), and *In a Dark Dream* (1989), he has published forty-two novels, twenty-three anthologies and collections, and more than a hundred short stories; and he has no plans of stopping.

"The best thing about being a writer is being able to do exactly what I want to do, get paid for it, and be able to live comfortably. I get to do neat things like give interviews.

"The worst thing about being a writer is the void that your books drop into. You write a book and it goes away; it's published, and then it goes away. You never know if anybody has read it, aside from your friends; and you are never really sure about your friends, because you never know if they are telling you the truth or not. So these things disappear, and then someone like you comes along, and I don't understand why. All I'm doing is what I like doing. I certainly don't make a lot of money from my writing, and I don't sell hundreds of thousands or millions of books, and I don't get fan letters. Felicia Andrews gets fan letters, but I never do.

"All I do is the best I can do, and I really don't see why that's special. I don't get it, but it's nice."

T. E. D. Klein

"There's something singularly uninviting about
a book that proclaims it'll keep you awake nights biting
your nails. Where's the fun in that?"

Evening has cloaked Manhattan; it is the perfect time to journey through Times Square, an urban dreamscape of bright lights and disquieting shadows. Stern-faced, suited businessmen mingle with panhandlers and prostitutes, while overhead, movie marquees are aglow for promisingly titled skinflicks and Italian gore extravaganzas ("Make Them Die Slowly!" reads one—adding, as if an afterthought, "The Most Violent Film Ever!"). As I walk this surreal borderland of fact and fantasy, it seems only appropriate that I am meeting T. E. D. Klein, the editor of *Twilight Zone Magazine*.

Klein and I have agreed to meet at a mutually favourite haunt, Hotaling's international newsstand on Forty-second Street – a cubbyhole for magazines, newspapers, and paperbacks from around the world. It is the publication date of his long-awaited first novel, *The Ceremonies* (1984), and Klein exits Hotaling's clutching a copy of the *Washington Post*, sceptically eyeing its rave review of the book. When I ask how it feels to be a *bona fide* first novelist, he shrugs.

"It should probably feel better than it does. I was walking with my girlfriend the other night, and she said, 'Let's see if your book is in the stores yet.' She took me into Doubleday; it turned out that she was setting me up, because she knew the book was there. She led me around until I saw it, over by the front counter—a big pile of *The Ceremonies*. And I have to admit, I got a real kick out of it.

"But at the same time, my thought was, 'How soon will it be gone? How soon will it be off the shelves?'"

This ambivalent reaction is typical of Klein: he describes himself as "a born pessimist—the kind of kid who, on Christmas morning, unwrapping the presents, would suddenly realize when I was half-way through that the excitement was almost over, and that there were 365 days to go before it would happen again."

Thanks in part to the pressures of his work at *Twilight Zone Magazine*, Klein has never been a prolific writer. With but a handful of published novelettes—"The Events at Poroth Farm" (1974), "Petey" (1979), and "Children of the Kingdom" and "Black Man with a Horn", both published in 1980 anthologies—he is nevertheless one of modern horror fiction's most promising and intelligent writers. The release of *The Ceremonies* has solidified that reputation, but Klein wonders at the cost: he worked on the book, on and off, for more than five years.

"I remember getting the original contract in July and assuring the publisher that I would have the book ready by September. And later I would aim to have it done by every Christmas, every New Year's Day, every April Fool's Day, every Fourth of July, every Halloween.

"It went through a number of different versions, both in outlines and rough drafts, and I made further changes in the galleys. I was literally revising the final page as the elevator took me up to the publisher's office. And as I sat waiting for my editor to come out, I was finishing the final sentence.'

His experience reminds him of a family story. "During the war, my father had a book that he read in his foxhole at night—a collection of Sherlock Holmes tales. And as the war drew on, he began to get very superstitious about it; he became afraid that if he finished the book, he would die. He told me that, toward the end, he would read only a couple of sentences each night, rather than finishing it. I sometimes think I had that feeling about completing *The Ceremonies*.

"Months would pass without my working on it. I'm one of those people who will do anything to avoid writing. Anything!

I would walk around the house in my underwear and I would read hi-fi magazines. And I don't even *like* hi-fi—I know next to nothing about music—but I would read them cover to cover. I would read catalogues of camping equipment and weapons and electronic gadgets. At one point, I got it into my head that I absolutely had to memorize T. S. Eliot's 'The Waste Land'—and then, that I had to read every book *about* Eliot.

"My friends would say, 'Hey, how's the novel going?' and I'd just groan. After a while, they learned not to ask. That book was like an open wound, or like some huge term paper that was years overdue. All the pleasure had gone out of it. I was just sick to death of the whole thing.

"It took years at a shrink, plus an investment in an early-model word processor, to get me over all that. But what really helped was reading a review of a best-selling Eric Van Lustbader novel that quoted some of its incredibly crude writing. I was encouraged by that. I thought, 'Jesus, if this stuff gets published and even treated respectfully by some readers, then I should just go ahead and finish the fucking book."'

Klein himself encounters more than his share of bad prose, because of his job at *Twilight Zone*, which often involves reading dozens of manuscripts a day, many of them by newcomers. "It can be curiously beneficial," he says. "The experience of reading something just awful and saying, 'God, I can do better than that,' sometimes stimulates my own writing. But more often it has the opposite effect: reading too much bad work makes me forget how a *good* writer pulls it off. It suddenly seems an impossible task to get a character out of a room, down the stairs, into a car, and off to the next scene."

Klein's susceptibility to the style of whatever he has read last has given birth to a superstition of his own: "It's that someday I'm going to find the perfect book. All I'll have to do is read three or four paragraphs in it, just to get the rhythm down, and immediately I'll turn to something I want to write, and it will just *flow*."

Has he had any luck so far?

"The closest I've come have been certain passages in Orwell, Updike, and Virginia Woolf. But the magic always tends to wear off."

Born on St Swithun's Day (15 July), 1947, Klein grew up, with a younger sister, in Woodmere, New York, part of the predominantly Jewish suburbs on the south shore of Long Island: "a fairly unromantic place with a lot of split-level homes. That's why going to college in Providence, Rhode Island, just bowled me over. The neighbourhood—Lovecraft's old neighbourhood—was so terrifically Colonial. When it snowed, I felt like I was living in a Christmas card. I still have fantasies of going back there eventually, buying one of the old houses, and just living out my days."

Of the years on Long Island, he says: "I would be lying if I said there was anything particularly awful about my childhood. In fact, it was a very nice one—very sheltered, very traditional, with more than my share of toys, ski trips, summer camp, and so forth. There was certainly nothing I lacked. But I'd also be lying if I described my childhood as happy. And the things that I write about, that still scare me today, are the things that scared me as a child."

He believes that the same is true for most horror writers and readers: "The press is always trying to make neat connections between an interest in horror fiction and various current events—fear of the bomb, the pressures of modern society, things like that. Personally, I don't think the sociological explanations make much sense. I suspect that the fascination with horror begins back in the playpen, right in the bosom of the family."

He recalls one of his own first contacts with the genre: "I was probably around five or six, and a friend brought over a magazine with some pictures from a horror movie—I think it was *The Creature from the Black Lagoon*. I was too young to have seen the film, maybe even too young to read, but I recall being terrified of those pictures. I remember that I didn't want the magazine in my room. I wanted my friend to take it back. But he wouldn't, because *he* was afraid!

"During my grade-school years, I had a voracious desire to read horror comics and to see horror movies—by day. But when night came, I would invariably regret this indulgence. I'd be so scared that I would have to keep the light on all night. I'd lie awake waiting for some kind of monster to come into my room—at the same time scaring myself with the idea that maybe there was a secret door in the wall behind my head, as well as something under the bed. It's crazy, because during the day, I couldn't get enough of this stuff. It was like the binge-and-purge syndrome.

"I wrote quirky, eccentric horror stories even then—stories about time travel and weird inventions and stories with simple twist endings. I grew up loving pulp magazines like *Amazing* and *Fantastic, If* and *Galaxy*—which is one of the reasons I've held onto this job at *Twilight Zone*, even though it's taking time I should probably spend writing. The money doesn't interest me, I just get a kick out of the job. I love the fact that I'm actually editing a genre magazine. It's the kind of thing I dreamed of back in high school, when my face was buried in those pulps."

He had no real religious upbringing.

"I think I'm a bit like H. P. Lovecraft in that respect. When I was four, I said, 'Is there really a Santa Claus?' And I like to think that when I was five, I said, 'Is there really a God?' And though I really don't remember, I suspect that, both times, my parents looked at one another and shrugged and said, 'Well, no, not really.' That was the end of my religious training, and I sure as hell don't miss it. I'd *like* to believe in all that stuff—I mean, a belief in God certainly provides solace for a lot of people, and the rituals must be comforting—but it all strikes me as nonsense, an institutionalized form of wishful thinking."

He is equally suspicious of "wishful thinking" in art— "things like *Close Encounters of the Third Kind*, which, as I see it, tends to Disneyfy the universe. It says, 'They're up there, but they're not inimical at all. They're really nice and sweet and cute and they *like* us'. I find it hard to accept that sort of thing."

Does he find solace, at least, in fiction?

"Well, I certainly don't find it in horror fiction."

What scares him?

"The actual nightmares I have are embarrassingly trite, like being chased by a bear or a lion. And even in waking life, the essence of horror is for me, quite crude—downright primitive, in fact. It's as simple as an ugly face. It's when suddenly the trunk is unlatched, the closet door is opened, or the trap door in the attic flips up, and there's a horrible face with teeth and a kind of leathery skin and staring eyes. That sort of thing scared me when I was four years old, and it scares me today.

"It's funny, because the horror stories I most enjoy reading are anything but crude. They're subtle, cosmic, oblique. They're by people like Arthur Machen, M. R. James, and, today, Ramsey Campbell."

Most modern horror fiction leaves him cold. "Even when the writing's good, the payoff is always pain, violence, cleverly depicted gore. That's what these stories derive their so-called 'power' from—that little core of sadism. They can be fun to read, but they're like pornography, they just fire away with both barrels.

"It's so easy to affect readers through the sheer awfulness of what you're writing about. Certain subjects are intrinsically powerful, even in the hands of a hack. I remember a professor back in film school saying that it's not very hard to make an audience sit on the edge of its seat if you've got two men fighting to the death at the top of a cliff; but it takes a truly great film-maker to make the audience sit on the edge of its seat during a game of cards, or a simple conversation on the beach.

"I'm no longer interested in simply being scared, or in scaring other people. Personally, I don't think I do it very well. My stories don't strike me as especially frightening; I suppose I'd be content if they just delivered a tiny shiver here and there, and maybe a laugh or two. And that's really all I'm looking for in other people's work.

"I guess that's where I part company with most fans of the genre. To me, there's something singularly uninviting about a book that proclaims it'll keep you awake nights biting your nails. Where's the fun in that?" (Ironically, Klein later shows me, with amusement, the quote from a *Los Angeles Times* review that appears on the cover of the Bantam paperback of his novel: "If unspeakable horror is your dish, take a whirl at *The Ceremonies*. You will never sleep too well again.")

"When it comes to scary movies, I'm an easy mark. I remember leaving *Alien* and wondering why my left arm was aching; finally I realized that I'd been sitting through the whole movie with my hand in front of my face! I admit it, I'm a real chicken the first time around. I closed my eyes so much during the remake of *The Thing* that I missed a lot of great special effects. The second time I see a film, I know when the creature is suddenly going to burst onto the screen, and I can watch."

What is it about the horror story, then, that appeals to him?

"I like the little shudder, the hairs prickling on the back of the neck, but I value more that certain feeling you get at glimmerings of something huge and strange—you know, 'beyond our ken'. Lovecraft used to provoke that feeling in me; now I find it more often in Machen. Certain images can actually make me get a bit misty-eyed. It's not really fear, you see; it's more a kind of awe. That's why I think I prefer 'supernatural fantasy' as a phrase to describe what I like, rather than 'horror'."

Klein first came upon the writings of H. P. Lovecraft when he was in junior high school. "I was the perfect age, I guess, because I was a complete sucker. I believed that somewhere people actually worshipped Cthulhu, and that the *Necronomicon* actually existed. There's a bit of that in *The Ceremonies* – manufactured myth that ultimately, I hope, attains a certain credibility."

His interest in Lovecraft was one of the things that drew

him to Brown University in Providence, Rhode Island. While there, he wrote his honours thesis on Lovecraft and edited the campus daily newspaper. "During my years at Brown, I was primarily interested in Lovecraft's fiction, especially the dreamy Dunsanian stuff, but lately I've begun to find the man a great deal more interesting than his stories. Like a lot of fans, I'm attracted to the personality you see in Lovecraft's letters—the hang-ups, the obsessions, the solitude, the quaint poses, the passion for the past."

Klein's favourite horror writer today is Arthur Machen, a Welshman whose fiction, written around the turn of the century, probed an everyday life interpenetrated by the mystical, almost sentient, forces of nature.

"What interests me most are really trivial little images, like light falling from a window on a tree branch outside, or the shadow of moonlight on a lawn. I don't mean to sound like a haiku master here; I'm just saying that certain little touches tend to excite me more than an actual story. You know, one of my favourite things in life is talking about movies—not so much the plots, which I often have trouble following, but specific shots and the feelings they evoked.

"It's something like that with Machen. All Machen had to do was write a phrase like 'the dark woods' or 'the bright and shining pool', and I'd feel a kind of excitement.

"I remember reading a memoir by the British poet Louis MacNeice in which he said that, as a little boy, he was obsessed with the phrase 'the green grass'. He'd found that simple phrase very evocative; it seemed to him, then, like a poem. I can understand that.'

"I had a very dismaying talk with my second editor on *The Ceremonies*, before it was pulled from Morrow, the original publisher, and given to Viking. She said, 'What the hell are you trying to do in this book?' And I wasn't able to come up with any pat answers, though I'm usually pretty glib; but I did mumble something about wanting to base the story, as much as I could, on certain phrases that chilled me—very simple, fairy-tale phrases like 'the dark woods'. I said,

'Doesn't that move you somehow?' And she shrugged and said, 'No, it's just three words.' "

The Ceremonies is perhaps the classic novel of urban man's confrontation with the dark power of nature. A Manhattanite studying supernatural literature takes summer accommodation in a rural religious community, and soon learns that both civilization and fiction cloak disturbing truths alive in nature. Klein comments:

"I'm not at home in nature. I'm the quintessential urban man. I keep kidding myself that I really love the country, and sometimes when I'm in the city, I'll long for this little house in Vermont that Bobbie owns, which is really isolated, miles up dirt roads that are impenetrable during the mud season. I keep telling myself that there's something so peaceful and liberating about this. But the truth is, I find it very unnerving to be there for long periods of time. My idea of going to the country is to go to Providence or Boston on a Greyhound bus; for a New Yorker, *that's* the country.

"I like being close to civilization. I like living near bookstores, and going to restaurants at night. I've occasionally gone back-packing with a friend—the White Mountains, the Wind River Range in Wyoming, the Pecos Wilderness in New Mexico—but I'll tell you, marching up a trail with a forty-pound pack on your back is about as much fun as moving heavy furniture up a narrow flight of stairs. And usually, after about half an hour in the wilderness, I have to fight off the panic. There's a sense of 'Christ, where am I going to get my Dannon yogurt?' (I've had coffee Dannon yogurt for breakfast for the past fifteen years.) I'm uncomfortable being cut off from civilization. My idea of pleasant isolation is to take my phone off the hook in my apartment and just hang around."

Klein has lived in New York City for most of his adult life. After graduation from Brown in 1969, Phi Beta Kappa, he spent a year escaping the military draft by teaching high school English in Dexter, Maine. When he received a high draft lottery number, he returned to New York in 1970 to study film history at Columbia University.

"It was a complete waste of my time. I don't know what the hell I thought I was doing there except sitting around watching movies and then bullshitting about them. I was on a free two-year fellowship, though, so I stuck it out. I thought I wanted to be a movie critic. My fantasy was that I would get a degree and return to Providence to review movies for the *Providence Journal*. But instead, I found myself despising most of the film students around me—solemn, wimpish types who'd spend their nights doing frame-by-frame analyses of cavalry movies. Whatever they saw, they loved; there was absolutely no sense of discrimination. They'd have made great Zen monks.

"By a fluke, thanks to a friend from Brown, I began working as a reader in the story department of Paramount Pictures here in New York. It was just three days a week, at the top of the Gulf & Western building; I sat reading novels, scripts, manuscripts, and treatments all day long, or sometimes just watched the ships sail up the Hudson. I loved the job, but I was terrible at it. I turned down—or tried to—all kinds of things that later became enormously successful movies, like *Death Wish, Semi-Tough*, and *All the President's Men*, and I recommended all sorts of things that didn't have a chance. Meanwhile, I was writing horror stories, occasional pieces for the *Times*, beginnings of novels, and failed attempts at movie scripts that are now sitting in my bottom drawer.

"*Twilight Zone* is the first full-time job I've ever held."

Our conversation winds up in the magazine's offices, further along Forty-second Street at its intersection with Second Avenue. *Twilight Zone* was founded in 1980, and serves as a forum for both original fiction and reprints of scripts from the cult television series for which it is named. The magazine shares office space with the men's magazine *Gallery*, published by the same company, but its quarters would no doubt disturb the fantasies of that publication's readers: they are the austere, maze-like workspace typical of the publishing industry, with only occasional pinups of entries in *Gallery*'s "Girl Next Door" contests to suggest the specific nature of the enterprise. Inside Klein's office, where framed *Twilight*

Zone covers and an array of humorous fantasy art erase even these minor traces of the other magazine, we settle in on either side of his cluttered desk. He pulls a half-empty bottle of cheap Scotch from a filing cabinet and fills two coffee cups.

The interview turns inevitably to his memories of the *Twilight Zone* television programme.

"Carol Serling, Rod's widow, who's on the board of the magazine, tends to admire most the episodes that showed a lot of the social consciousness. But I was watching when I was about twelve or thirteen years old, so my memory is just that the show was scary. Even when it turned out that a story had a kind of moral message, you didn't know that until the end. Like 'The Monsters Are Due on Maple Street': it may have been intended as a parable about mob violence, but that was lost on me. I was too busy waiting for the arrival of the monsters.

"I'm convinced that what was special about the *Twilight Zone* series was not, in fact, the stories. There've been plenty of other anthology series on television, and they've all had clever twists and ironic moral messages of one kind or another. I think that what made *Twilight Zone* different was the presence of Rod Serling himself as a kind of avuncular story-teller who would interrupt the flow of an episode by walking out onto the set, like a counsellor at the camp-fire who reminds you, by his very presence, that it's only make-believe.

"I never met Rod Serling—he died in 1975—but I did see him once when he gave a lecture at Brown. He was an extremely good speaker, very witty, and clearly not a saint, though some of his admirers like to picture him that way."

Klein finds the *Twilight Zone* name "both a commercial asset and a burden". He notes: "We're a bit constrained by the wholesome image that the name conjures up. I mean, we're dealing with readers who practically deify Rod Serling. One poor guy wrote in that he'd been in the hospital with an inoperable brain tumour, and that he saw a vision of

Serling standing at his bedside. The vision reached out, touched him, and bingo! he was cured.

"Personally, I wasn't the world's biggest fan of the series, and I seldom watch it today, but I think I'm the perfect editor for *Twilight Zone*. The kinds of stories we were designed to publish are precisely the kind I like best. I like—well, I guess you'd call them *winsome* stories, if they're not too cloying. I like happy endings. I'm a real sucker for sentimental stuff, stories that leave me with a lump in my throat. We tend to avoid really graphic violence and stomach-clutching horror. Although I've sometimes described *Twilight Zone* as simply a horror magazine, we specialize more in light contemporary supernatural fantasy. Our new spinoff digest-sized publication, *Night Cry*, which I also edit, is probably a better vehicle for straight horror."

Twilight Zone Magazine receives as many as two hundred stories a week, but in a year, it is able to publish fewer than fifty. Klein relies on his two-man staff to screen the slush pile, but ends up reading a lot himself.

"I'll tell you how I spent my summer vacation: with two shopping bags of *Twilight Zone* submissions in that little house in the middle of the Vermont hills. Day after day, just reading stories. And on those camping trips out west, my back-pack was literally stuffed with manuscripts. I ended up scribbling rejection slips in a little tent in the middle of a thunderstorm."

Klein's editorial work has given him an unusual perspective on current fiction. "When I was at Paramount reading my way through piles of books, I'd come across various articles about the death of the novel, about American fiction being in the doldrums—and all I can say is, the people who wrote such things just weren't reading widely enough. They were generalizing from just a few well-known novels. The truth is, there's terrific stuff out there.

"It's the same on the magazine. We have three times as many good stories as there's room for—not merely publishable stories, but memorable ones that deserve to be seen. And there's just no room for them; it's really a shame. Every day, too, I get a different artist coming up to show me his or her portfolio. I could choose seven different artists for each issue without ever going back, and I could always find good people. The limitations on the market are really a shame. Frederik Pohl once said that when he was starting out as an editor, back before World War Two, there were at one time nearly five hundred different pulp fiction magazines on the newsstand. Today I have writers saying, 'If you reject this story, where else can I send it?'' '

Despite the abundance of good material and a total circulation that, at times, has reached as high as 150,000 readers, *Twilight Zone* has yet to show a profit. "If anyone ever tells you how ruthless and efficient capitalism is, just whisper our name. We've been carried for the past four years by *Gallery*, and let me tell you, it's demoralizing as hell. Every day when I come in, I assume it will be my last; but then, I'm naturally fatalistic.

"Despite it all, I like to think of *Twilight Zone* as the last, best hope of contemporary fantasy and horror; we print more first-time stories than anybody else. Of course, we also feature name writers whenever we can get them, even if the work isn't first-rate; anything to keep the magazine alive. And you know—this is the discouraging part—our readers invariably write in praising those very stories as the best things in the issue. I used to think they were immune to the star system, but they're as snowed as everyone else."

There is a pause in our conversation; Klein refills our cups. There is something he has wanted to say, and now is the time.

"Something occurred to me this morning. As I was climbing into my clothes, I thought, 'Gee, I want to tell you something.' I suddenly thought, as I looked at myself in the mirror, that I wanted to confess something. And what I wanted to confess is that I really don't *like* horror. I'm turned off by most of it. You're including me in this book with a bunch of horror writers whose work I respect, in so far as I'm familiar with it, but most of whose work I'll probably never read.

"I remember looking at a recent listing of horror novels

that you yourself compiled. It was sort of like looking at baseball scores—and I'm not a baseball fan. I thought, 'Jesus, I wouldn't want to read one in fifty of those things.' I read horror stories all day at *Twilight Zone* but when I get home, I'd rather read a Victorian novel or a poetry collection or a book about polar exploration—anything but horror.

"Maybe I'm just feeling my own mortality; at any rate, I'm much less patient than I used to be. Now, when I read for pleasure, I'm looking for wisdom, good advice, information, a little bit of comfort, a refreshingly original point of view to help me get through the day.

"I guess it's obvious that I tend to have a pretty bleak view of the world. I see it, really, as a crusher of dreams—a place where most living things experience a lot more pain and fear than pleasure, and where most hopes and ambitions are ultimately disappointed. It's not a place I'd care to bring a child into.

"Let's face it, most lives turn out to be a series of sad little compromises—and all the time you're getting older, and eventually people are talking about you in the past tense. It all seems to go by pretty fast, and to no particular purpose.

"I suppose all we can do is try to alleviate a bit of the suffering, animal as well as human—and my sympathies usually lie with the animals. Though it sometimes seems to me that the simplest solution of all is just to melt the whole damned planet down into one great big ball of molten glass. I'm probably one of the few people around who were actually relieved when they didn't find any life on Mars. So much the better for Mars.

"Another solution, of course, is to just thumb your nose and laugh at the whole situation. I find this, in some ways, the noblest response of all. Like the hero of that Peter De Vries novel, *The Blood of the Lamb*, whose little daughter dies of leukaemia, after he's spent half the book praying for her— and who takes a pie, goes to the church, and slams Christ right in the face with it. Or like the TV commentator in *Dawn of the Dead*, putting on this earnest grin in the midst of all the carnage and saying, 'We really mustn't lose our sense of humour.'

"You can see why, feeling as I do, that so much horror fiction just seems beside the point."

Does he himself mind being called a horror writer?

"No, I'm comfortable with that, because it seems kind of unpretentious. I remember something Lafcadio Hearn once said—how he was not sure he dared woo the muse of literature, because she was so demanding, so he chose to woo the muse of the grotesque, because she's a more forgiving mistress. It's simply easier to work within a genre; people expect less, and it's a wonderful way of easing yourself into writing. It also gives you a certain tradition to react against.

"So when people ask, 'What kind of book is *The Ceremonies*?' I say it's a horror novel. I'm trying to be accurate in terms of marketing, and I'm admitting that it's just a genre novel—you know, the kind of thing that comes out in paperback with a lurid-looking cover."

Writing, for him, remains a "private, almost shameful" activity: "I don't chum around with other writers, and I don't think I could be best friends with someone who wrote precisely the kinds of things that I do. I'm not the kind who corrals friends and reads them selections from his current masterpiece; I just don't like to talk about my work very much. I don't really want to be part of a writing community— I had enough of that in college, reading stories aloud to the assembled group. I guess that's one reason I've come to dislike conventions.

"I still find writing fiction terrifically hard. I think I'm an extremely good editor of other people's work, at least when I've got the time for it—I can go through a story very carefully, making corrections, suggestions for revision, improving the language, weighing the nuances of the words, and so forth—but it's awfully hard work producing anything of my own. I sometimes wish I could just jot down stray little thoughts in a notebook, and that someone would be willing to publish *that*."

"In part, it's simply an act of recreating for myself—or

attempting to—some of the pleasure I've felt in reading other people. *The Ceremonies* is, in many ways, an attempt to update Arthur Machen; it's almost masturbatory, in that it's about the same things that pleased me in Machen. It's like a guy who has read a lot of porn sitting down and writing it himself, and finding that he gets off on it.

"But writing's also something I've been rewarded for and encouraged to do, and that's certainly important. I never expected that I'd be able to earn much money by writing, but now I see that it's possible. And sometimes I have fantasies that, if I gained enough of a reputation, I might eventually be able to do some good, especially on behalf of animals. You see, I'm secretly Albert Schweitzer!"

When we talked, Klein had just signed a contract with Viking, the publisher of *The Ceremonies*, to complete a novella, "Nadelman's God", for his collection of stories, *Dark Gods* (1985), and then write a new novel, *Nighttown*, for publication in 1986. It will be, he says, "a paranoid horror novel set entirely in New York City."

Will he finish them on time?

"As a matter of fact, there's a penalty built into my contract. For every month I don't get the novella in, I owe Viking $500. For every month I don't get the novel in, it's $750. And they also send some guy around to cut off another digit of my left hand each month, like the Yakuza.

"It's going to be hard to type after a while."

[T. E. D. Klein subsequently resigned as editor of *Twilight Zone Magazine* in order to complete his second novel. By the close of 1989, he was not finished. So far as we know, his fingers are still intact.]

Alan Ryan

"There is just not a lot of art without commerce."

"Some years are better than others," says Alan Ryan, "but I have to live pretty close to the edge, actually."

For the working writer, success is a relative term. It could mean a first sale, a fan letter, a first novel, an award, a story collection, a motion picture sale, a bestseller—or the mere satisfaction of having created something out of nothing but one's imagination. The implications of success are likewise varied. While a first sale rarely brings significant financial reward, its emotional impact may be unforgettable. A single bestseller, on the other hand, could mean that a writer will live comfortably for the rest of his or her life.

For the working writer, however, merely making a living by one's writing is an extraordinary success. A common assessment is that only five per cent of this country's working writers write full-time. The real number is probably even lower. Just ask Alan Ryan, with four published novels and more than forty short story sales.

"Even people in publishing are likely to say to a writer whom they know is a published novelist, 'Yes, but what do you do to support yourself, to make a living?' For me, writing full-time has been a very tenuous sort of success—you can never predict anything with any kind of security. You don't make much money to begin with, and you can't predict what you'll make next year, let alone two or three years from now. Financial success? It's in the hands of the gods.

"But there are other kinds of success."

*

Alan Ryan was born in the Bronx on 17 May 1943; he grew up two blocks away from the apartment building where he lives today, in an Irish-Jewish, working-class neighbourhood. He has two four-room apartments in the building; one is his office, the other his living space, although it looks more like a library, with books and videotapes stacked neatly on the shelves, the tables, the sofa, the chairs, the floor. He slips the ever-present pack of Dunhill cigarettes from his jacket pocket, and our interview, the first he has ever given, begins:

"My childhood was different from the norm, but maybe everybody would say that theirs was different from the norm. Everybody thinks that somebody else had the proper sort of childhood.

"My father died when I was an infant, and I never knew him. My mother went out to work. My grandmother, who was sixty-four when I was born, raised me like her own son and lived to be ninety. So essentially, I grew up in a household with two women, which does indeed make a difference. I certainly grew up bookish. I never had the slightest interest in sports or those traditional kids' sort of things. I once owned a baseball mitt, and once, at the age of twelve or so, I went to Yankee Stadium and couldn't wait for it to be over. It all seemed pointless—probably about as pointless as the books I was reading seemed to my friends.

"We didn't starve, but we were very poor. My mother was able to manage, on her secretary's salary, two weeks at the Jersey shore each summer, but that was the extent of our luxury. What extra money there was, she spent on me, so that I could buy books and records.

"I was deprived of a couple of things. I am an only child. I don't quite understand the relationship between siblings; I don't know what it is like to have a brother and sister, to have that kind of relationship, good or bad. I really don't know what it is like to have a father, or to be a child growing up with a father figure in the house. My male role models were some of the teachers, and Jesuits whom I knew as teachers, at Regis High School. And partly because of them, I am sure, from the time I was fourteen, I wanted to be a teacher; it would also put to use, as it were, my interest in books."

Upon graduating from high school in 1961, he attended Fordham University, also a Jesuit school, majoring in English. He graduated from Fordham in 1965 and moved to California, entering the graduate division at UCLA; he left in the middle of his second year. "I came back to New York and looked for a teaching job, because by then, I was so sick of being in school that I just couldn't take it. So I looked for a teaching job—which, alas, I found."

From September, 1967, to June, 1976, he taught English at a Catholic high school in the Bronx. In his ninth year, he decided to quit: "I was making less money than it was possible to live on, and I had great problems working in an environment that was not aimed at teaching. The Catholic Church is not interested in education; they do this to hold on to people. I had done, within the structure, everything it was possible to do as a teacher, and I reached the point where I just couldn't see myself doing this any longer. And there was nowhere to go—I was a big mouth and openly critical of the system."

He took a job with an off-Broadway theatre. "It was all very exciting and I was just thrilled to death and six months later I had terrible pains in my stomach, because I just couldn't stand it. The dream was shattered.

"I was thirty-three years old, and did not really know what I was going to do for the rest of my life. I was totally unfit to do anything that could be called gainful employment. I took a notion that I was interested in television, and I bought a lot of books, and I bought *Broadcasting* and *Advertising Age*, and I tried to read them. They meant nothing to me. I also knew that I was about twelve years too old to be looking for a job there—and it didn't really interest me at all. Nothing really interested me, nothing that looked like gainful employment that would not drive me berserk.

"I really just sort of drifted from December of 1976 to the summer of 1977. At that point, I was getting pretty desperate. I had no money. The woman I was living with, Virginia, was bringing in some money. My mother was helping me to pay the rent. And I realized that I had to think of something—and fast—to do with the rest of my life.

"Psychologists say that creative people often reach just such a crisis at that age, and, if the circumstances are right, such a person will literally create himself. This is pretty much what I did. After all, it was crazy idea to decide one day that I would be a writer, that I would be successful enough to make a living at it, that I would begin making sales very quickly.

"What actually happened is that Virginia mentioned in a casual conversation that somebody she knew had written something and been paid money for it. And I thought, Gee, that sounds like a swell idea.

"I had written some stories in high school, winning a prize and what-not, and during college I sent stories out to magazines and collected rejection slips; but I had no serious intention then of trying to make my living as a writer. Anyway, I'd done a little writing, so this looked like a possibility. And I made up my mind that I was going to do it; I began consciously writing for publication in August of 1977. Looking back on that, it seems startling, because that wasn't like me at all. I had never in my life been ambitious or aggressive; for the first six or seven years of teaching, I was quite satisfied, even though I certainly was not being rewarded financially and it limited my life a great deal. So this was a very unusual way of thinking for me, but once it happened, I knew it was the right thing."

His first sale came six months later; it was a parody of poetry anthologies, "Collected Prefaces", which he placed with the *New York Times Book Review*.

"It had been rejected several times. I figured this would be another dollar in postage lost—you know, what the hell. So I put it in the mail, and about two weeks later, on 16 February 1978, at about 3:40 in the afternoon, the telephone rang. A strange man's voice said, 'Mr Ryan?' and I said yes very cautiously, because I owed a lot of money to a lot of people. And he said, 'This is mumble mumble at the *Book*

Review'—that registered—'and we read your piece and I passed it on to the boss and if it's OK with you, we'd like to publish it. Now I'm not certain about the amount of money, and we'll have to talk about that . . .' And I said, 'Hold on, hold on, you have to give me a minute to catch my breath. You want to buy "Collected Prefaces"?' And he said, 'Why, yes.'

"I said, 'That's my first sale.' There was a long pause, and then he said, 'Oh. Oh, well. Hmmmm. What can I say? It's not every day that I speak to a virgin.'

"And the rest, as they say, is history."

He was then asked to review books for the *New York Times*, and he is today a leading reviewer and member of the National Book Critics Circle, publishing regularly in such newspapers as the *Cleveland Plain Dealer* and *Washington Post*. But his fiction career also blossomed when, one month after his first sale, he placed the first of several short stories that would be published in the science fiction field.

"I began by writing science fiction for a number of reasons. I read SF extensively when I was younger, and thought it offered exciting possibilities to explore ideas. Also, I wanted to write short stories—partly because I love the form, and partly because I didn't feel ready to write a novel—and the short story, of course, really only exists in the realm of SF and fantasy.

"I sold all but one of the SF stories I wrote, but I was never completely comfortable with SF. For one thing, I don't know any science and don't have much interest in it. More important, my stories more often than not had very dark endings, not at all the hopeful and positive view that most SF editors seek."

His transition to writing horror fiction was speeded when he took a part-time job in the menswear department of Macy's during the 1978 Christmas season. "I hated the job. But I made a few dollars, my girlfriend stopped complaining, and I survived by watching Christmas coming closer and bringing an end to it all. On 23 December, Macy's fired all of the thousands of temporaries they had hired for the season—

except for five others and me. We were the lucky ones. We were offered part-time work in the linen department for the January White Sale.

"I still needed money. I went to work selling sheets and instantly became convinced that I was in immediate danger of losing my mind. The work was stupefyingly dull, most of the time there were no customers, the temperature in the place was absolutely tropical, and the full-time workers were like zombies, content to stare off into space all day long. When customers did arrive, they came in hordes, all at once, and they had questions about sheets. Until then, I hadn't known it was possible actually to converse on the subject of sheets. They wanted patterns that were in the sales catalogue but were nowhere to be had in the department. They wanted sizes and shapes not on display. The stockroom never had what they wanted. They yelled at me, they refused to pay the sales tax, they demanded to know why the shipping charges were so high, they wanted to know why I was glaring at them with murder in my eyes."

He wrote a short story based on this experience—titled, appropriately, "Sheets" (1979); it was reprinted in the 1980 DAW *Year's Best Horror* anthology, and Ryan suddenly found himself a writer of horror fiction. "I didn't realize that I was writing a horror story. It was only when somebody called it a horror story that I realized that it did indeed fit into this category."

He had, by then, become close friends with Charles L. Grant, who encouraged him to move further in the direction of horror. Dissatisfied with science fiction, he soon wrote horror almost exclusively, gaining a reputation as one of the bright new talents in the short story form, and appearing regularly in a variety of magazines and anthologies, including Grant's *Shadows* series. His best short horror fiction has been collected recently in *The Bones Wizard and Other Stories* (1988).

Why does he think that he is able to write successful horror fiction?

"I suppose because I have a very dark view of the world.

I don't know. I feel like I ought to have a good answer to that question, because I'm forever reading interviews with writers who always have a coherent and carefully articulated answer to the question of why they write horror fiction. I really don't have one. I don't think in terms of a position. Some writers say, 'I would never write a story in which . . .' or 'I write horror fiction because my feeling is that there is a dark, supernatural world and it is out to get us.' I just don't think that way. Each story, it seems to me, is something new. Now, as it happens, there is indeed a pattern, because I have written an awful lot of stories that can indeed be called horror stories.

"I think there is a lot of nastiness in the world, and I think that is interesting to explore thematically. Evil characters are generally much more interesting than good characters—this is not a profound new truth. And there's a certain amount of fun in talking about unpleasantness and the people responsible for it. Hemingway said that the interesting thing to do in fiction is to take a character and put him up against the wall—put him in a critical situation and see what he does. And horror fiction offers some pretty extreme critical situations—extreme in the sense of being even more than life-threatening. It offers a set of conventions that allow a character to be challenged in a way that threatens perhaps everything he believes in—very basic things, including his grip on reality. I'm interested in seeing what characters will do when confronted by some ultimate evil—not something as trivial as losing a job or a girlfriend, the sorts of things that so much mainstream fiction is about—but really dark, unfathomable evil, evil that is cruel and random in the way it frightens and inflicts pain."

He also enjoys the demands that horror fiction places on the writer:

"There's no such thing as the easy way in this kind of literature, not if you mean to do it well. Stories of this sort absolutely demand the highest standards of writing, in creating strong, believable characters, a vividly believable setting, a powerful atmosphere, and a convincing portrait of evil.

If all these things are not done extremely well, the story is just silly.

"If you have all these dreadful, surprising things happening, and then you find out later that the lights kept flickering because there was a short circuit in the wire in the basement, the viewer or reader will have the feeling he's been had. Why did we take this whole journey if there is nothing there? And the viewer or reader is then forcibly reminded that he is in fact being told a story, and you don't want to do that.

"When you buy a book, you're acknowledging that you're going to be told a story. When you open the book, you've already agreed to be fooled—but fooled consistently and in a thoughtful and intelligent fashion. You don't want to see the wheels turning. You don't want to go backstage at the ballet and see how the magic is made."

When I ask whether he has ever been scared by his fiction, he puts me off with an anecdote, then owns up: "I guess it would be nice to say yes, but I really don't think so. I'm not sure that horror fiction is really about scares. I know it's popular to say that, and it's fun to have a really good scare, but I think it offers a metaphorical structure for dealing with evil—and in a larger, more traditionally literary sense, a metaphorical structure for dealing with challenges to a character. And I think it's the strength of these metaphors that appeals to me."

Despite his seeming emphasis on evil, a strong religious underpinning informs much of Ryan's work, from some of his best stories—"Following the Way" (1982) and "Pietà" (1982)—to his first anthology, *Perpetual Light* (1982), which collected a variety of horror, fantasy, and science fiction focused on the religious experience.

He summarizes his religious beliefs with a sardonic smile. "I'm a devout ex-Catholic. This is partly the result of having been brought up and educated as a Catholic; partly the result of my Jesuit teachers, who taught me to think and challenge and ask questions; partly the result of working for the Church for nine years as a teacher and seeing the Church's terrible indifference to the problems of mankind. I can't live with any institution that places its own interests and self-preservation, which it believes to be commanded by God Himself, above the interests of humanity."

Does he believe in the supernatural?

"Do I believe in Heaven? Yes. Do I expect to go there? Yes. A very famous Jesuit theologian at Fordham taught me one of the most valuable things anyone ever taught me—and it's a point easily made: if all God's chillun go to Hell, that doesn't make a great success of God, does it? His point was with reference to the distinction in Catholic canon law between venial sins and mortal sins. Venial sins are piddling little things. Mortal sins are literally that—they jeopardize the very life of your soul. And most of us simply are not equipped to commit a mortal sin, to commit an offence against God. After all, to commit an offence that was wounding, as it were, in some way to God, takes a person of tremendous size—and specifically, of tremendous knowledge. Father Gleason made the point that he was infinitely more capable of mortal sin than any of us sitting out there listening to him. And by that reckoning, the holiest man on earth is the one in the greatest danger of committing a mortal sin. And this all leaves me reasonably satisfied that, if I am careful, I am likely to end up in the good place.

"I occasionally do go to church—midnight mass is nice at Christmas—but the appeal is the ceremonial and traditional values, and the communal experience of doing something like that. I believe in God. I don't necessarily believe in the Roman Catholic Church's version of God, but their version is no more or less valid than anybody else's. I guess I am really a humanist. I'll choose the human value every time over some imagined spiritual value.

"I am very leery of theories and positions and all of that, and I think my stories show that, by being rather varied."

His career as a horror writer has grown "by indirection", he says. "Writing is not the sort of thing that has entry-level positions and a sort of structured passage to the top. It's a terribly disorganized business, the publishing industry, and writers tend to be terribly disorganized by nature—and possibly by inclination. So things just sort of happen."

A case in point is his first published novel, *Panther!* (1981), which he began in 1978 after reading newspaper reports of a phoney sighting of a great white shark in Long Island Sound just after the motion picture *Jaws II* was released. He wrote a proposal—three opening chapters and a seven-page outline—for a novel about a motion picture producer whose ill-fated publicity stunt looses man-eating panthers on Manhattan. At the time, he was working as a free-lance "reader" for editors at major New York publishers, providing written evaluations of manuscripts that were submitted for publication. When he did similar work for a literary agency, one of the agents was so impressed with his reports that she invited him for a meeting with the president of the agency.

"We sat for about an hour in his very impressive office, where I was mesmerized by this sky-blue silk ascot that he wore. Finally he looked me right in the eye and said, 'What do you want to do?' And I thought very fast and said, 'I want to get rich and famous by writing good books.' He smiled, leaned back and nodded once, and I became a client.

"I gave my agent part of a novel that I had been toying with, and she said, 'I can't sell this, it's a love story.' Which probably tells us a lot. Then I gave her the proposal for *Panther!* I knew it was impossible to sell a first novel from a proposal. But she said, 'I can sell this in a week.' And she did."

After completing *Panther!*, Ryan turned to his first two horror novels, *The Kill* (1982) and *Dead White* (1983), promising excursions in atmosphere that were set in the fictitious upper state New York town of Deacons Kill. Again, both books were sold on proposals.

"You have to have money. If you don't have the money to buy yourself the time to write a novel, then you are compelled to sell novels from an outline. Artistically, it is infinitely more satisfying to write the novel on your own. Working from an outline is like trying to direct the lives of strangers; all you have is stick figures moving on something that is no more exciting than the board for a game of Monopoly.

"You have an idea that, after a lot of thought, you decide is good enough for a novel. You get excited, and you start writing—you get a few chapters done, fifty pages or so, and you're having great fun. The characters are talking, they're becoming clear in your mind; you're getting tangled in what will develop into a plot. And then you have to stop and figure out where it is going to end, rather than how it is going to get there. And this bare outline is then sent off by your agent, and it's offered around town, and perhaps three months later, after heated negotiations, complete with hard feelings and bitterness, the contract is finally in condition, and then perhaps two months later, the publisher pays one-half of your advance. You are now six, seven, eight months away from your original excitement; and new ideas for other books are burning in your mind."

In 1983, Ryan wrote his fourth novel, *Cast a Cold Eye*, from start to finish, without a contract. It is undeniably his best book, an evocative mood-piece, striking both in its emotional violence and utter lack of physical violence. And it is the rarest of breeds, a horror novel in which no one dies.

"The experience of writing that book was extremely different from the writing of the three previous novels, and it was largely because it was not written from an outline. Certainly, I was more experienced—I had grown as a writer. But without an outline, I could let the book grow in a way that seemed natural; I could feel my way through it. I could let the characters act in a much more natural way, by letting them act in the writing of the book. I didn't feel the pressure to keep things moving at a rapid pace; I finally felt close enough to the characters to trust them to move at their own pace.

"I knew where it was going, and I knew what kind of crisis would be faced, but everything along the path to that crisis was discovered as I wrote. It was exciting."

Following the publication of *Cast a Cold Eye* in 1984, he edited the anthologies, *Halloween Horrors* (1986), *Vampires* (1987), and *Haunting Women* (1988), while also working on

Quadriphobia (1986), a collection of four horror novellas written in different genres—hard-boiled detective, western, romantic suspense, and jungle adventure—and *The Coffin Chronicles*, a generational saga spanning eighty-five years in the life of a family uniquely susceptible to vampirism, and thus dedicated to fighting vampires.

All of these books were sold on proposals. Despite the critical success of *Cast a Cold Eye*—and a substantial paperback printing—its economic impact was sufficient only to buy him a little more time to write.

"Let me give you some figures. When I signed my contract to teach for my first year, and this was in the spring of 1967—so anybody who cares to can adjust accordingly for inflation—my salary was $5,000, and that didn't seem so terrible to me. That summer, the salary scale was raised, and when I actually began teaching in September, my salary was the magnificent sum of $5,300, and I thought I was living pretty high on the hog. Nine years later, in 1975–76, my salary was $10,900. For my first full year of writing, in 1978, I think I made $1,200, maybe $2,000 in the following year. For *Panther!*, I was paid double the going rate for that kind of book—you know, giant bugs and crabs. I got $6,000. I have done rather better since, but do I feel financially secure? Nothing of the sort.

"In terms of knowing or even being able to begin to guess at what I might be making in the current tax year or next year or the year after that, I couldn't. I entertain myself with the notion of feeling reasonably secure in the knowledge that I will think of something—that, when the chips are down, I will think of something. I will always have ideas and I expect I will always be able to sell books.

"But I have no sense of security, nothing like the sense one would have in a regular job. I hear some writers talk about how they won't sell another book to such-and-such a publisher. It doesn't seem possible to me for a writer to talk that way with any grasp of reality. This is the order of thinking in those handbooks designed for beginning writers, which always have a chapter entitled 'How to Choose a Publisher'.

You don't choose a publisher, unless you are a brand-name author. You offer a book for sale, and you hope that an editor and publisher of your liking will like the project as much as you do.

"The satisfactions and rewards are elsewhere. The reward is in knowing that you have written as well as you know how to; and of being master of your own fate, and being self-employed."

Would he continue writing horror fiction if it were not selling?

"I would be very hard put to answer that. If I weren't selling, I'd have to go back to work at Macy's, and that wouldn't leave me a great deal of time or energy in which to write.

"You know, there's a total misconception out there about what it means to be a writer. Sometimes people will say to me, 'Oh, I'm a writer, too.' And I ask, 'Oh, really? What have you written?' And they say, 'I keep a diary.'

"I make my living as a writer. And any writer who tells you that this doesn't matter to him is lying to you.

"I suppose that it is entirely conceivable that, if I could no longer sell, maybe I would stop writing or continue to write only in a small way; but writing is a means of communication. If you are writing for your own amusement, that's all very well. But that's not writing the way that a professional writer writes. A professional writer writes in order to be read, and the satisfaction comes when a large number of people read what you write, because one gets some sense that you have communicated with somebody."

He pauses, shaking his head. "But there's a great deal of misconception. At a recent World Fantasy Convention, a fan told me how much he had enjoyed *Cast a Cold Eye*, which is set in Ireland. And he went on at some length, some very pleasing length, as had a number of reviewers, praising the believable setting and atmosphere of the book. And then he said, 'How long did you live there?'

"I said, 'I never lived there. I have *been* there once.' And he said, 'Oh, you must have been there quite a while.' And

I said, 'No, I was there actually eleven days.' And he was horrified; he went off, visibly in a huff—he thought he had been made a fool of.

"Well, when he put his money down to buy the book, he was asking me to entertain him. To tell him a story. I'm a writer, I make up stories—that is my business. It seems to me that if he wanted to be a really decent fellow, he would have been all the more impressed that I could convey the sense of place to him and convince him so effectively after having been there only eleven days.

"I don't know how he would have felt if he knew that I had only stayed in the specific setting of the book overnight."

The misconceptions, Ryan says, are also held by other writers who pay no attention to the business side of their work.

"It is the obligation of the writer to learn his business. I work very hard on what I write, and I want to see that it is treated commercially, in a business sense, with the same degree of care and concern that I put into it when I'm sitting in front of my keyboard. I am very impatient with writers who don't know what is in their book contracts. Or say that that's their agent's job. It's *their* job; the agent works for the writer, and the writer has nobody else to answer to but himself.

"There is just not a lot of art without commerce. I'm always tempted, when talking about anything like this, to remind people that the concept of art is a relatively new one in the history of mankind. It's a nineteenth-century concept; until the early nineteenth century, there was no such concept as art. There was craft. Bach didn't pick up his pen—and Michelangelo didn't pick up his chisel—until money had been laid on the table. It was work designed for a purpose: music to be played in your garden while your guests drank wine, or to be played at church and to elevate the spirit and to let all the other churches see that this church was better and therefore closer to God. A sculpture was work designed to elevate one's stature and decorate one's Florentine mansion in a more lavish fashion than somebody else's Florentine mansion.

"Some of it was so well crafted and so informed by the intelligence and sensitivity of the artisan that it has stood the proverbial test of time, and we now label it as art. Shakespeare had no sense that he was a great playwright, that he was creating art; it's only through the merest happenstance that his plays even survived. They survived not because some editor or literary society thought they were great art and worth preserving, but because some old friends put a collection of his plays together—an unheard-of thing at the time—as a tribute to someone who was good at what he did. Shakespeare was interested in making money, not art; and, indeed, he retired and bought the best house in town.

"The notion of an independent artist is a very modern concept, and leads people to live in cold garrets. I don't think very good art is made in cold garrets."

Horror fiction, he stressed, is a popular form of literature, intended first and foremost as entertainment.

"I consider myself, above all else, an entertainer. If I don't entertain the reader, and keep him entertained, I lose him. I have no desire to write 'literary' novels that are read by two thousand people and then lost to oblivion. I do not believe that good writing and the bestseller lists are incompatible. The more people I can reach—by writing well and thoughtfully in a popular form—the happier I'll be.

"I have no patience with academic novels and with all the whiny women who write them—Anne Tyler and that sort. The world doesn't need another novel about a college professor who is always in either the English or the Art department, who is married and has two children and a cocker spaniel but who is having an affair with one of his graduate students and it changes his life.

"Story-telling is just that: story-telling. If I want an introspective study of my deep inner feelings about art or something, I'd rather read an essay that's honestly labelled as such than an essay fitted out as a short story. So-called 'literary' writers have forgotten what stories are about, and what they produce is nothing more than masturbation. They're amusing no one but themselves and their inner circle. And that's not why people have the talent to write.

"I don't think it's embarrassing to make money. I don't think it's embarrassing to be on the bestseller list. I don't think it's embarrassing to be popular."

He lights another cigarette; it is time for us to quit. We talk about his future projects, and his sense of frustration is clear. "Each time I find something interesting, I want to do something with it, touch it somehow, react to it, respond to it in written form. Maybe that's how the writer's mind works, responding to the real world."

He is anxious to return to his book in progress, *The Coffin Chronicles*, not simply because new ideas are waiting, but also because of a new sense of ambition.

"I remember once watching *Gone with the Wind*, and it came to the end of the first part, right before the intermission, where Scarlett O'Hara is silhouetted against a blazing red sky, and she raises her fist and says, 'I'll never be hungry again.' And I thought, 'This is corny and tacky . . . and wonderful.' The grand gesture. I think that any writer has to go for that, to risk that.

"I have a recording of Jascha Heifetz playing the Prokofiev Violin Concerto—the articulation of notes is so precise and clear that the first time you hear it, it's hair-raising. To see a dancer like Nureyev—there's tremendous risk in what he does; he doesn't always succeed in a combination of steps, but the attempt itself is exciting.

"And to go beyond that, to spill over into tacky, yes, but effective. I've been a fan of professional wrestling for years now, precisely because of the exaggerated drama, the boldness of its colours, and the sheer *size* of its characters. Or take the scene in the funeral parlour in *Pet Sematary*, where the father gets into a fight and the coffin is knocked over. Is this tacky? Absolutely. But it's *unbelievable*—it's exciting, it's entertaining. And writing novels is entertainment, nothing else.

"This sense of risk is essential to any artist, and I've been slow to learn it; I've been reticent in my early years of writing. But now I have a better sense for the creating of drama."

He talks with enthusiasm about the opening chapter of *The Coffin Chronicles:* "In the first chapter—a birth, a death, a vampire, and a howling blizzard."

Then he pauses, gladly acknowledging the risk:

"Whether it's tacky, whether it's successful, remains to be seen."

[It does indeed remain to be seen. After an ill-fated marriage, Alan Ryan withdrew from the writing of horror fiction and has not completed *The Coffin Chronicles*. He writes occasional travel articles and regularly reviews the music and books of Africa, the Caribbean and South America].

John Coyne

"Publishing has nothing to do with literature;
it concerns commodities."

John Coyne is leaving horror fiction.

He announces his intent in a matter-of-fact tone, sitting across from my wife, Lynne, and me at Dobson's, a restaurant near his Manhattan apartment on the Upper West Side.

We had first met at a reception a few years before, when Lynne, startled, pointed him out across the crowded room; he was a virtual *doppelgänger* of a friend who had died that spring when Air Florida Flight 90 plummeted into the Potomac. He was sitting alone at the bar, and we struck up a conversation that lasted for hours, talking about travel, restaurants, life in Washington, DC—a welcome relief from the usual publishing small talk. In his mid-forties, his dark hair and beard salted with white, John Coyne seemed withdrawn, out of place, in that gathering of horror writers. Today, it comes as no real surprise that he has decided to leave the field after but a few years.

In 1979, he became one of horror's most well-known "brand names" with the one-two punch in paperback of his first novel, *The Piercing*, and his novelization of the motion picture *The Legacy*. That success was a long time coming: writing is his sixth career. Born on 10 October 1937, the youngest of six children, he grew up on a farm south of Chicago, dreaming of becoming a professional golfer. He was, and is, dyslexic: "In those days, they just thought you were dumb. I didn't start reading until very late."

At age eleven, he discovered Daphne du Maurier's *Rebecca*.

"When I read that first paragraph, that romantic language, I thought that to be able to write like that is power and that, therefore, someone who writes like that is powerful. So I decided to write—that was it. On weekends, I started writing. I wrote for the high school newspaper, the usual stuff. At St Louis University, I met a professor named Albert Montesi, who was a great enthusiast for literature. I started writing seriously then, but I had no success."

After college, he entered the Peace Corps, then attended graduate school at Western Michigan University, where he received a master's degree in English. "Then I went into the Peace Corps again and wrote a novel. I went to Spain and wrote another novel. Then I took other jobs to survive. I worked for the government, I was the dean of a college, all sorts of things, until 1971, when I finally decided to write full-time. I wrote some short stories for *Ellery Queen* and *Alfred Hitchcock* magazines and a lot of novels that were not published. Then I wrote several non-fiction books on alternative education that were published and were successful in a limited way."

Intent on making a living through his writing, he approached his next fiction project with unabashed commercialism.

"I wrote *The Piercing* because I wanted to write a book that already had a built-in audience. I had written six other novels that hadn't been published, so I sat down and looked at predetermined categories like the CIA-Washington novel, the romance novel, the detective, the western."

The increasing popularity of the horror novel proved irresistible: "I had known the story behind *The Exorcist* before it was a novel, when I was at St Louis University. I wasn't smart enough then to realize that it was a great idea for a novel. Blatty was ahead of the game—and it was a very good novel, a well-constructed, well-written book that deserved everything it got. But it's also more than just a scary story. It came out at a time when women were saying, 'I don't want to take care of the kids. I want to get out and work. I want my freedom.' And it's an anti-feminist book because it says that if you go on your own and try to have a career, look what's going to happen to your kid."

"I had just written a hundred pages of a novel based on a true story about a diplomat in Africa who goes crazy and kills his partner. My editor didn't like it, so I sat down and said, 'What do I know that could play into this predetermined market?' I actually looked at the bestseller list and decided what to write about. And no one had really written about stigmata."

The result was *The Piercing*, written in the mould of *The Exorcist;* it concerned a Catholic priest whose faith is challenged by a young woman manifesting stigmata—the bleeding wounds of the crucified Christ.

"The idea of people who bleed is not unusual—it's a fairly common phenomenon, actually. When I toured for the book, in every town I visited, somebody would call the radio or television station and say, 'We've got some woman down the street and she bleeds.' The power of the mind is so overwhelming that it can produce this. It is unusual in contemporary societies, but a woman in Rhode Island had it, and a French-Canadian in the 1940s. There is a woman in Wisconsin who bleeds, and a small cult has grown up around her. There was also a woman at the turn of the century in California—and these are the ones we know about.

"I was living in Washington, DC, and I went to the Old Jesuit Library at Georgetown and got all these great books about stigmata. Most of them said that it was all nonsense, that these people were crazy. I interviewed people at Georgetown. I interviewed a priest by the name of Father King— no relation—who really believes that the Devil can possess your body. He was one of the technical advisers on *The Exorcist* movie.

"And I just took it one step further. Originally, I was going to have it be all true—have it be the act of God. But then it's another kind of book. I think I was the last person in the world at that time who could write a book about the Devil. We had gone through enough of them, and *The Exorcist* really used it up. I have friends who have been in psychoanalysis, and they say that what we really mean by evil is a mental disorder.

"You don't need the Devil," he laughs. "You just need mental disorder."

He refuses to believe in stigmata in the religious sense: "I think that stigmata are the result of a hysterical neurotic who has what they call 'conversion syndrome'. For example, if I thought you were Christ and I wanted to identify with you so strongly, then I would emulate you in some way. There are proven medical cases.

"I *do* believe that some of these people are so religious that they believe they have been gifted by God. Except for that, they are not crazy; they *are* crazy, but they would still be able to work for a law firm. It's that intense sort of identification with Christ.

"Do I think it is a miracle? No."

What is a miracle, then?

"A miracle is getting on the *New York Times* bestseller list."

The Piercing sold to Putnam in 1977, with a substantial advance for its paperback rights from Berkley. Coyne was promptly asked by Berkley to write a novelization of the motion picture *The Legacy*, produced by the same conglomerate that owns the publisher.

"The idea was to promote the movie by writing and selling a paperback. The movie was obviously done in six weeks. The novelization was written in three weeks. The movie didn't make any sense in terms of motivation. I found I had to write my own conclusion to the film."

The movie disappeared, but Coyne's novelization sold nearly two million copies; it is now in its seventeenth printing. When the paperback edition of *The Piercing* hit the bookstores six months later, the reading audience was primed, and John Coyne became a brand name.

"Publishers do not spend any real money promoting books. Hollywood thinks differently. They took I don't know how much money and pushed it into the promotion of *The Legacy*—remember those TV spots with the girl swimming up into an invisible barrier? Incredible—that's everybody's fear, right? Every time people saw the commercial, it sold books; but apparently it did not sell the film.

"Now, I am worth something to a publisher because I can write books that have a proven record. It's all by accident, but it happens to be true.

"You really have to look at this as commerce. There's an audience of approximately 650,000 people out there who will buy my books. But they don't know who John Coyne is, they just know *The Legacy*, *The Piercing*, and so forth, and they know that if they pick me up, they'll get a similar satisfaction."

Coyne followed his early successes with *The Searing* (1980) and *Hobgoblin* (1982), which had small hardcover sales but massive paperback editions. Confirming that his audience was the paperback readership, his next novel—and what he intended to be his last horror novel—*The Shroud* (1983), was published only in softcover. Gaining and sustaining the kind of popularity he has enjoyed is less a matter of good writing, he urges, than of marketing.

"Publishing has nothing to do with literature; it concerns commodities. If you are perceived in a certain way, then you are promoted that way. It has nothing to do with whether you are good or bad as a writer.

"Paperback audiences are word-of-mouth audiences. Book reviews are unimportant. Reviews satisfy or upset the writer and the publisher, but they have nothing to do with who buys these books. People who read paperback horror novels don't read reviews—they buy books because of the cover. That's why you have a cover like this—"Coyne flourishes the paperback of *Hobgoblin*, with its sparkling emerald lettering"—which makes people pick up the book just to give them another reason to see what's inside.

"Half the battle is to get people to pick up the book. So it's like selling soap; it's advertising. Thus, you won't find my name on the cover of *The Legacy*. On the cover of *The Piercing*, my name is below the title. And with *Hobgoblin*, my name went above the title.

"When you get above the title, then you know you've

arrived. It's brand recognition; just like you know that if you buy Dial soap, it will treat your body a certain way, the publishers offer horror writers as if they're ingredients that are going to scare you.

"For writers, you buy the product. You do not know the writer—which is fine. Stephen King is getting more visible, but in that sense he's his own worst enemy. You really shouldn't be known. J. D. Salinger has probably sold a lot more copies just because no one knows who J. D. Salinger is. If King or I wanted to play this game really well, we would be totally anonymous. We would be sending books in via UPS. King's problem—and it's a problem for all of us—is, what if he wants to write a love story? If he writes it under his own name, he'll disappoint his readers, because they're expecting, if nothing else, that one lover will chop off the other's head or whatever."

A writer's talent, he observes, is meaningless in a modern publishing industry that must compete with television, film, music videos, and even computer games. He insists that his own abilities are relatively meagre.

"I don't have a world view, and I'm not at all a serious writer. I am an example of someone who took a limited talent a long way.

"I think I have a good prose style—one that is clear and that allows me, as a writer, to go for the jugular of the audience. I'm very much influenced—as all contemporary writers should be—by television. The reviews of my books are terrific because they say, 'He must have been writing for the movies.' I wish to God they *would* buy one of my books for the movies!

"I think I can write very clear scenes and good dialogue, and I think that I can tell a story. I don't think that I'm particularly good at scaring people, nor do I think I am particularly good at descriptive writing. My writing is a plain song.

"I try to write every word and every sentence on every page as well as I can at the time. People come along and say, 'Well, I read that book. That's a simple book. I can write that.' They can't. They can't do it because the simplicity of it, which makes it work, is the genius—and no one can just *do* that. That's the gift. But I never think of my stories as having value beyond. I don't sit and decide to write about man's inhumanity to man. If I did, I'd never get anywhere."

Instead, he writes to events: "It is never a problem for me to start a book. The first line is always easy. The middle is really the hard part. I will say, 'Well, in this chapter, the girl's head is going to get chopped off.' And I try to write to that and then pull away, so that the reader, at the end of every chapter, says, 'Well, I have got to at least read the next page.' I try to create page-turners, because the audience that I'm writing for wants page-turners. They're looking for entertainment. They're a sophisticated audience in the sense that they know what the gimmicks are. So it's me against them, all the time, and I try to outsmart them at every turn, and if I fool them completely, great. That's the fun of it for me. Otherwise, if I knew the story and I knew what was going to happen. I wouldn't want to write it. It wouldn't be any fun.

"I try to create characters. I take what I perceive to be a gimmick, and I try to work the characters around the gimmick and see what comes out. And I'm always the last one to know. I never know what the ending is because I don't want to know."

Coyne's search for a "gimmick" has seen him base *The Searing* upon Eric Von Daniken's pseudoscientific *Chariots of the Gods*, investigate the "Dungeons & Dragons" phenomenon in *Hobgoblin*, and capitalize upon renewed publicity about the Shroud of Turin in *The Shroud*.

"There are few new ideas that come along for a writer in this particular genre. You can't write any more books about exorcists. You can't write any more books about poltergeists. You can't write anything more about extra-terrestrials or aliens. You've got to be able to figure out something new. And I'm out on the street looking around, but there is nothing out there—unless you revert in some way, do something different.

"These books do not have new plots, not that there are

any new plots. You come up with a new twist on them. Most of the ideas have been done by horror writers years ago, but you are able to package it again and market it in a different way, as a different kind of book.

"What you do is go back and figure out how to write *Dracula* again. How do you turn it around and write '*Salem's Lot*? You think: Why do we have characters like Dracula who stay with us since Stoker created him? Why does he have meaning today, just as he did when it was written?

"The writer just carries it one step further. That's what we're all trying to do—carry whatever is real one step further. And the reason that this whole thing came back as a popular genre is that Blatty and King and others moved it into the colloquial and made it commonplace, so that we're not talking about vampires and Dracula, we are talking about the girl next door or the girl in the next seat. And that was a significant jump of genius.

"There are a limited number of people who like these novels, and the recent surge in popularity may have run its course. Of course, there will always be people who will read horror novels. But I don't read them, for two reasons. First, I don't read them because they don't interest me. And two, because, if I am dealing in the field, I don't really want to know what other people have written."

He pauses, then admits that, in addition to Blatty and King, he has read Peter Straub and Charles L. Grant. "But they're the exceptions," he says. "I think King is successful because he's colloquial, and because of *Carrie*, which was a terrific idea. It's every little girl's nightmare and revenge, and it works in the same way that Charles Bronson works in *Death Wish*—it's nice to get even. I'm surprised that Peter Straub is so successful, because of his language. I can understand why people appreciate him. I can't understand why he has been able to catch the market. Straub's language must be difficult for the audience that reads these books, unless the letters I receive are entirely wrong. I mean, people have written that I have replaced Erich Segal—the author of *Love Story*—as their favourite writer."

He views his writing abilities as secondary in importance to his knowledge of the business of writing.

"I see myself primarily as a writer who writes a lot of different things but who currently is writing horror fiction. I may only be able to write horror fiction. I have an ability to write that kind of fiction, and I do not know why. When *The Piercing* came out, a lot of people I knew who wanted to be writers said, 'Well, if Coyne can do it, anybody can do it'—which is not so far wrong. But none of them could do it. I have other friends who *are* writers; they said, 'If Coyne can write a horror novel, then I can write a horror novel.' They couldn't do it either.

"It is not easy to write horror fiction. But if you have the ability to understand the marketplace, you can do it. One thing I know very well is the business of publishing. And the business of publishing has more to do with what is published than what is written. The problem that a lot of would-be writers face is that they don't understand the business.

"Literature and fine writing have nothing to do with publishing. They have nothing to do with the commodity—with what the people will buy. It's harder and harder for someone new to come along and sell a book. If *The Shroud* were my first book, I could get it published, but it would be difficult. I wouldn't make as much money, because the paperback market is tightening up. We're in a transitional stage. What they call the 'middle book'—the book that is very well written but about nothing in particular—just doesn't fit in. Because it's not a particular kind of book, it's not going to get published. And that's too bad. It's a question of economics."

He doubts whether his novels, successful as they have been in the marketplace, really fulfil the purpose of horror fiction.

"The essential element of a horror novel is that it scares people. That's what the audience wants, that's what they buy it for. The problem with horror novels is that they have to compete with movies. In a book, you have to spend pages building suspense—and there is a difference between suspense and shock. Shock is easy. Shock is opening the cabinet door and having a head fall out. But for suspense, you have to be able to capture the reader's attention and move him along. In a way, it's using the familiar in a new way—like in *Shadowland*, when the image comes out of the mirror.

"I have a friend who, when she sees a window with a curtain that is blowing in, is just automatically scared. The *idea* of it scares her. We all have different thought-cycles that make us look under the bed or not read certain books at night. Now I'm always surprised at people who are scared by my books, because I don't think that's involved. I don't think that they should be scared.

"When I was writing *The Piercing*, having had no experience in this field, I kept saying to myself, 'No one is going to believe this.' I was laughing at these scenes. You don't know, really, until you do it, whether you are going to get away with something. But you have to try it. Nothing I write scares me, and I think that's the difference. If I was scared by the right prose, I could then scare the reader.

"I would love to write every page to scare, but I don't have that ability. I don't think Peter Straub is really like that, either, but I *know* that Charles Grant is like that. Charles Grant likes to scare people. He gets up in the morning and he says, 'How many people can I scare today?' And I think King is the same way."

One of the things that Coyne likes to write about is sex. He wise-cracks that he is the man who brought sex to the modern horror novel; it is certainly true that he is one of very few contemporary horror writers who regularly include graphic scenes of sexual behaviour in their novels. "It's probably a detriment to my prose; but so many horror writers are not interested in sex, at least in terms of their fiction. I tend to be very clinical about sex—not explicit—and clinical sex bothers people. But I'm also clinical about someone walking across the street. No one else really dealt with sex in horror novels the way I dealt with it—as normal sex."

His clinical approach also extends to his depiction of violence, and he shrugs off the occasional criticism that horror fiction and film exploit violence.

"It is the age-old problem of the chicken and the egg. I

used a lot of violence in *Hobgoblin* because it is the nature of fantasy role-playing games to be violent. The games involve transferable violence; you create a character to undertake adventure whose essential purpose is to do your violence for you. In that sense, the games are good, because someone else is exercising your violent emotions.

"And in a roundabout way, that is what violent films and books do. I remember, years ago, seeing a movie called *Willard*. I could not believe that people would go see a movie about rats. But the reason, I learned, that people went to see the movie was because it gave them a chance to scream. There is no place in this society, other than a movie theatre or a roller-coaster, where we can actually scream; and teenage kids were there, screaming their heads off. It is a great thrill to scream, to get it all out. It is almost like laughing or crying.

"The violence that one sees in these movies is totally harmless. People go to see the films because it's like going to see a funny movie. It doesn't mean anything to the viewer when an actor or actress plays dead in a splatter of special effects. There is much more violence if you look at the evening news in Washington or New York, where they show dead bodies. I find that very offensive, because I know that I am seeing real people who live down the block, and the camera just lingers on them.

"The kind of violence that horror films and books depict has reached almost a ludicrous height. When I was a kid, the violence in movies and books was much more credible, much more real. Now, it has reached the level of fantasy. It is like the kid brought up on television who says to his father, 'Are you real or on tape?' And it's that kind of understanding of the world, not the violence of films and books, that becomes truly frightening."

As our conversation draws to a close, Coyne talks about his decision to stop writing horror. It is a time of change for him; he has recently been married—to the editor of *The Piercing*, Judy Wederholt, presently an editor at *Redbook*—and they now have a son. He talks of his shift to the "mainstream" in a lengthy family saga, *Brothers and Sisters* (1985).

"I don't see myself writing these books endlessly. I don't see myself writing ten horror novels. I want to do other kinds of books, because I am interested in whether I can work with other kinds of techniques. I may fail. Maybe this is all I can do. I don't know, but I am going to give it a try.

"Now I want to write this family book. I grew up in a large family, and I want to show the dynamics of a family, brothers and sisters, over a twenty-year period. And it presents problems in the writing—the kinds of problems I can't get out of by having someone stalking up the stairs.

"Writing a novel today is a tremendous feat. It requires a lot of discipline, a lot of work. Writing a novel that gets published is much more of a feat. It might be luck—it might be circumstance that you never get anything published; and then you turn around and the world's worst writer, who still must have something if he can complete a book, will sell two to three million copies of a book. Most people who write books that get published sell two or three thousand copies, if they're lucky, and there are no reprints. And no one has ever heard of them. They'll disappear off the face of the earth. I have a lot of friends who have written first novels, and sold a couple of copies. Good writers. And it's really very sad. They can't figure out why their book isn't selling. And it's because there's no audience out there. There's no audience for the maturation novels, the sensitive novels."

What about art?

"There is no art. The audience that we are writing for is people who cannot read books. That's a dilemma. They read a lot of horror novels, but they don't read anything else.

"I don't read horror books," he repeats. "I'm interested in other kinds of material. I grew up when literature still had a capital L. I gave up reading Edgar Allan Poe when I was thirteen. I think Edgar Allan Poe is a great sixth-rate writer. I think that I am probably a great twentieth-rate writer. That's the pecking order.

"I read all the horror stuff when I was eleven, twelve, thirteen. But I was also reading J. P. Marquand and Thomas Wolfe. I was always in love with what I would call fine writing.

I was interested in the power of writing. When I was growing up, my heroes were Faulkner, Fitzgerald, Hemingway, that whole period of the 1920s in Paris and all that stuff. I wanted to be an expatriate. I was interested in literature, but as I grew older I found out I couldn't write well. I didn't have that capacity to say something new in a new way.

"Now, we live in a visual world. When I was going to college, you'd say, 'What books have you read? What have you been reading?' Now we say, 'What movies have you seen?' And that's the difference. Soon, novels will be as obscure as poetry. Nobody reads poetry anymore and I read poetry every day when I was in college. Now I don't have the time, the patience, or the inclination."

We talk about how the "brand name" process and categorization of fiction as "horror" help in marketing books, but tend to place horror in a ghetto-like genre as potentially inescapable as that which has trapped and trivialized science fiction.

"Interview with the Vampire shows it's possible that the people who are writing horror novels today could write a piece of literature with that capital L. The genre works against itself. You have to go beyond it, break through into another area. King and Straub did it. They were able to get wider audiences than the die-hard fans, the people who read only these books, like people who love bowling to the extent that they bowl every Thursday."

But Coyne doubts whether, ultimately, such breakthroughs make a difference: "People, for the most part, do not recognize fine writing. If you want to say 'I cross the street', and you write the most pedestrian sentence and then you write it with grace and style, most people can't tell the difference. They'll say, 'Well, the sentences say the same thing—I cross the street.' Most readers are in that sense language-deaf. They don't read for the language, but for the meat of the material.

"I got into writing because I was interested in the way words and combinations of words sounded. And I still am. But I try to write as if my language were a plate of glass and the readers are looking through it at the material. I never try to draw attention to the writer. Grace and style are more often perceived than noticed; they're part of the plate of glass—if it works."

What is the most important thing he has learned about being a writer?

"That it's all done with discipline. That I sit down every day and write a certain amount of pages. But I have no idea what it is that makes me a writer—in other words, what makes my stuff sell.

"You can learn how to write, but you can't learn how to be a horror writer. That's why, when people say, 'Well, I've got an idea just as good as that and I could have done it if I wanted to,' chances are that even if they did start to write, which takes a tremendous amount of discipline, it wouldn't have worked anyway, because there's something else.

"I have no idea what it is. It's not genius. It's just a knack. It's the same way somebody can throw a baseball and make it break one way or the other—it's that kind of gift, like being able to sing or dance. I can't do any of these things. But I can create situations in which there's either suspense or horror.

"I treat writing the same way that a plumber treats doing his job. You go in there and you do a good job, you put all the pipes together, and if you work it out right, you get water—and if you work it *really* right, you get hot water and cold water. Being a writer is no greater than being a plumber and no less.

"I was thirty-six years old before *The Piercing* sold, so I invested a whole lifetime in a real longshot that paid off— not only personally but financially. A lot of people can publish books but can't make a living out of it. I just happened to hit everything right."

Will he be disappointed if his other projects bring him less financial success than his horror novels?

"Yes, I would be disappointed, but I also realize that I'm lucky that I could write something, that I have some corner of the market. You can't do it all. I would have loved to have been Arnold Palmer, but I'm not that good as a golfer. There are a lot of things that you would want to do, but you can't; so you make a decision about what you're going to do and then do it. I spent a lot of time doing it and it worked."

Is anyone an overnight success?

"No, no one. First, it just takes a lot of work. But the big difference is that, for instance, in your case, you knew that if you took all these courses and passed all these exams, you would be a lawyer. You might not work for the great law firm that you work for, but you could chase ambulances. I knew that if I wrote, took all these chances, did all this stuff, I might not have made it. That's the big difference.

"That's the real difference."

[John Coyne's departure from the realm of horror fiction was short-lived. He has since published *The Hunting Season* (1987) and a novel of "new age" horror, *Fury* (1989)].

V. C. Andrews

"If your life is sweet heavenly bliss,
it will never be told by me."

Do women write horror fiction?

Check the shelves at the local bookseller, and you'll find that the modern horror novel is seemingly the enclave of the male writer. Despite a rich tradition of influential women writers—Mary Shelley, Ann Radcliffe, and Shirley Jackson perhaps most prominent among them—the horror story today has but a handful of women among its proponents.

There is Chelsea Quinn Yarbro, who has successfully mingled the macabre with richly detailed historical fiction. There is Tanith Lee, whose writing is packaged, most often correctly, as fantasy. There is Marilyn Harris. Kathryn Ptacek. Lisa Tuttle. Bari Wood. The occasionally horrific psychological suspense novels of Mary Higgins Clark and Ruth Rendell. The brilliant ventures into the field by Anne Rice in *Interview with the Vampire* (1976), Anne Rivers Siddons in *The House Next Door* (1978), and Suzy McKee Charnas in *The Vampire Tapestry* (1980).

And then there is Virginia Andrews.

She is the bestselling woman writer identified with the field of horror; indeed, she has been called the "fastest-selling" writer of *any* kind of fiction in the 1980s; more than fifty million copies of her books have seen print since her first novel, *Flowers in the Attic*, appeared in 1979. Her novels, a mingling of adult fairy tale and psychological terror, fall into no currently existing genre, earning the label of "horror" more by default than by design. She is best known for her series of books about the Dollangangers, four blonde and beautiful children who are locked away in an attic for years by their mother so that she can obtain an inheritance. Begun with *Flowers in the Attic*, the series includes *Petals on the Wind* (1980), *If There Be Thorns* (1981) *Seeds of Yesterday* (1984), and a "prequel", *Garden of Shadows* (1987); it is animated by nightmarish passions of greed, cruelty, and incest, yet is told in romantic, fairy-tale tones, producing some of the most highly individualistic tales of terror of this generation.

V. C. Andrews lives in Virginia Beach, Virginia, her large contemporary home hidden in a wooded cul-de-sac on Lynnhaven Bay, comfortably distant from the town's tacky beach-side strips of motels and souvenir shops. Her mother, who lives with her, greets me at the door and ushers me through a stylishly appointed living room to an enclosed porch overlooking the bay. There, Andrews offers me a wary smile; she does not like interviews, but she has consented to this opportunity to tell her story in her own words, without the embellishments of personality journalism that she believes have distorted other reports.

"The first interview I ever had was with *People* magazine. And they told me, quite frankly, that they come to get dirt. They ask all of your friends and everybody they can find, 'Tell us the dirt about V. C. Andrews.' And when they don't find any, they make up things. For instance, I wouldn't tell her my age. So she went around and found somebody who told them I was older than I was. I said, 'You must have found an enemy.' And the reporter said, 'What are you trying to hide?'' '

Andrews likes to call her birth date "a big mystery", though she knows full well that the matter could be gleaned from public records. "But perhaps," she laughs, "I was never born." The matter is not one of conceit, she explains. She loathes the notion of being judged on such simplistic facts as date of birth:

"I get older and younger as I want. It bothers me that people dig so much into your life for all the wrong reasons. When I was young, I made some new friends and they liked me a lot. They asked me my age, and when I said nineteen, they seemed disappointed I wasn't sixteen. I decided then that I was never going to tell my age again. People judge you by your age—if you're young, you're immature or impulsive, and if you're old, you must be senile and dotty."

She particularly resists the notion of viewing her novels as autobiographical. The predispositions of interviewers and reporters, she says, have been consistently literal:

"They see me as an abused child who has really suffered. They feel sorry for me, terribly sorry that I have gone through this awful abuse and was then locked away. A lot of them say, 'Don't be ashamed that you are in love with your brother.' All of these kinds of things."

What do they feel when her mother greets them at the door?

"Shock. How could such a sweet lady do all of those awful things?"

Her childhood years, spent in Portsmouth, Virginia, and Rochester, New York, were, if anything, too mundane. Born in Portsmouth, she is one of three children. Her father was a career Navy man, but he retired to a tool-and-die business after her mother demanded that he settle down and support the family.

"I didn't have a terrible childhood. The most terrible things about my childhood probably were those that I created in my mind, because my childhood was so ordinary, and I wanted it to be more exciting. But it wasn't exciting. A lot of people think I was tortured, but my parents didn't do anything. They didn't beat me. They didn't whip me. They didn't lock me away. I didn't even go hungry. And I had a lot of pretty clothes.

"I don't know how I suffered, except that I wanted a life much more adventuresome, and I didn't think it was, so I used to play exciting games with my friends. They told me I was the best instigator of the plots for our games."

She found much of her excitement in reading.

"I read everything. I read the Bible when I was seven. I didn't know what it was really about, but you kind of glean something from it. I think I read every book in the school library, including adult books. I would read my father's books. I would read anybody's books. I read books that were way beyond my years and I didn't know what the words meant. And I would ask my mother, 'What is a harlot?' and she would say, 'Look it up in the dictionary.'

"I found girls' books dull. I liked boys' books better— Alexandre Dumas, adventure stories. I loved science fiction and fantasy. I loved the fairy tales. But there is an element of horror in fairy tales, so that when I would go through the woods, I was always looking for something—a witch, an ogre, something scary—and it was never there, and that was a little bit disappointing. I didn't want a real horror, like a rapist or a murderer, but I wanted a fairy-tale horror.

"I read Edgar Allan Poe and I was absolutely fascinated with him—I can't read him today, he's too dull. But at the time, I adored Poe because he gave me the chills, made me shudder. I liked *Frankenstein*. My uncle bought me a first edition of *Dracula* when I was twelve, and he said, 'Now this is valuable. Keep it and treasure it.' That book scared me so much I would put it in the closet and cover it up, and I would put a little piece of garlic at my windows. I even bought a crucifix to keep Dracula away from me."

She wrote stories at an early age, winning a scholarship at fifteen for a parody of Tennyson's *Idylls of the King*. "I was creative in the rough. If I didn't have anything to read, or if I wasn't able to sleep, I would make up stories. I made up stories as I walked to school and back. I was never me in these stories. I was a princess or somebody else, living out all sorts of adventures until I got to school."

But her creative impulses were channelled into art rather than writing. "I was a child prodigy in art. You know how, in school, you are asked to draw representations of your family and home? Well, most kids draw a house straight on, and put mommy and daddy and brother and me right in a row. Well, we had a house that had an interesting design, and I knew you couldn't see it if I did it head on, so I drew it three-quarters and in perspective. And my people had necks and arms and waists. The teachers were stunned, because seven-year-olds don't know how to see in perspective and how to go toward a vanishing point. They began to send me to junior college art classes when I was seven. I would sit on *Webster's Unabridged Dictionary* so I could see over these huge desks. I think my nose just used to clear the desk. And I would draw with all these great big kids.

"Art was just something that I did so naturally. I used to draw on all my books; I illustrated everything that I read. Even when I had library books, I would deface them like that; I thought that readers would appreciate it. I used to colour the black-and-white funny papers, because I wanted them to be coloured. I even tried to colour the bedroom wallpaper because I thought it wasn't lively.

"In grade school, they gave me my own easel at the back of class, because I would finish my work so quickly and then sit there and distract the other kids. But that didn't work either, because the kids would turn around to see what I was drawing or painting. So then they sent me out of the class to help the principal. I think that he really put me on the road to writing. When we left Rochester to move back to Virginia, he said, 'Remember you've got the talent to do anything you want to do as long as you stick to that one branch. Decide which one you want to follow and lop the other ones off.' And every time I would falter in my writing, I would think of him."

She grew up in the Southern Baptist Church. "My grandfather was fanatical about his religion. When we moved to Portsmouth, my mother fell under his control, and he insisted that everybody go to church on Sunday morning and Sunday night and on Wednesday, and she resented it, she didn't want to go. And she didn't go, but she made me go.

"At first, I liked it. (When I was in Rochester, I went to a Methodist church, where they didn't seem to have all those fire-and-brimstone speeches.) And I was kind of enthralled by how many women just worshipped the minister. Later, I got a little disgusted. I think the people are hypocrites—that they go to church mainly to show off their new clothes. They turned away from religion and into things like clothes and gossip and malicious rumours."

Today, she no longer holds with any organized religion. "I don't think, right now, that I am very religious. I believe in God, but I don't believe in going to church. I think you can have church in your own heart or make your own little temple. Maybe I am just making it convenient for myself, though; I don't know.

"I think I have a free-wheeling religion all my own. I have all kinds of beliefs. I happen to believe in reincarnation. And I know I'm an old soul. I tell my mother that she's a new soul.

"When I was a little girl, particularly when I was very young—three or four—I would look at things like automobiles and skyscrapers, and I would say. 'They didn't have those when I was here before.' I was sort of expecting horses and carriages. And then I would feel strange thinking this.

"I would often get flashes of other lives when I was a child. But as you grow older, and you hear adults say that you are crazy if you mention this or that, you begin to shovel it all under and you don't think about it or let it happen to you as much."

She found, in reading and writing—and in ambitions for a stage career—ways of living other lives; but she was thrust into art as a vocation, against her wishes. "Teachers pushed me into art. Mother enjoyed my artwork; there, she could see what I was doing. Now, when I'm typing or writing on the computer, she can't see a thing.

"Even though the paint brushes were pushed into my hand, I really wanted to be an actress. I think it's very boring being one person. And when you are an actress, like when you are a writer, you can be all the people that you create. I always felt thwarted just to be Virginia Andrews. Maybe that's why I wanted to be everything. Then, when I had arthritis, I couldn't go on the stage; so I just accepted what I could do, and that was the art."

Her dreams of the stage were dashed in her late teens, when she was injured in a fall. "I was coming downstairs at school when my heel caught on something, and I fell forward and twisted to catch the banister. Later, the doctors found that the twist had been very violent, and that it tore the membrane on my hip and started little bone spurs."

The bone spurs led to arthritis, which—combined with complications resulting from botched orthopaedic surgery—have forced Andrews to use a wheelchair. "I really don't like to talk about it a lot—I get too emotional. A newspaper once said that I was 'paralysed'. It made me really angry, because I am not paralysed. They think that if you are in a wheelchair, you are paralysed, or else you would be up on your feet. And I do walk; but since they don't see me walk, they don't think I can."

When I ask how I should describe her condition, she replies: "Why do you have to describe it? I'm just another writer.

"Whenever I talk about it in interviews, whatever I say seems to be the wrong thing. If, for instance, I talk about the arthritis, then they say I dwell on it too much. If I don't talk about it, then I am reticent. My editor asks why I don't write about doctors. I can't write about doctors—I still need doctors. But I could write a book about all the things that have happened to me. And if I told you about it, you might think I was obsessed with that."

She is quick to agree, however, that her disability has played an intrinsic role in her fiction.

"Naturally, I think anything that affects you affects your writing. I don't have active arthritis now. They tell me it is sleeping, and I hope it stays asleep, because I don't have the pain I used to have. But it is very traumatic—particularly when you are young—to be yanked out of the main stream of life because you have an illness that comes on you so unexpectedly.

"Suddenly, you are not in control anymore. You are made helpless by circumstances that you don't have any say about. It's not justly dealt to you. I always felt that if I had done some terrible thing, this would be a punishment; but I hadn't done anything yet. I thought, 'Why don't you give me a chance?'

"So it does affect you, and that's why I write. When I wrote *Flowers in the Attic*, all of Cathy's feelings about being in prison were my feelings. So that, when I read them now, I cry."

She states her unsurprising world view precisely: "I think the world is cruel. You find pockets of kindness, but you have got to make it yourself and be very careful that you have the right people with you, or it is cruel—particularly when you are young and, I imagine, when you get very old."

Despite the frustrations and bitterness that resulted from her physical impairment, Andrews persisted in her work as an artist. In the midst of a gruelling series of surgical operations, she completed a four-year art school programme at home; soon, she was supporting herself respectably as a commercial artist and portrait painter.

"Fine arts doesn't pay a lot of money—I had two or three gallery shows and so forth—so I did commercial art in between painting at the easel for exhibitions. I later drifted into portraits because a doctor asked me to paint his daughter's portrait; after that, a lot of work came my way because he showed it to all his friends. After my father died, and his income went out of the house, I started doing commercial work for the department stores, drawing bridal gowns and accessories and so forth."

When her father died in the late 1960s, the family moved to Manchester, Missouri, a suburb of St Louis; there, her childhood urge to create stories began to reassert itself. "I am somebody who has to be busy all the time. And I've got to have something material that I've created, not just a piece of cooking that everybody eats and then it's gone."

She began working at night—a "closet writer", hiding her work from her mother. Her first book was an autobiography, which she later tore up. "I'm a Gemini, and I've got a tremendous need for secrecy. I don't want to tell people all about myself. I decided that I would put bits and pieces of me in all of my novels, and they won't know which parts are really me."

In 1972, while living in Apache Junction, Arizona, Andrews began to devote all of her time to writing, completing her first novel, a science fantasy entitled *The Gods of the Green Mountain*.

"If I turn all of my interest and concentration on one thing, I am usually successful. Problems begin only when you do a little bit of this and a little bit of that. I was a successful artist, but because I kept moving around, I would lose my clientele. Then I would start investing in the stock market, and that made me stop wanting to paint. Then I moved again, and there weren't stock market quotations available on television, so I said, 'Now it's time to write.' I just didn't want to paint anymore, and I thought I was old enough then to have something to say.

"Also, I had grown tired of reading. I had read voraciously all of my life, and I grew bored with the stories that were being published. I had finished most of the classics by the time I was twelve; then I started reading modern novels. Eventually they became repetitious, and I think they are what bored me, because they were not writing I wanted to read. I didn't think they were truthful. Families were always too perfect, and I would look around at families, and I didn't see them as that perfect. So I decided to write the kind of book no one else was writing."

It took seven years of writing—some nine novels and nearly twenty short stories—before her first sale. "I wasn't persistent about sending my manuscripts out. If they were rejected once, I thought, 'Oh, that's a complete failure,' and I would put them away and begin a new one. Momentarily, I would think that I wasn't going to write anymore, but then I would go right back to the typewriter and do it again.

"I just kept right on going. Every time I heard from an editor—and I did hear from them, not just receive form rejections—they would say. 'If you get gutsy, you'll be sold. You're not gutsy enough.' And I really didn't know what they meant, to get on the gut level, so I began to think about it.

I thought, 'Well, I guess I'm writing around all of the difficult things that my mother would disapprove of.' So once I brushed her off my shoulder and got gutsy enough, I sold. I decided that I would have to be embarrassed and write these things. That's how simple it was. Now I don't feel embarrassed at all."

Flowers in the Attic—dedicated, appropriately, to her mother—was the result; it was, she notes, the fastest book she has written. "I like to amaze my editor and tell her that I wrote it in one night. I did. I plotted the whole thing in longhand—it was eighteen pages. And then I typed it into ninety."

A revised and considerably expanded version was purchased by Pocket Books in June, 1978; upon its release in 1979 with an aggressive marketing campaign, *Flowers* promptly spent fourteen weeks on the *New York Times* bestseller list. The announcement of an impending sequel caused Pocket to advance the publication date of *Petals on the Wind* by months, and it soared to the number one position. Each of her novels, including the single non-series book to date, *My Sweet Audrina* (1982), has topped the sales of its predecessors, with the final Dollanganger novel, *Seeds of Yesterday*, ranked by the *New York Times* as the top-selling fiction paperback of 1984.

The reason for her success, Andrews says, is simple: "I think I tell a whopping good story. And I don't drift away from it a great deal into descriptive material. I wanted my new book to be published in hardcover, and my editor said that if I wrote in a more boring style, I would go into hardcover. When I read, if a book doesn't hold my interest about what's going to happen next, I put it down and don't finish it. So I'm not going to let anybody put one of my books down and not finish it. My stuff is a very fast read.

"But," she laughs, "I said to my editor, 'The next one you are going to get will be my most *boring* book.'

"I write mainly to entertain. I don't think people want moral lessons; in fact, they come up to me and say, 'You never make a moral judgement.' That is one of my assets.

Readers like the fact that I don't say whether I am for it or against it. But if you read between the lines, you can tell . . .

"My books also offer more of an honest viewpoint about families and the conflicts within them. I think families can be about the most destructive element in your life. Southern families are more tightly knit, and not always for the better, because people are inclined to keep themselves away from having lots of friends because they've got family. I know my mother feels like that—she needs family, but she doesn't really need other people. I feel I do. Family sometimes are so close to you; they are opinionated. When you break the pattern they've fixed in their minds as to what you are, they are disbelieving. But you don't have to face that with other friends and outsiders and people that you meet."

What does her mother think about her writing?

"She doesn't read it. She tells me she hears so much about it that she doesn't need to."

The principal reason for Andrews' success, however, is probably the degree to which she herself is present in the books.

"I don't think anybody who is perceptive can read my books without knowing me somewhat, although they would be wrong to presume that every main character I write about happens to be me. I have only one life. Even though I try to pretend I have many, I don't. I may be Cathy or Audrina for a while, but I always have to come back to being me. Although I give those people little bits of me, they are their own selves, too. For instance, sometimes when I am talking through Cathy, she says things I wish I *could* have said. You don't always think of those things in life, but when you are writing you can be very clever . . .

"I put so much of myself into writing that I feel like I'm in the book. I weighed one hundred and ten pounds when I began *Flowers in the Attic*, and when I finished, I weighed ninety-four. I live all of my books. When I go into my office, I lose touch with my conscious; I come in tune with my subconscious and it turns on like magic. So as I begin to push the buttons on my computer, I am also programming myself.

"It's a very powerful feeling. It's like being a little god, manipulating a small world. You are furnishing the houses. You are making the whole milieu and giving life to the characters. And you can wipe them out—and sometimes, after they die, I bring them back to life, not supernaturally but through believable things. How many people can do that?

"I like that feeling, because I can live so many other lives. I have an uncle who came and said, 'What do you write about, the things that you miss in your life? Things you can fulfil in your books?' And I said no, because a lot of the things that happen in my books, I wouldn't want to have happen to me. But I enjoy the awful things, because they are kind of fun."

Those "awful things" have led her to be classified, more often than not, as a writer of horror fiction—a category with which she is not entirely comfortable.

"I have to admit I resent that sometimes, as an author, I am lumped into the horror genre. But there is an element of fear that I deliberately maintain throughout my books. They tell me I am very good at that, keeping you on edge—because I like to be kept on edge.

"I don't write about the supernatural; in fact, when a so-called 'horror' story takes on too much descriptive material, including mutilation, torture, blood, and so forth, I feel uneasy and quickly put down the book. I like the horror without graphics. I like the build-up and the suspense, but don't give me bloody details."

When she first seriously thought about writing, she began to study psychology: "The crime wasn't nearly as fascinating as the motivation. 'Why, why, why?' was the question foremost on my mind—and that's what I write about. The whys, the wherefores, and the results.

"I like to place ordinary people—some with extraordinary talents—in bizarre circumstances. Once, when I was given an award, I was introduced as the writer who fires life at you like bullets. My characters do have life's calamities fired at them like bullets when they are helpless and can't dodge. They are wounded, but live to struggle on, and before my book is over, they have suffered perhaps, grown, become stronger undoubtedly, and have learned to cope, no matter what the circumstances."

The fundamental element of terror, she believes, is lack of control. "All of us have a few things in common. We all have primal fears of being helpless, caught or trapped in a situation beyond our control. Don't we all like to think we are captains of our own ships, masters of our own fates?

"Unfortunately, the people most likely to be caught in circumstances beyond their control are children. Children, out of necessity, live on faith: faith in mommy and daddy, in grandparents, in aunts and uncles and friends and teachers, in drivers who stop to let them cross the street. So many to trust—and so many who can betray.

"And when I began, as an aspiring author, to consider the genres of fiction, there was something in the air—spores, perhaps—burgeoning out of the collective subconscious, attaching themselves to the antenna I ran up. It was an odd sort of coincidence that I would start writing about child abuse right when it became very popular to write about it. There are so many cries out there in the night, so much protective secrecy in families; and so many skeletons in the closets that no one wants to think about, much less discuss.

"I tap that great unknown. I think my books have helped open a few doors that were not only locked, but concealed behind cobwebs.

"The face of fear I display in my novels is not the pale spectre from the sunken grave, nor is it the thing that goes bump in the night. Mine are the deep-seated fears established when we are children, and they never quite go away: the fear of being helpless, the fear of being trapped, the fear of being out of control.

"The perfect life is the one in which we are the captain of our ship, and we are the master of our fate—certainly that's the ideal way. And for a lucky few, the ship sails on without squalls, with our own hands at the helm; but life does get out of hand, accidents do happen, the wind does whip up and crash the waves, and death does strike before its time, and bad health does occur, and the bridge does collapse, and the tornado and hurricane do eventually come.

"What do we do when we make a wrong decision on a lonely highway and take the shortcut full of perils? How do we cope with a stalled car in the middle of nowhere? What to do when you make the wrong choice in a spouse? Cry, scream, pound ineffectual fists on the wall or floor? Not if you're one of my characters—you fight on, learn to cope. And that's what I write about—life and the unexpected curves it throws, showing my reading audience how to stay on top and guide a rudderless ship to home port.

"And if that is 'horror', then it's a horror most of us have to face at one time or another. And if your life is sweet heavenly bliss, it will never be told by me."

Why does she think so few contemporary women writers have written horror fiction?

"My response is based on the viewpoint of the women who read my books. I meet them all the time, and there are women who are crazy about my books but who always say, 'When are you going to write a romance?' I think women are basically concerned with romance. There is this basic urge—they have to have the man-woman thing all the time. They don't understand why I personally like to write the way I do. To me, it's more challenging than writing about romance. I don't think romance is enough. Women should have romance and careers and the thrills and chills, too.

"As I was growing up, I had to put the thrills and chills into my imagination, because they weren't there. Truthfully, I didn't want anything bad to happen, but I thought it would be exciting if I could get away with doing all of that. I think that I was thinking more like a boy. I read in the newspaper that boys like fantasy and science fiction, and girls don't—but I always did. I had no other masculine interests—I liked dolls, but it wasn't enough. I always wanted something else.

"I don't see why women have to lead dull lives in fiction,

just having romance. I say, 'just romance', but most women think it's *all* romance."

It is notable that it was not Andrews' decision to use her initials instead of her first name on the books. Her experience is no different than that faced some fifty years ago by women writing for pulp horror magazines, who often found that neutering initials or pseudonyms were necessary when writing stories of horror and violence.

"The publisher sent me a copy of the galley of *Flowers in the Attic*, and it read 'Virginia Andrews'. Then, when they sent me the cover, it said, 'V. C. Andrews'. So I immediately called up and complained. And they said, 'It was a big mistake by the printers, and we can't change it—we've already printed a million copies of the cover and it's too expensive to throw them away.'

"Then later, I learned the truth. It was an editorial decision. Men don't like to read women writers, and they wanted men to read the book. They wanted to prove to men that women could write differently—that we don't write only about ribbons and frills and kisses and hugs, that we can really write something strong.

"A lot of my readers don't know I'm a woman. They write fan letters that begin 'Dear Sir'. They also send me photographs in skimpy little bikinis—or nothing. 'I am willing to come to be your secretary, to be your anything.' Of course, they don't write like that when they write to me as a woman.

"Without the initials, I think it's very likely that I would be discriminated against as a woman in a man's field. And I think some men may feel I have trodden into their field now."

How does she feel about that?

"I think it's *my* field. I've got it all to myself. Because I don't think anyone else writes the kind of novel I do. Although now that I'm successful, some people try."

Although she would like to try her hand at writing supernatural fiction, her publisher has discouraged her. "I am supposed to stay in this niche, whatever it is, because there is so much money in it. I mean, I have tapped a gold mine and they don't want to let go of it. I don't like that, because I want to branch out."

With *Heaven* (1985) and *Dark Angel* (1986), she remained firmly in the tradition of her Dollanganger books, instituting the "Casteel" series of novels about the adventures of five brothers and sisters growing up in poverty in the West Virginia mountains. Andrews's experiences of precognitive dreams tell her that the series will more than fulfil the expectations of her audience.

"I perceived my father dying two weeks before he died. I dreamed he was going to die of a heart attack, and he did. I woke up and I was crying, and I told my mother, and she said, 'Don't tell me, I don't want to hear it.'

"If I had a dream that the aeroplane I was taking was going to crash, I wouldn't take it. So before I take a flight, I try to remember what I dreamed. When I sent *Flowers in the Attic* off to my agent, I had a big house dream. This is the thing that has happened every time I have a big hit. I dream I buy a house so huge: it's beautifully furnished, like a palace, and it hardly has any walls, and I drive through it in an automobile.

"I just had another house dream; in this one, I bought two! So I know this next book is really going to be a smash."

But she also dreams that she will indeed "branch out". We talk of her hope to direct a motion picture based on one of her novels following Wes Craven's adaptation of *Flowers in the Attic*. She also hopes to publish the first novel that she ever wrote, *The Gods of Green Mountain*; it would be a major departure for her, a fantasy trilogy aimed primarily at the young adult market. And she tells of plans for even more different books:

"I have a medieval novel that I would like to get published, and a fantasy that is going to be published. And I would like to write a book about someone who has a little bit of the same kind of clairvoyance that I have—the ESP experience."

She pauses, adding in afterthought: "But I don't want to write that as autobiography."

Why not?

"My life isn't finished yet. I wouldn't have a good ending."

[This was Virginia Andrews' last published interview. She died in 1986. Her name is still a fixture in bookstores and libraries, with the publication of *Fallen Hearts* (1988), *Gates of Paradise* (1989), and *Web of Dreams* (1990), which rumour has it were "completed" posthumously by sometime horror writer Andrew Neiderman.]

Michael McDowell

"I need a novel about underwater Nazi cheerleaders
and it has to be 309 pages long and I need fourteen
chapters and a prologue."

"I like being published in paperback," says Michael McDowell. "That's important to me."

He is the master of the "paperback original"—the novel published its first and only time in softcover—with an amazing twenty-five books, about half of them horror fiction, in print in the six years since his first novel was published in 1979. And notwithstanding his prolific pace, his writing is of such consistently impressive quality that Stephen King has rightly called him "the finest writer of paperback originals in America today".

Michael McDowell lives in Medford, Massachusetts, a few miles north of Boston. As I greet him at the front porch of his house, he stands very much at ease, although his eyes are alive with interest—this will be the first interview he has ever given. His close-cropped, fiery hair and beard surround his face like a truncated lion's ruff. Although seemingly stern—his appearance was once described to me as that of a New England lighthouse keeper or whaler—he is, in fact, warm and inviting. When he speaks, in a lilting accent that only faintly echoes his southern upbringing, he is precise and possessed of a charming wit; the recurring description of his work is "fun".

His house is filled with photographs, posters, and other curiosities from the nineteenth century whose principal themes are the circus, children, and death. We talk on Valentine's Day, in a pleasant, recently remodelled kitchen with a prospect of the snow-covered lawn through its windows. Later we would ascend to the attic room where he writes, a word processor poised incongruously amid nineteenth-century books and prints, presided over by a life-size bronze skeleton.

Born on 1 June 1950, in south-eastern Alabama, Michael McDowell grew up in two small towns, Geneva and Brewton, near the state's border with Florida.

"I did not have an unhappy childhood, although I was an unhappy child. I had parents who loved me, and grandparents who loved me. I didn't go through any major disasters. We were not poor—but we were not rich. But I was not a happy child. In fact, I don't know anyone who was a happy child.

"Now I did not grow up in suburbia; I grew up in a relatively poor, rural area of the country. I saw a lot of poverty, the likes of which you don't see any more. And southerners *are* Gothic—there's no other word for it. They're warped in an interesting way."

After graduating from high school in 1968, he moved to the Boston area to attend Harvard, planning on a career as an English teacher. "I took a number of writing courses where I didn't learn a whole lot, except being able to read aloud and to have people criticize and to take that kind of criticism in good form." He soon became a committed New Englander; upon his graduation from college, he entered the Ph.D. programme in English at Brandeis University. "By the time I had started to write my dissertation, I realized that I didn't want to teach. I had written my first novel by then, and had got it rejected, and was starting on my second. And I decided to try to write for a living."

He took work as a secretary: "I discovered that teaching used the same sort of energy as writing, so that I couldn't do both seriously. So I made a decision—and the decision was a brave one for me—not to continue in the chosen profession, not to take the easy way out of teaching and finding a job somewhere at a junior college. Being a secretary provided a certain amount of money and allowed me to maintain the kind of energy that I needed to write. I would work my eight hours a day and then come home and write at night.

"It was, in a way, a foolish thing to do, because now I know how hard it is to make a living at writing and how few people succeed and what the odds are against you."

The lesson was learned soon, however, as he wrote six novels—none of which sold. He also tried his hand at screenplays, without success: "They were pitiful, I see now, because I didn't know what I was doing."

Then, one night in 1977, he went to the movies. "I went to see *Barry Lyndon*, and before it was shown, there was a trailer for *The Omen*—which was all I ever saw of *The Omen*. In it, the child is called Damien. I had just seen *The Exorcist*, and in that, the child is called Regan. And I thought, "Well, isn't it convenient that these possessed children have such diabolical names? What if you had a possessed child called Fred?"

"So then I thought, Well, OK, why don't I write a screenplay about a possessed child called Fred? And I went home and tried to work out a plot, and then started to write."

The result was his first published novel, *The Amulet* (1979), a blackly comic horror novel about a death-provoking amulet that is passed around a small Alabama town. His inspiration, Fred, made only a token—and non-diabolical—appearance.

"Before I started, I knew that I was going to have a sequence of deaths, and that the amulet would pass from one to the other. Beyond that, I didn't know what I was going to do, so a friend and I sat down one evening and thought. 'How can you kill people with things from around the house?' We came up with an icepick in the ear, and throwing a baby into a washing machine, and decapitation by a ceiling fan, and so on. So I wrote those down and then I figured out ways to connect them."

The first draft, written as a screenplay, totalled one hundred pages. "Then I doubled it in length, because I thought that if they made a movie out of it, maybe they'd want me to do the novelization." The "novelization", about two hundred pages long, was purchased by the first publisher to see it, Avon Books, on the condition that he double it in length. "What could I say? So I just doubled it in length, almost page for page."

McDowell then received a two-book contract from Avon that gave him enough money to quit his secretarial job in 1978. He also received a Ph.D. in English that year: "Not because I wanted a doctorate—not because I thought I was going to do anything with it, but because so many people had been good to me at Brandeis, and had just shown so much faith in me that I couldn't very well back out on them just because I realized that I had made one wrong choice. There was no point in not finishing it out. Also, there was the fear that if you don't finish something, you will never finish anything again in your life. So I went ahead and did it."

The subject of his dissertation?

"Death," he laughs. "Death in America between 1825 and 1865."

He followed *The Amulet* with novels impressive in both variety and number. *Cold Moon Over Babylon* (1980), an atmospheric tale of supernatural revenge, quickly established him as one of the leading young horror writers. Later that year, he proved his skill in the historical mode with *Gilded Needles*, a psychological thriller set in the New York City of the 1870s. Then came his favourite novel, *The Elementals* (1981), whose irrational horrors reflect his grim world-view, and a second historical horror novel, *Katie* (1982). "It has some of my most gruesome murders in it," McDowell comments. "Certainly my most cold-blooded. It was a lot of fun to write." In 1983, his epic *Blackwater* was published in an unprecedented six-part edition, with one volume appearing each month from January to June of that year.

Outside the horror field, McDowell collaborated with Dennis Schuetz, using the pseudonym Nathan Aldyne, to write a series of wryly humorous mystery novels about gay bartender-detective Daniel Valentine and his sidekick, Clarisse Lovelace: *Vermilion* (1980), *Cobalt* (1982), and *Slate* (1984). Writing as Axel Young, McDowell and Schuetz have also published two psychological horror novels, *Blood Rubies* (1982) and *Wicked Stepmother* (1984).

Families are at the heart of McDowell's horror novels, and for good reason—he views the institution of family as the American nightmare:

"I don't believe in happy childhoods. I don't think they do anybody any good. And I believe in people growing up just a little perverted.

"I believe in strong upbringings—people kept in dark closets until the age of puberty. And then I believe in escaping from that, because that's what I've done.

"But not everybody can escape from it. Some of these people have to grow up to become parents, too, so that they can pervert their children, so that their children can escape and become like me.

"There is an ambivalence there. I have no interest in having a family for myself, and there have to be families out there—I just don't want to have anything to do with them. I think they're violent and I think they're oppressive and I think they're manipulative—and I think they're interesting because of all those things. I don't have a family now—I have a family in Alabama, but I don't have a family around me. I do have friends around me, but friends tend to be more or less your same age or within your generation. And even if you have friends who are twenty-two and friends who are fifty-five, it tends to be a horizontal life.

"A family life is the opposite. A family life is vertical. You're dealing with children, parents, grandparents, nieces, nephews, and those are all vertical relationships. I think you get more intensity from vertical relationships than you do from horizontal relationships. In the horizontal, you can stave them off and push them farther back. But vertical relationships go right through you. They're like girders stuck in you, and there's more possibility for drama in something that has staked you through to the top of your head. And that's why I write about families."

His novels are not often autobiographical, however.

"Those six novels I wrote that did not get published were

all about me and my friends, and I got it out of my system. In the past few years, I have grown to dislike autobiographical writing—writing that spins out of the author like a web out of a spider, in the sense that the author is using himself up to write a story. I find it more interesting to write about characters who are not like me. I'm proud that I've never published a novel that's principally about a writer or even a schoolteacher. I also don't write about people in the arts. I much prefer to write about people who are mechanics and real-estate agents—people who just do the most mundane sorts of things—because I think it's harder to write about them.

"It's a temptation for an author who works alone at home to write about authors who work alone at home, for several reasons: one, because they understand the psyche; and two, because it's easy to get them going. A writer can take off in the middle of the day and do whatever will help the plot along. That's harder to do if you have a character who works nine-to-five.

"This sounds picayune, but it's not. It's a real problem for someone who writes a lot. You have to decide what your characters will do for a living. I tend not to believe books that are written about authors, because how many writers are there? I know a lot of them, but most people don't.

"The most interesting thing about a writer is his work. His life tends to be rather dull or else showy in a false sort of way—authors can be very sweet, but I don't know that they lead very exciting lives.

"I really am not interested in writing about myself. There are things in the books about me, but I mine myself in the way that I mine friends and people in restaurants. If there's something I can use, I'll use it, but I don't go out of my way. If I have to fill up a paragraph about what a character thinks about so-and-so, then I may just put what I think about so-and-so because it's easier than trying to figure out what the character really would think. And if it fits, I'll use it—so to that extent there's autobiography, and I think any writer does it to that extent, but that's just taking shortcuts.

"Certainly nobody can go to my work and read it and say 'This is the man who stands behind it,' because I write southern horror novels, and novels about New York in the 1870s and 1880s, and novels about a gay detective, and psychological horror novels, and male adventure novels. It really is as if different people wrote them."

There are, however, clear links between his books—one of them is a beguiling sense of black humour.

"I mistrust writers who talk about things philosophically, and yet so much of what I do has a philosophical base. The humour comes because I see life as basically ridiculous, and almost everything as funny. I think it's impossible to write a book without humour. If you do, it doesn't come off realistically—that is, it doesn't come off as having anything to do with real life. I tend to play up the humour, and the horror comes off as more horrible if it's played against an absolutely mundane background.

"It's strange—I've never thought of myself as clever, and I panic if someone comes up to me and says, 'Say something funny.' I would panic if I ever thought, All right, you've got to sit down and write five pages of material with laughs in it. That would send me into a panic, because I don't think of myself as having a jokewriter's imagination. And yet I can sit down and write five pages of clever dialogue."

Another link between his novels is the repetitive theme of revenge. I ask him about the importance of revenge in his books and in his life.

"Revenge is an important emotion, but it really works only in books. It doesn't work in real life. I suppose that's why it's so satisfying when it works in books—simply because it does not work in real life. If you try it in real life, the object of your revenge suddenly becomes pitiful to you, so you've lost. Or else the revenge doesn't quite come off, so you've lost. And the world is just too wide. There are too many factors. By the time you've formulated the revenge and implemented it, things have changed and you don't get the satisfaction.

"The only real revenge in real life is being above revenge—

just saying, 'Life is like that. This person screwed me and there is nothing I can do.' Not being wimpy about it—I just prefer going up to the person and saying, 'You screwed me, and so far as I'm concerned, you have no business living. Good-bye.' And that's about as far as I'll go when it comes to personal revenge.

"I have been known, however, to trip little boys who run up and down the aisles of aeroplanes.

"But in books, you can make revenge work, because you can focus life to the extent that someone can formulate and carry out revenge. And I think that's fun. It's certainly more enjoyable than love, and more satisfying."

McDowell finds no real fear in vengeance. What is his deepest fear?

"I'm still pretty easily frightened. What I convey of fright—or what frightens me as I'm writing—are childhood fears, specific things I remember and ways I remember of being frightened. Specific examples are variations. I do lots of variations on themes. A common theme in ghost literature is the face looking in at you through a window that you didn't expect to see. I tend to find looking *into* windows to be more frightening—that is, the viewer being on the outside, looking into a house or building. Or doors that are locked when they should be unlocked, and unlocked when they should be locked. The elements—excessive elements, in the sense of too much sand or too much rain or too much heat or too much wind. Anthropomorphism—door-knobs that look like faces.

"But most of all, the thing that I find frightening is vibrations in houses. It can even be outside—I've felt it outside. It is a feeling that something is wrong, that something is *here*, and that frightens me a lot.

"I've had a development that came with writing *Cold Moon Over Babylon* that has stayed with me and still works. It worked yesterday. In planning our scary book, I do the plot, but I don't plot the scary scenes. I don't decide that I have to have a scare here. I just follow the plot, and then I'm sitting at the keyboard thinking what to write next, when suddenly I lose contact with the plot and I start to type and it goes into a scary scene—something that I wasn't thinking about writing at all. And, in a way, I lose control. Those are the most frightening scenes—the ones that I had no planning for. And as I type them, I honestly don't know how they're going to end. I don't know what is going to happen, and if I'm talking about, say, looking in a window, I actually don't know what the characters are going to see until I'm typing that sentence. It's a creepy feeling.

"When I was writing *The Elementals*, I was working on the first draft between midnight and two o'clock every night, upstairs in my study, and never knowing what was going to come out, and having to stop because I was so frightened of being alone, having written things that really frightened me.

"That's good so far as I'm concerned—that I can pull these things out of the subconscious without planning and without knowing how they're going to end. And I think they're the better for that."

Does this fear arise from the fact that these occurrences cannot be understood, or from something else?

"It's not because they can't be understood. That doesn't bother me. I think there are things that we can't understand, and that's just the way things are. It's actually the danger— the fear of getting hit over the head by something that looks just *awful*"—he begins to laugh—"and that's the fear.

"It's a childish fear, in the sense that they were fears that I experienced as a child—I'm talking about the time until I was seventeen. I lived with my grandmother for a time, and her house was filled with these vibrations—it was just a nasty, nasty place. It frightened me very much to be in that house alone.

"I discovered recently that I wasn't the only one. My sister just refused to be in the house alone, and would sit out on the porch until someone came along. My aunts felt the same way about it, and my mother and father and everyone—the whole family hated the house. And a lot of horror I write about comes from the feelings I had inside that house, and still did until . . . It's sold now, I'm happy to say, but a lot of what I feared came from that house. And when I realized that—and I didn't really realize it until my grandmother's death and her funeral—I decided that I would write about it in *Blackwater*."

McDowell was raised in the Presbyterian Church. "Now," he says, "I'm anti-religion." He discusses his view of the supernatural.

"In *The Elementals*, two characters have a philosophical argument throughout the book. One is willing to believe in ghosts if she can be convinced that the ghosts will operate in a straightforward manner—that is, if they will either do the things that ghosts are supposed to do or else act in some rational manner. The whole point—that of the other character—is that they won't. That they are evil spirits and they will do anything to trick you, if indeed that's what they're doing. But there is no way of knowing. There is something out there that is malevolent and there is no way of making whatever it is conform to our petty beliefs in rationality and in things going along as they should. Things don't go along as they should.

"When it comes down to it, if you stare at the locked door, you will never figure out whether it's locked or unlocked. If you think it's locked, you go over and it's unlocked. If you assume that it's one, then it's the other. And that's what the Elementals were—what I consider to be quintessential evil. The point of the book was that there is something out there that refuses to go by our rules. I find that frightening because that's a major insecurity—if you realize that not only are we small, but we're powerless and insignificant."

At bottom, why does he feel that he writes horror fiction?

"Because it sells,"he laughs. "That is to say, I make my living at writing. It would be self-indulgent at this point to write something I couldn't publish. I suppose the question is, what is there in me that *allows* me to write occult fiction?

"I do feel that the universe is a joke, and that we are the butts of that joke. And horror is one of the best ways of saying that, of saying that there are things out there and forces and vibrations that are simply malevolent. They strike without warning, they strike without reason, they strike without our being able to do anything at all against them.

"The wrong people die. Your best friend is crippled when he's twenty-one and never recovers. Your mother hates you. And a way of putting order into this disorder is by postulating the stuff of horror—by saying that there is something in the cellar with seventeen arms and that *that* is what is making you unhappy.

"Writing is a way of putting order into life. Certainly it's the way I put order into my life, by creating a semblance of things going right. Even if a book ends unhappily, at least it ends. So within the context of writing being a way of putting things into order, writing about horror is a way of pointing out that even within this order there's disorder—that the world that we live in, Earth, is an aberration.

"We say that the temperature on Earth is hot and cold, and yet it wavers between minus 150 and plus 125 degrees Fahrenheit, when you're talking about the Sun being 2,000,000 degrees and Pluto being minus 650 degrees. Now *there's* a variation—when we talk about variation, we're talking about nothing. So there's a kind of order that is fake, and we live our nervy little lives as if we were plummeting between extremes, when in fact we're just moving straight along in grooves. The best writing about horror gives a sense that there is a void on both sides of those grooves, and that there's more than unhappiness—there is malevolence and annihilation. And I don't mean death—I mean nothingness. And I think people should be reminded of that."

Is he comfortable with being called a writer of horror fiction?

"Sure. I don't care what they call me. I don't like reviewers—I'm speaking to a critic, which is different. When I see a review, it's like a fan letter, in the sense that it is one man's opinion—and that's the only way I look at it. And I say, 'This man liked my book, or this man didn't like my book,' and that's as far as it goes. There is a secondary thought that it will help sales—whether it's good, bad, or indifferent, it will help sales. But basically I don't care what they say . . ."

McDowell feels the particular influence of two writers: "Eudora Welty— I don't know if she'd want to hear that— and H. P. Lovecraft. A lot of the extravagance of speech that I allow my characters comes from Welty, from seeing how she did it.

"It's quite popular to cry Lovecraft down, and to say that he's overwritten and overpraised and that nobody over the age of thirteen reads him or ever has read him; but he taught me several things, and the one that appears most prominently in my own work is the sense of place—his region. I adopted the South to be the equivalent of his New England, and that works very well for me. Also, he taught me how to depend on sense, and the senses that you might not normally associate with writing, such as smell—particularly smell, with Lovecraft. And hearing, too. Those aesthetics are very important to me.

"He *is* overwritten, but I got from him—because it was so obvious what he was doing—that the sound of a sentence may have as much meaning as the contents of the words that make up the sound. That is, there are fifty ways of writing 'the gun fired' to convey that information, but there is only one way that's right. In a particular paragraph, you may want to take up two seconds of the reader's mind or you may want to take up a tenth of a second, and you have to decide which one. You may want it in a paragraph of its own, so that you have more blank space on either side. A good writer will think about things like that.

"Think about the difference between horror movies and writing about horror. You have real time in film, so that you can have a suddenness of something happening—someone's hand bursting through a door happens in real time. But in a book, it doesn't happen in real time. So how do you stall a reader and how do you speed him up and how do you make him go quickly? You have to learn to do that, and it's hard. Stephen King is very good about that, and I think that I am, too. And you do that, to put it cheaply, by big words, little words, big sentences, little sentences; and with the sounds of words—with clipped words or with stretched words—and that's what you get from writing a lot. Some people don't ever learn to do that, no matter how long they write, but good writers do."

One of McDowell's strengths as a writer is his vivid visual images. Film has had a major influence on him, particularly the work of Erich von Stroheim, "because of his skewed moral sense and his absolutely controlled, absolutely telling tableaux. I'm thinking particularly of *Foolish Wives*, *The Merry Widow*, and *The Wedding March*. And Japanese films: *Onibaba*, *Kureneko*, and *Double Suicide* really changed the way I look at things, and at horror in particular. As for American, or rather western horror films—I like the grade Z epics: *I Eat Your Skin*, *Wrestling Women vs. The Aztec Mummy*, *Drive-In Massacre*. The cheaper the better.

"I am, by the way, absolutely terrified by horror films, and am embarrassed to go to the theatre with anybody, because I usually end up screaming and clutching in the really scary parts. I suppose, along these lines, I ought to mention another big influence, and that was the cellar of Oona Goosepimple's house in the 'Lulu and Tubby' comics. Everybody I know still has nightmares about the things that lived in Oona Goosepimple's cellar."

It is such visual imagery rather than story that animates his imagination and his fiction. When he writes, "I don't harken back to stories that influenced my life, but I do harken back to film tableaux that influenced my life. Things like Max Schreck in *Nosferatu*, just single frames that I have seen in my favourite movies. I like the sense of creating a tableau in a book, just a real flatness with characters pasted across it. You can set that up, and then go on and give it depth with dialogue and with description. And that's how I usually set up my scenes—like a photograph taken with a long-distance lens. It comes out very flat, and then suddenly it's given depth, to see what's really going on. In a strange way, it's the way I think about dialogue and speech. I like dialogue to be clear-cut."

Not surprisingly, McDowell has a special interest in photography; the nineteenth-century photographs that decorate his house are part of a substantial personal collection.

"I like photographs because I think they're perverse. A photograph is a single moment, a single precise positioning of five of all the trillions of random elements in the universe. They're arbitrarily aligned and then preserved. I look at a photograph—any photograph—and I think, 'Why *this* moment rather than any other?' That arbitrariness is intriguing to me.

"For the same reason I like daguerrotypes, tintypes, Polaroids—because the images are made without negatives and therefore they're unique. Only one copy of that image exists in the entire world. If I destroy it, it's gone forever. There's something very powerful, very melancholy, very perverse in that. That's why I like photographs."

He collects with a particular emphasis on death: "I did my dissertation on death, and I'm a collector at heart. It was easy, when I started, to collect death, because not so many people were collecting it; so there was an opportunity to pick things up at a reasonable price. Things are starting to disappear now, for whatever reason. I don't think that there are so many more collectors, but that what little there is has been bought up. I have a fair collection of . . . death artefacts, shall we say?"

Blackwater was McDowell's last horror novel to see print in the mass market. When his editor left Avon to work elsewhere, "I left with him. I had lost three editors in succession in a year and a half. I didn't want to live with that." He wrote eight male adventure novels under a pseudonym; he declines to identify the pseudonym publicly, with a laugh: "From the point of view of the publisher and of sales, you wouldn't want it known that the writer of these books was a member of the National Gay Task Force." He also wrote several teleplays for the George A. Romero television series *Tales from the Darkside*, and one original stageplay and two stage adaptations that were produced in the Boston area by a feminist stage company, the Double Edge Theatre. The first book to bear his own name in two years, the surreal novel *Toplin*, was published by horror specialist Scream/Press in 1985.

"It wasn't exactly an unproductive time, although it felt strange not being published under my own name for a while." He then started a series called *Jack and Susan*. "It's very unlike anything I've ever done: the adventures and misadventures of a couple in every decade of the twentieth century—one book for each decade, and they're always the same age." Books in the series include *Jack and Susan in 1913* (1986) *1933* (1987), and *1953* (1987). McDowell soon returned to writing horror, with a decidedly comic twist, with the screenplay for *Beetlejuice* (1988).

How does he see himself, ten years from today?

"I would like to be doing exactly what I'm doing now. But how do I see what I'm doing now is the question—and that's a hard question. I love writing. I've been lucky, because I started publishing in 1979, only a few years ago, and I've published twenty-five books under five different names. I get published a lot—and that's how I read. If I like an author, I want him to have forty books so that I can read every one of them. And that's how I see myself—as someone who writes constantly, and who writes lots and lots so that people who like me can have lots and lots to read. It seems to me that that's a simple pleasure and one I like to fulfil. I would certainly not want my reputation staked on any one book and not even on any one genre.

"The fact is that I'm a very quick worker, and I concentrate on my work. I write something like six drafts of every book, but they're minor drafts: the book at the sixth writing looks substantially like the book at the first draft. The concentration comes in the first draft and I just get a lot done. And I like publishing that much. It might be better for my career if I didn't publish so much and asked the publishers to concentrate on one thing every eighteen months. But what would I do the rest of the time? I don't know. I like publishing this way, and I'd rather be judged on the basis of forty books than on the basis of three. So, in ten years, I see myself doing exactly what I'm doing now, I hope—and making a lot more money; but that's really the only difference I see. This is what I always imagined would be the best kind of life, that is, working at writing and not having to do anything else."

He revels in being a commercial writer.

"My God, I was trained as a graduate student, trained in a literary way of life, and I've grown so far from that and dislike it so much that, in my own small way, I am contemptuous of it. There is no reason to read except for pleasure. You can make excuses that you are learning about things, but when it comes down to it, there is no reason to read but for pleasure—and that's why I write. I write so that certain people can read my things with pleasure, and will want to pick them up, and will have a good time, and will not have to delve.

"I am a commercial writer and I'm proud of that. I am writing for people *today*. I am writing things to be put in the bookstore next month. And I think that's important. I think it is a mistake to try to write for the ages. I seriously doubt there will be anyone here in one hundred years. If someone is here, there is no way of telling whom they are going to be reading. I tend to think they are going to be reading good writers, but more important, writers who are *typical*. They are going to see in those books some of the things that we don't see. They are going to see what is most indicative of the '80s—attitudes toward work, for instance, or the East Coast-West Coast dichotomy. They are going to look for things that we take for granted within a book. They will also be reading suspense or humour that holds up. I don't think that they will be reading the books that were written now to be read a hundred years from now. That's a terrific mistake. I am not talking about myself, because I am not saying that I think I will be read in a hundred years, but I think that the writers who will be read in a hundred years are the writers who people want to read now.

"I enjoy being a commercial writer. I enjoy being published in paperback. And I'm a craftsman. I'm very much concerned with crafting, very much concerned with improving writing, with making it clear and concise and saying exactly what I mean, exactly what I'm thinking, and of improving my writing and doing the best I can within the genre.

"I tend to think that the best art comes out of being structured. I don't think that great art comes from experimental novels. I think it comes from novels that are written within clearly defined limits, and that do the best possible within those limits. You get something that is in the shape of every other novel but has all new colours—and that is what pleases me. It is not a stricture working within the genre of the horror novel or the detective novel. Those are simply givens; you take care of the limits, and then you make the writing flower outside of them. It is like forcing bulbs—putting them in a very small pot and then making them have larger blooms than they would have out of doors. And I like that sense; I would be perfectly willing if a publisher came up to me and said, 'I need a novel about underwater Nazi cheerleaders and it has to be 309 pages long and I need fourteen chapters and a prologue.' That's a charming kind of challenge, and I think I could do a lot with that.

"And who knows? Now that I've mentioned it, perhaps I will . . ."

Whitley Strieber

"It's too bad that Franz Kafka never
got to read Stephen King."

On a hot July afternoon in 1966, a college student named
Whitley Strieber was walking across the campus of the University of Texas in Austin, when he passed beneath the
shadow of the Texas Tower.

"I had just had a Coke. I was walking from the student
union to the academic centre, which was an open-shelf library
near the Tower, when I heard a sharp bang that echoed off
the University co-op across the street behind me. And the
reason I am alive today is that I didn't turn around. I thought
it was coming from the Tower. Maybe I saw some movement
out of the corner of my eye. All the people in front of me
thought the sound came from the co-op in front of us, not
the Tower behind.

"The next thing I saw was a little boy on a bicycle coming
toward me—his head just exploded. I didn't hear that one. I
knew then that it was coming from the Tower. The other
people all took cover that shielded them from the co-op, but
left them exposed to the Tower. They were all killed, shot.
I ran to a little retaining wall about three feet high which was
near the base of the Tower building, about twenty yards from
it. And I lay down there.

"He shot two girls in the stomach right behind me, thirty
feet away from me. And they were lying there in the grass,
screaming, begging, pleading for help, trying to crawl along.
One girl's legs wouldn't work. The other one was vomiting
pieces of herself out of her mouth. And I could smell the

blood and odour of their stomachs, what was in their stomachs and their colons. The smell was horrible coming out of these poor kids, two young coeds. And he did that to get me and this other guy who was hiding behind this embankment to come out. I stayed there. I was sick with dread, watching them die, knowing that that gun was waiting. And the other guy suddenly went out and tried to pull one of them away and got shot in the head and killed. Whitman just shot the top of his head off.

"I stayed right where I was for a long, long time—until I saw them, with my own eyes, bringing Whitman's body out. The ambulance men came up to me and said, 'You can come out now, he's dead.'

"But I would not move until I saw him."

Today, some twenty years later, Whitley Strieber still lives in the shadow of the Texas Tower. He sits with me, the tears of these memories burning his eyes, and he is afraid; and the rifle of Charles Whitman, striking from its godlike height, is the relentless symbol of the terror that he has learned to expect from life.

Whitley Strieber is one horror writer who doesn't have to work hard to find fear: "All I have to do is take my next breath." No other writer of horror fiction lives in fear as obviously or as intensely. He shudders visibly at the very mention of his childhood bogeyman, Mr Peanut; he walks away from puppets and ventriloquist dummies; and he whispers with such fervour about conspiracies and secret government machinations that the unwashed might find him the quintessential paranoid.

"Fear is the basis of existence," he says. It is also the reason that he is a writer of horror fiction. "We have surrounded ourselves with this bright world because of death. If we did not have death to haunt us, if we had not eaten of the tree of knowledge—the knowledge of good and evil, the knowledge of life and death—we wouldn't be here. We wouldn't be surrounded by air conditioning, electric lighting, automobiles, and elaborate medical facilities to keep these tortured and frail, overly complicated bodies from collapsing in almost mystically difficult ways. But we are here and this is our condition, and when you read a good horror novel, you are being honest with yourself. You are doing something that is very important. It's cathartic and it leaves you more in control of your own experience of your inevitable demise than you were before—if it's a good, honestly written book. Great horror fiction enriches the reader with his own fear, the experience of his own fear."

And because of the horror novel, Whitley Strieber no longer cowers in the shadows; he has turned his utmost fears—those concerning the fate of the earth—against themselves. After novels like *The Wolfen* (1979) and *The Hunger* (1981) established him as one of modern horror fiction's most popular writers, Strieber created—with his long-time friend, science writer Jim Kunetka—the best-selling "nuclear gothic" novel, *War Day* (1984), an examination of life in the aftermath of limited nuclear war.

Our interview takes place on a park bench on a deserted college campus near Bristol, Rhode Island, where Strieber will be guest of honour for a convention of horror fans beginning that night. He smiles as we begin our conversation, noting that the date, appropriately, is Friday the thirteenth.

"I was born on the thirteenth," he says with a wry smile. "It has always been my lucky number."

Then, turning to me with a sudden frown, he adds: "Meanwhile, around me, the world fades."

Strieber has just returned from an overseas tour promoting *War Day*, and he talks about the global reach of his fear:

"I am very afraid . . . and concerned. I am very sad. Especially because of our inability, as a species, to address the great problems that we face. Problems of over-population, of political and military pressures resulting from over-population, and of ecological decline, perhaps irreversible, also resulting from over-population. Our inability to face these problems with a kind of planetary consciousness, and, more importantly, to act on them. We need hundred-year plans, but our governments change too much for there to be any plans at all. We are not conscious enough. But nature is saying to this species: if you want to make it, you have got to become more conscious.

"Since the middle of the nineteenth century, the human species has been tested by a continual growth of population that has gradually emerged as the central issue of existence. It is the primary reason why the twentieth century has been afflicted with so many wars. And the population of the planet is expected, conservatively, to double, in the next seventy-five years, while the population of the developed world will stabilize. There will be enormous friction—and radical Third World countries will acquire nuclear weapons.

"I wrote *War Day* not only because I am concerned about a nuclear war between the Soviet Union and the United States; I feel that there is an urgent need not only for peace but also for the two great powers to find a way to work together, because unless they do, they are both going to be gradually overwhelmed by problems coming from the outside, problems that neither they nor the rest of mankind can solve. The increasing mass of human beings, the tremendous and unchecked reduction of forest cover, the changing atmospheric conditions, all lead away from a healthier environment just at the time we need that environment to support the agriculture to feed more and more human beings.

"There is a distinct possibility that, as a species, we will be overwhelmed by these problems before the end of another hundred years. There is also the possibility that we will make some kind of breakthrough, but fundamental social change will be necessary."

Whitley Strieber was born in San Antonio, Texas, on 13 June 1945, the second of three children in his family. "I had a very strange childhood," he says. It is a characteristic understatement.

"My family was pressured by enormous difficulties throughout my childhood. I mean, destruction was right in front of me all the time as a boy. I came from a big, prosperous, and rather prominent family in San Antonio, Texas—a very proud family. And I saw it beaten to death by the inevitable forces of nature. In five years of my childhood, from the age of ten until the age of fifteen, here is what happened.

"My uncle was murdered brutally and his body left on his mother's own doorstep. My grandfather, the patriarch of the family and a man enormously respected by the poor and the rich alike in San Antonio, died very horribly and very suddenly of a devastating form of lung cancer. One day he had a chill, the next he had a cough, a month later he was dying; and he died right in front of my eyes in abject agony. Shortly after that, the wife of the uncle who had been murdered was burned in a fire from head to toe—seventy per cent of her body, third-degree burns. She had four kids. Shortly after that, my father, who was an attorney, a real estate operator, and an oil man, lost his vocal cords to cancer. He was ruined financially after two or three years without working. He had on his hands my family, my grandmother, my burned aunt who was in hospital for two years, and her kids, all of whom were young, desperate, and becoming juvenile delinquents. A lot of his money and my grandfather's money was mismanaged. My grandmother nearly went crazy. Right in the middle of all these catastrophes, our house burned down.

"It was just terrible. And it came from the outside. It wasn't because of the internal dynamics of the family. Nature was just striking us and striking us and striking us with these terrible blows from the outside.

"And I think that's where I get my passion for security and my overwhelming belief that if we do not act on our own behalf, we will suffer the full consequences. Every great human society of the past—Egypt, Greece, Rome—has suffered the full consequences of everything it was able to brush under the carpet during its heyday, as right now we brush under the carpet our rape of the environment. We think we can always find a quick fix. There's going to come a time when that habit, and our other bad habit of ignoring the problem of the Third World, are going to crush this society and leave this great and beautiful country a pile of bones. That comes from my own experience of life and from my own reading of history. You are never ignored by fate for long and you cannot brush your sins under the rug.

"They all come back to haunt you."

His first contact with fictional horror came through the discovery of E. C. Comics.

"The stories in them were like stories of my life, where there was unbelievable retribution for what I perceived to be the internal sins of the family. I looked upon this lightning striking us from the outside as happening because the family inside was doing things that were wrong, that were immoral or evil.

"The first horror movie I ever saw was *The Creature from the Black Lagoon*. And I remember coming out of that theatre feeling as if a terrible vice had been taken off of my head for a while. And gradually the vice came back again. But I understood instinctively even then, when I was about eight, that there was something good about this relief. That it wasn't prurient and it wasn't evil. That to experience these horrors moving and living before my eyes, the horrors that walked inside the shadows of my own mind, to see them out there and to see them defeated, was doing something wonderful for my subconscious. And I began to hunger for more.

"Then, when I was ten, I discovered the writer who I still consider the greatest horror novelist of all time, Franz Kafka. It was just love at first sight. I read everything that Kafka ever wrote. I read every letter that was published. I even wrote to Schocken Books, his publisher in the United States, asking for more.

"To me, Kafka is still the definitive and quintessential voice of our era. If he had only been born into this generation, there are certain things he could have experienced directly—the culmination of German Romanticism in Nazism—that would have enriched his vision tremendously. Also, he would have known how to personalize horror, how to make it flow in and out of ordinary life.

"It's too bad that Franz Kafka never got to read Stephen King."

There is no better description for Whitley Streiber's own

horror fiction—a fiction of twisting realities, dreamlike and menacing, that speaks to a popular audience. He began to write at age six, and to submit stories for sale in his early teens.

"I have always craved respectability. I wanted to be published in *The Atlantic Monthly* or *The New Yorker*. So at the age of thirteen, I tried to write very lugubrious stories and poems and sent them off and they all got rejected. At fifteen, I wrote my first horror story.

"In my teenage years, I went through all kinds of sexual upheaval. I was quite a gangly and ugly teenager. I came from this controversial sort of fallen family and was the butt of a lot of jokes among the elite kids in San Antonio. From the time I was fifteen until the time I left San Antonio to go to the University of Texas, I never had a date. No girl I knew would go out with me. And I finally took a job and worked on weekends and nights, so I wouldn't have to face it. But that also drove me more and more into myself."

An English major at the University of Texas, he went on to law school there. "In the middle of my second year, I was sitting in one of my classes and realized I just absolutely hated it. I was supposedly studying to become a lawyer, but I was thinking about writing and making movies. I had seen *Cabaret* the night before, and I longed to make a film as good. Law just wasn't for me. I got up and walked out. I left my books, my briefcase, my notes, everything behind."

He entered film school at the University of Texas; one of his instructors later became the best-selling suspense novelist known by the pseudonym Trevanian. Strieber then directed underground films in London and Texas, and became a Directors Guild Trainee, working on such films as *Diary of a Mad Housewife*, *The Owl and the Pussycat*, and *They Might Be Giants*. "But I was thrown out of that programme as being a hopeless wimp who would never be a successful assistant director. So I tried a flank attack on the film industry: I would write novels that people couldn't resist making into films."

To support himself and his wife, Anne, Strieber took work at a leading New York advertising agency: "Benton and

Bowles, because it started with *B*, and because N. W. Ayer, which started with an *A*, wouldn't hire me. I was in advertising, I think, because it started with an *A*."

He was successful in advertising, rising to a vice-presidency of another major agency, Cunningham and Walsh. "But my first love was writing, and I sat there and wrote every night. I would come home at about six. We would have supper. From seven until midnight, I would write. On weekends, I would write. I would collect my rejection slips and I would sit there and write, and collect my rejection slips and sit there and write."

He followed this routine from 1970 to 1977, finishing eight novels; none was published. With the reception given his ninth novel, a black comedy called *The Searchlight Horror*, the situation seemed hopeless. "It was about a little town in the California desert in which everything goes wrong. Inanimate objects turn against the town. The town turns against its people. No one knows why it has happened. It doesn't stop; it just gets worse until the town is virtually destroyed. The difficulty of the novel is that every catastrophe is funny. The novel wants the reader to jeer, and it pissed people off so much that one agent actually threw the manuscript at me when I went to his office to get it. The last time *The Searchlight Horror* went out, it came back in a bag. The agent who had got it had pushed the manuscript into a mailbox without even so much as putting a box on it. And some postal worker had found the damn thing lying there in the bottom of the mailbox, had put it back together, seen my address on the front cover, and brought it back to me personally on his time off.

"He had read it, and he said, 'I didn't think it was so bad.' "

In those years, the Striebers lived in a two-room apartment near Central Park. One night, after midnight, Strieber was strolling in the Literary Walk. "My theory was that there were no muggers in Central Park at that hour, because there was no one there to mug. I was right.

"But as I was walking, I noticed something near me in the

trees. It seemed to be following me. I recognized it, finally, as a dog, but as I walked toward it, I found nearly ten dogs. Their smell was horrible, and one growled as I approached. I realized that here, in the middle of New York City, there was a pack of wild, feral dogs.

"And I began to wonder . . ."

What if werewolves stalked the modern-day wilderness of Manhattan? *The Wolfen*, written at fever-pitch, sold immediately to Morrow in 1977—a film version, directed by Michael Wadleigh and starring Albert Finney, was released in 1981.

"The breakthrough that led to *The Wolfen* was primarily one of humility, in the sense that I began to write recognizing that while I have certain skills, I also have certain limitations. I was much more aware of the needs of the reader and of how my work would look when it was read while it was being written. And I guess that it was simply the accretion of so many years of failure and so much effort that eventually I would make such a breakthrough.

"But more important, I was writing with passion for the first time in my life. I am passionately concerned about animals, and wolves in particular. *The Wolfen* was conceived originally as a way of separating the myth of the werewolf, with its evil symbolism, from the wolves and placing it on a creature more correctly tailored to our own internal mythic needs. There was a certain intellectual breakthrough, in that I began to understand the significance of that. It serves not only the purpose of wolves but also the purpose of entertaining people.

"When I was working on *The Wolfen*, I was in a state of wonder. My external circumstances didn't matter; I knew I had broken through because the book was so exciting to me. Blood was steaming through my veins. I would come home from the office and eat my supper, Anne would faithfully withdraw into a book of her own, I would go to work and I would work until morning. During the latter part of the writing of *The Wolfen*, when I made the great breakthrough that I could write from the Wolfen's point of view—I could feel their feelings and experience their experiences, and I could express this from their point of view—that was so exciting."

Strieber quit his advertising position upon selling *The Wolfen*, and he has never looked back. "I shifted to horror fiction because I wanted to write 'important' novels. One of the most important functions of literature is to allow the reader to become an explorer in his own emotional world. To me, the best fiction allows me to learn about my own inner life as I read the story. But it is never didactic."

He then turned to an exploration of another of horror's archetypes—the vampire—in *The Hunger*. As with *The Wolfen*, he did not work within tradition, but re-examined the mythology of a creature of the night "in order to give the contemporary reader a reason to believe in them. My own work always follows a certain pattern: I want to go down in the cracks of life and find there a complete reinterpretation of our world, one that somehow satisfies the old dragon at the bottom of the soul."

It is not with mere irony that the film adaptation of *The Hunger* (1983), directed by Tony Scott and starring Catherine Deneuve, David Bowie, and Susan Sarandon, begins with the cult punk band Bauhaus singing "Bela Lugosi Is Dead". Strieber's novel studiously avoids use of the word "vampire" to describe the blood-hungry Miriam Blaylock, precisely because she may as well be a next-door neighbour, one of the faceless thousands whom we pass each day on the city streets. Like the Wolfen, she is our immortal dark side, a monstrous manifestation of our craving for the shadows of death and forbidden desire.

He followed *The Hunger* with *Black Magic* (1982) and *The Night Church* (1983), which also concerned the invasion of our society by alien races and powers that were disconcertingly capable of a parasitic co-existence; he sought to explore "the eerie interior of human experience and our *alienness* for all other living things. We are never at home with ourselves: because we understand that we must die, we are a species alone. Mankind, the knowing shadow, haunts this innocent planet."

His intent is a "new wave" Gothicism, focused upon life in death and death in life—and inevitably to stay the progress of death. Darkness and chaos are at the root of reality, the source of life, and the fate of our future. His images conjure an apocalyptic vision of evil, an assurance that the order created by man is worthless in the face of the shadowy secrets of the creatures who walk among us.

But the story itself, he recognizes, is a way of creating at least an appearance of order.

"On one level, horror fiction puts the reader back into the seat of power. It is the same seat in which the Romans sat as they watched people done to death, struggling for their lives, in the arena. We forget, nowadays, that the gladiatorial fights, which later became an amusement, were originally a religious ritual. And the Romans were attempting to grapple in their own direct and rather mirthless way with the very same issues that are grappled with when a person opens a horror novel. We are much more civilized now. We do it on the printed page and on the movie screen. And we are going to keep doing it on and on and on until we have succeeded.

"But horror novels don't replace religion. Horror novels are about the search for acceptance of one's own death—to find a way to deal with the fear that underlies all human life."

In this search, Strieber pinpoints a reason for the success of men, rather than women, as writers of horror fiction.

"The experience of reading horror fiction is a matter of being guided through the terrors by a hero. The hero is, on one level, the person in the story around whom the events take place. But in many horror novels the hero is really the author, because there is no one in the story who isn't either acting or being acted upon in such a terrifying way that they can claim the title. In *The Hunger*, Miriam is certainly not the heroine. She is not guiding you through the dark; she *is* the dark. And Sarah is not a heroine because of the fact that she is victimized. We see her victimization.

"There is, however, a hero. The hero is the one who gets us through the story to the very end, and that's the author.

"In western culture, we are accustomed to identifying our

heroes with the male. Therefore, it has been hard for women to be successful as guides through the netherworld. Certainly, as our culture becomes more balanced between the sexes, there will emerge women who are effective guides and who can be believed in by the readers. Incidentally, when you look upon a horror novel as a trip through the netherworld, with the novelist as the guide, then it becomes clear why so many rather technically bad books can succeed, because it's not the fictional artifice that matters, it's the presentation of that world. The novelistic structure and so forth very distinctly take second place to the journey itself. The relationship between the reader and the writer becomes the most important thing."

Strieber is obsessed with the search; when I ask him to describe his religious beliefs, he replies: "I am a searcher, a seeker." A devout Roman Catholic until about the age of twelve, his religious convictions "fell apart in a tide of Kierkegaard, Kafka, Heidegger". For nearly fifteen years, he studied with the Gurdjieff Foundation, then found that "the Foundation began to invalidate itself through an odd combination of zealotry and a curious lack of passion. The generation taking over were intellectual zealots but emotionally dead. We must find ways to open up to every belief and to every possibility, not to be zealots about our various beliefs."

As he begins to outline his feelings, it is clear that they defy definition: "Certainly I believe in some kind of unifying force in the universe. I once had a conversation with a great Zen master named D. T. Suzuki. He told me that the universe is God's effort to create a companion—that this companion of God is the process of birth, and will eventually emerge out of the physical universe. And he said that God is the receptacle of time in which all things happen.

"If I have religious beliefs, perhaps those are my beliefs. You could say that there are elements of Zen in my thinking religiously, strong elements of alchemy and esoteric western Christianity. I am a student of Meister Eckhart, the great thirteenth-century German mystic. I am a fractious, contentious, rebellious Catholic, sometimes an Episcopalian. I have been a witch. I have experimented with worshipping the earth as a goddess/mother. I think that the Green movement in Germany is tremendously important, because it looks upon the planet as a unified single being, and all of us as parts of that being, but also includes trees, plants, flowers, animals, the air, the water, the stones, the body of the earth itself as part of this one enormous, extraordinary creature which is striving to become conscious. It has created mankind, which is, of course, the consciousness it is seeking. You can look upon mankind as the earth's effort to become conscious of itself. And as we mature as a species, our consciousness will expand to go beyond just ourselves as individuals and then as a whole species, and come to include the whole planet, and eventually, the solar system and the galaxy and the universe. I think then we will truly join the world."

These views—which, as a member of the Green movement, he also holds as political principles—came to Strieber during the writing of *War Day*. He attributes their evolution to the documentary style of the book, which not only mingles non-fiction with fiction, but uses both Strieber and his co-author, Jim Kunetka, as characters.

"Most fiction is faithful to its lies, as it should be; and it draws truths out of them. *War Day* is as faithful to its truths as it is to its lies; it recognizes the outside world in a very real and immediate way.

"I learned how to be naked before my readers in the sense of being exactly as I really am inside. When you read *War Day*, you are reading me, as I understand myself, and perhaps even beyond that. And one of the things that gives the book its appeal is that it's got real people in it, real live human beings.

"But there was a great breakthrough in consciousness. I found myself able to think and to feel in ways I have never been able to think and feel before. And other human beings and other creatures at once began to obtain a certain similarity to me and to each other that was quite startling and beautiful. In other words, I began to see all beings as a kind of an expression of some sort of a life urgency that pertains equally validly to the tree, the wolf, the man, and to their shared plight. And to see myself much less as a separate personality, and much more as a part of a great collective whole. An enormous passion of love for the whole appeared in me and I began to write on its behalf."

Although he has talked of possible sequels to both *The Wolfen* and *The Hunger*, Strieber followed *War Day* with further cautionary tales: the post-apocalypse *Wolf of Shadows* (1985), and a realistic inquiry into environmental disaster written with Jim Kunetka, *Nature's End* (1986).

"The whole focus of my career has changed in the past few years to address more directly the problems that I see. And I feel that the horror field is a very natural jumping-off point for that kind of work.

"My early novels, like many conventional horror novels, dealt with horrors interpreted into the real world. But the definition of horror has changed for me, and I no longer wish to identify it simply as a medium of entertainment. As terrifying as any horror novel may be, time and history have caused what I used to think of as horrors to become—more and more—realities. There's never been a horror novel written as horrible as the camp at Auschwitz."

The fundamental purpose of horror fiction, Strieber holds, is no longer one of scaring its readers. "The new wave is saying that we can go beyond the exploitation of fear and start dealing with something real, the evocation of the most furious and powerful of interior human states.

"The most important things that happen to people happen inside. The greatest fears and the greatest dreads are internal. There is no fear in the outside world as great as the fear that can be generated by a nightmare, because a nightmare is a direct confrontation with whatever it is that we come from, and wherever it is we are going. It is so terrifying that any ordinary individual walking the streets has generally known the greatest terror that mankind can know. In this we are all brothers and sisters.

"What does a nightmare do? It frightens, but it also releases something inside you. After it is over, you usually sleep a deep and peaceful sleep. A really good horror novel offers that whole experience—the fright as well as the release of energy that accompanies it.

"I want to take my books even beyond that. I want the books to speak directly to the problems we are facing today. I draw them out of the genre in which I grew up, but I am maturing, and so far as I am concerned, I am still in the genre—which means the genre must be maturing also. The horror novel ought to have significance politically, emotionally, culturally—and literary significance. It should have an impact far beyond entertainment, but be important on that level, too.

"Horror novels are about a release of tension; there will always be room for the conventional entertainment novel that is terrifying. However, I believe that the genre can expand and that it must make its own massive breakthrough. *War Day* is a horror novel. I was quoted in the *New York Times* as saying that I was no longer interested in horror novels and that I disdained the works of my past. That is not what I said. What I said was that I felt a good bit of disdain for horror novels that were sticking to the conventions of the past and weren't making the kinds of breakthroughs that I feel are essential to the future of the genre—and also essential to the future of its readership, in a sense."

His views of "new wave" horror, like his religious impulses, represent an urging rather than a descriptive definition.

"When you talk about the various things that are loosely connected under the sobriquet 'new wave' in terms of motive or structure and not mystery, the meaning becomes elusive. New wave is anger, defiance, black laughter, the resigned human being with a blade in his hand.

"Fiction that pushes things to the limits has always been the most important fiction. It's the comfortable fiction that the English professors feel confident in analysing that is now the so-called important fiction. I think most modern literature is trivial; academic interest tends to trivialize. The only way that it is going to get back to the centre of the moral controversy of the era, which is where fiction belongs—because, to me, all real fiction is moral fiction—is by being revolutionary, testing as many limits as it possibly can. And I am talking not about just social taboos. Those taboos have disappeared, because they were written to death in fiction.

"In the west, we have come to an era unlike anything since the sixteenth century. We have breathing space in terms of social taboos, real breathing space. And the moral questions of this era are very different now; they are just emerging—questions of what, for example, we should do to ensure that this planet will actually be capable of supporting our children and their children.

"As far as I am concerned, fiction that isn't at the centre of these issues is fiction that is simply being written by the lazy or the congenitally indifferent. The fiction that really matters will be guiding, directing, suggesting, disagreeing, but at the centre of these great issues."

If not writing, Strieber "would be in politics". He talks of the influence of *War Day* on the 1984 presidential campaign, and of the power of fiction, even in this so-called era of post-literacy, to influence the public.

"First of all, reading a book is an activity of a super-élite group. Less than ten per cent of the American public buys a hardcover book every year. If you include all trade books, everybody essentially who buys a book from a bookstore, it's about fifteen or sixteen per cent of the public. And one third of that group accounts for eighty per cent of all the books purchased. So about five per cent of the population of the United States is supporting the book industry. Even the readers of the most popular novels are part of this élite. These people range demographically on the high end of the economic scale. The average book reader is educated. The average American is not very well educated at all.

"On the other hand, thirty per cent of the American public sees a movie at the theatre once a year; three out of ten. And below the age of thirty-four, it's eight out of ten.

"My work reaches many more people through movies than it ever can through books. The definition of the difference between the élite and the other is very simple. The people who read the books, who have the money, are not passive. The farther you get from that little group, the more passive people become. And, of course, all passive people ever do is vote—and most of them won't really do that. So what do they matter in terms of the culture? They don't make the culture; the culture makes them. It's that five per cent who make the culture."

As we close, he talks again of his search, through horror, for a consciousness of peace and survival. He chooses a metaphor that echoes chillingly the day that he passed beneath the shadow of the Texas Tower.

"I am fascinated by the ant and the orange. If you hang an orange on a piece of string and put an ant on the orange, the ant will be perfectly happy to march along, not understanding its situation at all. What it understands is the texture beneath its feet and the odour it smells, and the colour of the orange. It has no idea where it is—no idea that it is being watched by an enormous consciousness that holds absolute power of life and death over it. The ant is willing to struggle for its life, not knowing the utter hopelessness of the struggle—hopelessness because it doesn't understand what threatens it. It doesn't understand what is behind the thumb that is pressing it against the edge of the orange. But if you leave the ant on the orange alone long enough, it begins to cross its own trail and begins to smell itself again and again. And finally it will be driven to the awareness that its world is not what it seems. And the ant will stop and raise its head, and begin to feel the air with its feelers, trying to touch some reality of escape.

"I am in that search with the ant; we are all in that search. And the parallel world that I write about, which is implicit in all of my books, is not the hidden otherlife of *The Wolfen* or *The Hunger*. That's only a mirror image. The *real* parallel world, the one that is implicit in *War Day*, is the much bigger reality that knows all about the orange and the nail and the string; its *the* reality that we're striving toward."

[Following this interview, Whitley Strieber called one night to tell me that he had encountered that "much bigger reality" in the form of apparently nonhuman visitants. He would later write of this experience in *Communion: A True Story* (1987), and in so doing recant the claim that he was present at the Texas Tower massacre. By the time of his sequel, *Transformation: The Breakthrough* (1988), he had determined that he was right the first time, and indeed had cowered beneath Whitman's gun. Strieber has returned to writing admitted fiction in a short story, "The Pool" (*Prime Evil*, 1988) and a UFO conspiracy novel, *Majestic* (1989).]

Clive Barker

"Give me B movies or give me death!"

"I wish you could see the look on your face."

Clive Barker twists in his chair with anxious pleasure, laughing as I force myself to witness each and every page of the newest addition to his library: a forensic casebook collecting colour photographs of the victims of grotesque accidents and violent crimes. "I found it in a medical bookshop," he says. "And at first, I couldn't bear to look at it. So I just had to have it." There is barely time for a breath before he proceeds to surpass its atrocities with vivid details from another of his recent entertainments: attending an autopsy.

For Clive Barker, the young turk of modern horror, "There is no delight the equal of dread." He is horror fiction's only superstar to emerge in the 1980s. In the space of little more than six years, he has seen ten critically acclaimed books in print—six volumes of his short stories, *Clive Barker's Books of Blood* (1984–85), and four novels: *The Damnation Game* (1985), *Weaveworld* (1987), *Cabal* (1988), and *The Great and Secret Show* (1989). He has also directed two major motion pictures, *Hellraiser* (1987) and *Nightbreed* (1990). It is an output matched only by his infectious enthusiasm for the gaudiness and grandeur of horror.

We have spent most of the morning sipping hot tea and talking about favourite zombie films at his flat in Crouch End, a section of northern London that seems a breeding ground for horror, both in fiction and fact. It was here, only thirteen houses down the street, that Peter Straub lived during his years in London writing *Ghost Story;* around the corner is the site of England's most recent sensational mass murders. Barker is clearly in his element; in faded blue jeans and sneakers, thin white tie knotted loosely over his shirt, he is quick to charm, compelling in his innocence and exuberance. "People always say I look like Paul McCartney," he tells me, but if so, they are wrong; he is thirtysomething going on nineteen, the brown-haired, strikingly handsome antithesis of a star of the past. Indeed, he may well be the future of horror fiction.

Born in Liverpool on 5 October 1952, Clive Barker grew up, with a younger brother, near Penny Lane, "though we never knew that, because the sign was always being nicked by Beatles fans". His upbringing, he says, was "very normal, very healthy. I don't perceive it as being out of the ordinary." He pauses in reflection, then laughs, "Though that may say something about me."

He isn't interested in explanations of why he or anyone writes horror fiction: "Because it seems to me that, although they may not always be spurious, they're always going to be reductionist. Motives are more complicated than one could ever express—so all you end up doing is telling part of the truth. If you say, 'Well, I had a terrible experience when my dog was run over, and I started writing horror fiction because of it,' that's never going to be the whole truth. I don't like the notion of hanging motive upon certain key events, as though the mind isn't—as I perceive it to be—a fluid, infinite series of associations.

"I wonder whether there are any ground rules about the way that minds are made. I don't feel that my taste was shaped by anything in particular that happened in my childhood. I remember strange things from my childhood, but there were no traumas. I was always an imaginative child, and my imagination had a considerable range—from very fanciful, light material to rather darker stuff. I know I had a reputation for being a dreamer; I had imaginary friends, and I liked monsters and drew monsters and so on. But I think lots of kids like monsters."

I ask him in what religion he was raised. "Church of England," he responds. "I went into church once, when I was baptized, but the font water boiled. They took me out and decided never to take me in again. I go to church for other people's weddings, baptisms, and the occasional funeral, and that really is it."

His religious belief today, he says, is "in system": "I believe in life after death. I absolutely assume the continuity, in some form or another, of mind after bodily corruption. I certainly don't believe in any patriarchal god—I don't believe in Yahweh, the vengeful Lord of the Old Testament. But I don't think we live in a universe in which anything's ever lost. Transformed, maybe, but never lost. I think that may be the bottom line of any religious belief. And that's probably as far as I'm able to go. But it gets me through the night."

He describes his childhood as that of an "overweight, spectacled youth, bullied by sixth-formers", who retreated into books and art: "It's the whole notion of commanding the world via what you created, and retreating toward a world where you knew the ground rules because you just invented them. But it was also a world where I could work through the problems.

"It seemed to me, from quite early on, that my formal education was not addressing the problems which I was really interested in. I didn't want to know the gross national product of Ghana. But I devoured books of mythology and books of paintings; I got something from those which I didn't get from school—a sense that I was delivered into a world where *ideas* had physical form."

He slips one of his favourite volumes, *The Book of Hours*, from the shelf, opening it to a detailed illuminated painting of medieval French country life invaded by three haloed angels. "I get a great thrill from that. It's what art does best—reminds me that we're living in a world which is full of metaphor, in which our dream lives are, any minute, about to break into our 'real' lives. Sleep is just a little way away; death is just a little way away; change is just a little way away. It's no use cleaving to the status quo—the status quo is a lie, because look, there are angels sitting in the corner, and one of them has a werewolf on its knee.

"That's not far from the basic notion of horror stories, in which the metaphor and reality are compressed into thirty pages. I think it's important that you get as many real things rubbing shoulders with the fantastical as possible. You should always be pressing the audience's acceptance level and saying, 'Look, you thought you understood? OK, now here comes another beast, another angel, another problem. Work this one out.'"

An effective artist and illustrator in his own right (skills inherited from both of his parents, who are talented amateur artists), he soon found that he could give physical form, in artwork, to the most fantastic of his ideas. Today, his study is filled with sketches, from cartoons to grotesques to highly sensual studies of the male. His early ambitions for a career in art were diverted, however, to the theatre: "It seemed to be a place where I could use several skills, where I could satisfy my desire to make pictures *and* my desire to write."

He wrote his first play at age eleven; it was produced by his mother at a local Boy Scout group. He soon became the school playwright: "We had the usual dry-as-dust productions of *Macbeth* or whatever, and I thought it was pretty boring. So I decided to write plays about magicians and dragons and mad Nazis—I've been consistent, you see—and they were pretty popular."

Horror and fantasy became Barker's constant companions after his first exposure to Edgar Allan Poe: "A two shillings and sixpence edition of *Tales of Mystery and Imagination*, which had a house and a lurid red sky and a skull glowering over it. 'The Masque of the Red Death' was always my favourite. I had three horror books, and I'd read them over and over again. I came across a couple of E. C. Comics, but my parents didn't really approve too much of that. And then the movies. I think the posters affected me long before I actually saw any of the movies, and it came as a great disappointment that often the films were nowhere near as good as I had imagined from the posters. I remember the poster for *Frankenstein*

Created Woman being hot stuff—capital H, capital S—and thinking, 'This has got to be some kind of movie.' One of my school friends, Norman, and I would have long debates on the implications of these posters.

"Movie posters contain so much of what I like. They're lurid, they're accessible, they can be great fun. They can be witty. I love hook lines—you know, 'Just when you thought it was safe to go back into the . . .' When *Suspiria* came out over here, one of the reviews said, 'This horror movie is the way that you always imagined horror movies to be before you could get in.' I had to be first at the box office to see this movie. Because invariably, your imaginings are much better."

But Barker's imaginings were more than fulfilled in his first experience with the horror film, in which he found his true impetus to write horror fiction. "There was a cinema in Liverpool which is now a church called the Shrine of the Blessed Sacrament. A double bill arrived there of *Psycho* and George Pal's *The War of the Worlds*. They both had X certificates. Norman and I were then fourteen or fifteen, and we decided that this was coming of age time. We rolled up handkerchiefs and put them in our shoes so as to appear taller. Norman, whose weight added a certain credibility, bought the tickets. I slunk in behind him, but we had mistimed it, because as we were going in, the descent into the cellar was just beginning—you know, a quarter of an hour before the end of *Psycho*. So we sat down, sweaty-palmed because this was an X movie, and we'd been in there a minute and a half when Mother Bates turns around.

"It was apocalyptic, of course: shrieks and screams filled the cinema. I'm thinking, 'Are X movies like this *all* the time?'

"We saw the end of the movie, and then the George Pal, and then *Psycho* started again. Four girls came in and sat in the row in front of us, giggling. And I remember thinking quite distinctly, 'I am in control this time, because I know what's going to happen. And these poor creatures in front of us don't.' And the feeling of, yes, *power* built up, as eventually the story caught up with the section we had walked in on. And again the woman was going down into the cellar.

"I wasn't looking at the screen. I was looking at the girls. I couldn't wait for the moment when they leapt off their seats. There was a distinct sense of *frisson*—not with the movie, but with what it was doing. And looking back, there was something muttering in my head, saying, *I want to do this to people*."

His feelings were reinforced a year or two later, when one of his classes at school was visited by Ramsey Campbell. "I think the lecture he gave was called 'Why Horror?' This bunch of snotty-nosed little kids all gathered around, and this guy came in, and I thought he was marvellous. For one thing, he was *weird* and that was great. And he did it—he did it, for God's sake! There were such people out there who actually *wrote* these things for a living!"

Although Barker's career path had turned to writing, it would be more than a decade until he embraced the horror story. He attended the University of Liverpool but spent most of his time away from school, working in theatre and mime. "I actually wanted to study art, and had a place in the College of Art. My parents said that they would prefer me to study something which would be of use to me. So I studied English and philosophy. I never took much notice of my courses. I got on with writing plays and making pictures and doing all the other things I had done beforehand. Academe didn't suit me at all. I was biding my time. I was preparing for whatever I was going to do when I got out."

After his graduation, he spent a few years in local theatre work before moving to London in 1977; it was break with his past, and the beginning of a time of accomplishment? He produced a number of comedic histories and *grand guignol* plays, including *The History of the Devil, Subtle Bodies* (in which a ship sinks on stage), *Frankenstein in Love, Colossus*, and *The Secret Life of Cartoons*. It was not until 1981 that he began to compose occasional horror stories at night as a diversion from play-writing. "I was writing them at odd moments and just enjoying doing them for the benefit of friends or my own pleasure." While browsing through a bookstore one day, he came across the thick horror anthology *Dark Forces*. "It had Isaac Bashevis Singer and Stephen King and Ramsey Campbell and Joyce Carol Oates—all these people doing completely different things, but they could all fit in one book. This was something of a revelation. I had been bound by what I thought were the conventions of the genre. Now I thought, The options are wide open. Let's see how far we can press this."

Thus began the series of short stories that ultimately saw publication in 1984 as the first three volumes of *Clive Barker's Books of Blood*. Originally structured as a single book, they sold to the second publisher to whom they were submitted, Sphere; and another set of three books was promptly commissioned and published in 1985. Word of mouth quickly established Barker as something of a legend in American horror fandom, well before the *Books of Blood* were published here in 1985 and 1986; it was a reputation that was deserved. What he offered was a unique and ferociously visceral vision of horror, one that pushed at the bounds of the genre, making the *Books of Blood* the most important short stories published in that decade. Their contents are striking in their variety—from such chilling renditions of "nasty" horror as "Midnight Meat Train" to the psychological terror of "Human Remains", from the gaudily fantastic "Skins of the Fathers" to the farcical "The Yattering and Jack"—but their common bond is an intensely intimate style that revels in overpoweringly explicit imagery of sex and violence.

Barker states his credo in matter-of-fact tones. "Horror fiction without violence doesn't do a great deal for me. I think that death and wounding need to be in the air. You've got to get the reader on this ghost train ride, and there's got to be something vile at the end of it, or else why aren't you on the roller-coaster instead? And I like to be able to deliver the vileness. There's never going to be any evasion. Whether it be sexual subject matter, whether it be violence, I'm going to show it as best I can."

He attributes much of his interest in violence to his background in the stage: "Because violence in the theatre has extraordinary power. My favourite playwright of violence is Webster; he's the grand master of the violent set-piece, in which there's a broad configuration of events, circumstances, relationships, which are leading inevitably to some dire conclusion. Brian De Palma's films are like that. I mean, the narrative falls apart in things like *Dressed to Kill*, but the films have poetry and incredible momentum. The extended sequence of pursuit, seduction, and finally death that begins in the art gallery and ends in the elevator stands as a whole piece, and it has a perverse grandeur, a baroque construction, which makes it interesting for itself. He's saying, 'Forget the plot. Give your eyes to this. This is going to be worth watching.' And that's what interests me about the violence: it *is* interesting for itself.

"To some extent, I approach the violence in my stories as being set-pieces, so when there are murders, or people are undergoing transformations or whatever, readers know we're not going to avert our eyes. We're going to *look*."

His views, he says, are exemplified by his reaction to reading *Heart of Darkness* at university: "It's a wonderful story, but when Kurtz eventually says, 'The horror, the horror,' I remember saying to my tutor, 'Well, what *is* it? What's going on here?' And she said, 'Well, it represents all kinds of things. It represents man's *angst* . . . you know.' I said, 'Look, cut the metaphysics—what's he been up to? What is *really* going on here?' And she said, 'It's important, isn't it, that these things remain vague, unfixed.' And I said, 'Why? What merit is there in not telling all that you know? Does Joe Conrad know something that we don't? And if so, why isn't he telling us?'

"Now everything that I know about *my* stories, I put on the page. So when something appalling happens, everything I can conceive of about the scene goes down in print. I want it to be imagined, in the reader's mind, as completely as *I* can imagine it. For me, the joy of horror fiction is pushing the boundaries of the imagination and saying, 'Let's confront the reader with something totally off the wall. How about two cities made of people?' " (referring to one of his best stories, "In the Hills, the Cities"). "Basically I have an image in my mind, and I'm trying to make the picture work. Those sorts of images, if they're to work, have to be imagined by me in great detail. I assist that by doing drawings along the way. I always know what these things look like. That's important to me. It's no use, for me, saying, 'And then the city lumbered over the hill, and it was made up of seventeen thousand people.' How? What were they doing? What did it really look like?"

Like a stereotypical Missourian, Barker's battlecry is "Show me". His taste in horror films is instructive: "I quite enjoy period horror movies, but I much prefer modern horror movies, because we're now in the era where it's show-and-tell time. I prefer the new version of *The Thing* to the old one, because you spend forever in the old *Thing* waiting for the monster, and eventually this guy in a rubber suit lumbers on. I don't like the monsters to be out of sight for more than the first quarter of an hour. For me, the joy of horror movies is the joy of *revelation*. It isn't the suspense of 'It's coming, it's coming, it's coming—ah, it's a guy in a rubber suit.' It's: 'Wow, look at *that*!'

"There is a very strong lobby that says you can show too much. Wrong. Not for me. You can never show too much. I'm sitting there with my popcorn and my enthusiasm, and I'm saying, 'Come on, man, do it for me. Whatever you want to do, *do* it.'

"There is also a school that says that suggestion is best, that understatement is best. And there are occasions, certainly, where that is true. But for me, as a viewer, a reader, I like it *there*—I mean, it's show me, show me."

What about the school that says that the depiction of too much violence is immoral?

"That's not a school. It's a madhouse."

Nevertheless, Barker finds censors and would-be censors vital to the well-being of horror. "Paradoxically, I thank God for them. I think it's important that there should always be somebody around who says that this is forbidden territory. We are, after all, trading on taboo.

"I don't support censorship for adults, but I do think children should be protected. It's surely common sense that there are a bunch of things you don't want to be showing to the average six-year-old. But as far as adults are concerned, there's no way I am ever going to be convinced that two dozen moral, upright citizens"—the British Board of Film Censors—"should tell me what I shall not see, though they have seen it themselves and claim they are so uncorrupted by the experience that they can continue in their work. This is bad logic, bad democracy.

"There are always going to be taboos. I think the interior surfaces of the human body are considered taboo—for the obvious reasons; the animal in us responds to that. Genital detail is for the most part taboo, though this does confound me a little bit—I never really understood that one. The sight of semen seems to be an absolute non-starter where most people are concerned, though again this confounds the hell out of me.

"There's nothing I can say about the absurdities of censorship that hasn't been said better by other people. It's self-evident in a way. You're not dealing with rational thought processes; you're dealing with a deep-seated Christian pre-occupation with the dirtiness of sex—hundreds of years of deeply ingrained tradition. You can fight it and you can shout loudly, but until we're free of Christianity I don't think we'll ever be free of censorship. And as I can't really see us getting rid of one, I can't really see us getting rid of the other."

But even if there were no censorship—if the taboos could be broken, as Barker has attempted in his fiction—he is certain that our need for horror would remain. "If you liberate the fiction, if you present as much as you possibly can of what was thought to be taboo material, it's quite interesting to see what you've got left. If somebody was totally at ease with their sexuality and the problems of the body and so on—if such a person could be conceived—what would they be scared of? What would work on them? Would they need horror fiction? Can we imagine Adam and Eve in Eden, sitting down and reading the collected works of M. R. James?

"I think we can. Because I think that repressed sexuality and so on, which is undoubtedly important to horror fiction, is only a small portion of the problem that horror fiction addresses. We all experience sex—sex presents its joys and its pleasures and, of course, its problems and its bad times to us regularly; but death is pretty much unexperienced, certainly on the most personal level, or else how are we here to talk about it?

"I'm interested in the places where sex reminds me of death, where sex and love and passion bring one close to thinking about death. It may be my own problem, but sex reminds me of death very regularly. Anything which transforms one's life, as the sex act does, for half an hour or half a day, makes one look at oneself afresh.

"Think back to our adolescence and the way that sex looked to us then. It was quite an extraordinary thing—and it wasn't just ignorance that made it seem so. Familiarity makes us lose focus on how subversive sex is. It comes into our lives and breaks down our normal perception of ourselves. It makes us realize that we can actually be out of control of our bodies for a little while, that our bodies can do things without us entirely comprehending how they work. Sex can give us incredible highs, and equally, it can give us incredible lows, and maybe it can give us those things side by side. The post-orgasmic sense of loss, or indeed the sense of escape or expulsion, seems to tie up very strongly with the preoccupations of horror, which are, very often, about the transformation of the body, which are about getting close to death but maybe avoiding it, which are about being out of control of oneself and one's feelings.

"Sex is about a little madness—how often is horror about madness? Sex is about a little death—how often is horror about death? It's about the body—how often is horror about the body?"

Although extremities of sex and violence play an important role in Barker's horror fiction, they are not the ultimate focus of his work. "I am doing what I think the genre does best—seeing how it best operates on me, how it best gets responses from me. When I write comedies, I do things which I think comedies do best. I go to a comedy, and something makes me laugh—and I try to recreate the *frisson* that I've been given, to do it again, putting my own angle on it. It's the same principle. I use whatever techniques work best on me.

"Now copious blood-letting works very well upon me. So does sex. So does humour. So does a certain momentum, a sort of a scruff on the neck, 'All right, we're going to go for it.' And so does blackness.

"I don't like horror movies with happy endings. Horror movies should not have happy endings, not in the classic sense. Hero and heroine should not walk hand-in-hand into the sunset. There has to be a sacrifice, probably has to be a lot of loss—love loss, limb loss. It's not that nobody will survive, but those who do survive aren't going to be in quite the same condition that they were in when they started. It's important that people be *transformed* in the action of the story. They may be transformed in a very fundamental way: they may begin alive and end up dead, they may lose limbs, they may lose their sanity.

"Within the context of my fiction, I think such changes are upbeat. People are given a moment of revelation, which, I think, is just about the most important thing in the world—moments where they see themselves in relation to the imaginative elements which have erupted into their lives. That happens again and again in the stories, though not as a conscious strategy. It's only as time has gone by that I've realized that the stories are very much about people accepting, embracing, celebrating the capacity for the monstrous in the world. I think it's very important to relate intimately to the dark, to the most outlandish parts of oneself, and of the world. That way, stories about fear may even teach one not to live in fear.

"The kind of horror I like drags things into daylight and says, 'Right. Let's have a really good look. Does it still scare you? Does it maybe do something *different* to you now that you can see it more plainly—something that isn't quite like being scared?'

"My stories are not written primarily to terrify, but to *excite*. I think of them as adrenalin stories—let's see how bad things can get and still want to go on and read, still want to turn the page to the next story."

The adrenalin flows in the writing of the stories as well as, hopefully, in the reading: "I often write stories in high states of excitement. I cry a lot when I write stories. I laugh a lot when I write stories. I read everything aloud as I write— I play every part—so I seldom write with anybody else in the house, because I hate to be overheard in rehearsal. I'm often disturbed by what I write. Sometimes I can even disgust myself with a notion. But I'm not often frightened by the tales."

What does frighten him?

"Absence. Nothing. Pascal said, 'It is the absolute silence of empty space which makes me afraid.' Or words to that effect.

"The worst monster in the world is better than a blank space, to my mind. Better a candle in an otherwise total darkness, even if it's illuminating something with a grin from ear to ear with one hundred and ten fangs. Better the light— whatever it's illuminating—because you can deal with something that's there. So the images which disturb me tend to be images which come very, very close to flickering out entirely."

This fear lies at the heart of *The Damnation Game*, which enacts his passion for the zombie. "Vampires don't scare me. Werewolves have had their moments, but they don't really do the job, either. One thing that's always claimed about vampires and werewolves is that they're about repressed sexuality. Maybe that's why they don't scare me. It's very difficult to see how a vampire would survive in the pages of my books.

"Now zombies are a different kettle of rotted flesh entirely, aren't they? Because, for one thing, they're mindless—and mindlessness terrifies the wits out of me. Joke.

"Zombies are the liberal nightmare. Here you have the

masses, whom you would love to love, appearing at your front door with their faces falling off; and you're trying to be as humane as you possibly can, but they are, after all, eating the cat. And the fear of mass activity, of mindlessness on a national scale, underlies my fear of zombies.

"Visually, their glamour lies in how close they are to something very like us. I mean, a werewolf is a total fabrication—a *fantastique*. Vampires have a certain gothic *élan* which takes them rather outside our experience. But there's nothing faintly exotic about zombies; it could actually be your grandmother, after all. Their exoticism lies only in the fact that they are one stage closer to corruption than us.

"There's no talking to them. There's no coaxing them. There's no praying to them. There's no asking for mercy or compassion. It's absence again, in a way. You look into their eyes and there's *nothing there*. It doesn't matter how much you reason, how much you cry. It goes back, I think, even to my school days and being bullied and being the boy with the spectacles, and feeling somehow that nothing would save me if the heavies got me."

Clive Barker has indeed escaped the heavies, creating for himself—and for a growing number of readers—lasting images of the conflict between dream and reality that he discovered in his youth. But he has not escaped his fear; indeed, in his sudden success, he has only found a new kind of terror.

"Success makes me nervous. I mean, it's great, smashing. But it makes me nervous. I didn't have any huge ambition for the books. I did them because I wanted to do them. And it's a little confounding to have the response that they've had. I've been working in the theatre for a long time, and doing illustrations, labouring without a great deal of cash. Suddenly to have things blossom in front of me—it's knocked my equilibrium a little bit. It's made me think much more closely about what I want to do. When they asked me to do the second three *Books of Blood*, I realized, 'These have to be as good as the first three, haven't they?' This is a new impetus, a new set of problems. Underneath it all is the sense that

I've got to work, I've got to sort this out, I've got to make sure it doesn't have control of me.

"I'm also aware that I'm stepping into an area where there is a lot of very, very considerable talent. And I feel I have, somehow or the other, to justify my presence. I have to continue to turn out good work—better work—and I mustn't disappoint myself, my publishers, and, most of all, the people who read the stuff."

His other projects include departures from the relentless horrors of the *Books of Blood*: a children's book that he will also illustrate, a lengthy fantasy novel, and a major West End production of his play, *The Secret Life of Cartoons*. His ambition has been bolstered, he says, not only by the success of his horror fiction, but also by the sense of liberation he has found as a horror writer.

"I feel most comfortable when I am free from the desire—or the insistence—that one produce *art*. I would prefer to pick up a book which is not covered in *The Sunday Times* reviews telling me this is going to be *the* subject of polite conversation for the next fortnight. I have more fun looking at the illustrations in *Playboy* or at comic strips by Berni Wrightson than I have in most galleries of modern art. It seems as though we're surrounded by people making claims for works. Hype is in the air all the time. We should read this because it's good for our minds. We should read that because it's good for our souls.

"We populists are made to feel—this is particularly true of horror enthusiasts—that we have to apologize for our taste. How many times have you been at dinner parties where people say, 'You *like* that stuff?' I used to go into a whole routine. I'd say, 'Look, this stuff has a very good pedigree. Horror is talking about the deepest concerns of the human condition.' And I would beat people into submission, not because they agreed with my argument, but because they wanted me to shut up. Finally I thought, 'Sod that. I *like* this stuff. If they feel so uptight they can't admit they like a good scare, so be it. That's their problem; it's not mine.'

"I think it would be much healthier if *The Sunday Times*

reviewed the books which people are reading, instead of those being read by a very small percentage of the general public. It seems to me spurious to argue that slim novels or volumes of verse may contain more art, more finesse, more metaphysical comprehension than a Stephen King book. Stephen King has sold more than forty fucking million books. We should look at how this guy is working on people. *That's* what's important. Horror fiction is shaping minds on a huge scale.

"And that's the final put-down of the snob at the dinner party. He may go to the recital of modern music, and he may feel wonderful about it. He may feel morally superior to the happy many who are listening to Bruce Springsteen. He may feel all kinds of things, but the one thing he isn't going to feel is in tune with what is actually shaping the world around him.

"So when all is said and done," he says, raising his fist in a gesture of defiance, "give me B movies or give me death!"

Peter Straub

"I value virtuosity . . . to be able to
do undo-able things."

It is often said that Peter Straub doesn't look like a writer of
horror fiction.

The presumption, of course, is that a horror writer ought
to look the part—sprouting bristled hair and pointed teeth
like a werewolf in transformation, perhaps. But the reality is
that the faces of fear are man-on-the-street average. If anything, writers of horror fiction appear younger and more
relaxed than the typical lawyer or banker.

The problem is that Peter Straub looks like a lawyer or
banker. In a subculture whose attire runs an informal gamut
from T-shirts to that height of professorial chic, the Harris
tweed jacket, Straub is rarely to be seen without suit and tie.
Tall, well-groomed, his serious face framed with no-non-
sense glasses, Straub seems businesslike, reserved, and
utterly respectable. But he laughs at the notion that he is a
perfectly normal person.

"I am a perfectly normal novelist, which is different. I'm
more rebellious and exotic than the usual description of me
would permit anyone to know. The way I habitually dress
often throws people off. But I can't help that, because when
I went to school, I had to wear a tie and a jacket every single
day, and that has stuck in my head as the way you dress.
Even when I sat at home all day long, I used to put on a tie
and a jacket or a suit—that was like breathing to me."

You must get close to Peter Straub before you begin to
see the werewolf; his is an intricate personality, and his public

persona, like his intensely styled writing, often seems at odds with the fiction to which he has devoted the last fifteen years of his life. As we talk in his Manhattan apartment, he is relaxed, informal—wearing no tie with his crisp white shirt and tan slacks—sprawled on a couch with a glass of wine in hand. But there is a sense of restless energy, manifested in nervous shifting and an occasional stutter, and in his passionate devotion to jazz.

With the publication of *Ghost Story* in 1979, the name of Peter Straub became inextricably identified with contemporary horror fiction. Besides making him a fixture of the bestseller lists, *Ghost Story* and its successors—*Shadowland* (1980), *Floating Dragon* (1983), and a collaboration with Stephen King, *The Talisman* (1984)—established him as the premier stylist of the modern supernatural novel, a writer of rare wit and intelligence in a field beset with cynical potboilers. But before there was Peter Straub, brand-name horror writer, there was Peter Straub, poet and mainstream novelist. Throughout his career, he has walked the uncertain—and often unbreachable—line between popular fiction and "serious" literature. It is a tightrope act that started as early as childhood.

"I was a famous story-teller—always called upon by other kids to tell them stories. In grade school, whenever I saw a chink of daylight—the tiniest possibility to justify it—instead of actually writing the theme I was supposed to do, I would write a kind of wild invention around it. I dreamed up plays and the neighbourhood kids would put them on. They had extremely didactic themes—moralistic, with a lot of violence.

"In high school, I wrote a couple of stories, but by then I was affected by 'literature', and these stories had become studious imitations of *New Yorker* stories. I remember being worried, at about the age of sixteen, by the undeniable fact that I wanted very much to be a writer and to write novels but that I had nothing at all to write about. This made me suffer to some extent, since I was aware that there was a category of beings that you could call failed artists—those people given the temperament and character to be painters, writers, musicians but who lacked the talent. This is like being a pig with a view of heaven. A pig staring at heaven is a pig in pain, and I had no idea whether or not I was like that—whether I would be someone who could do it or whether I had everything except the ability, the conditions but not the soil."

The path to Straub's true direction was a winding one. "It seemed to me that what I needed was a conventional career that could fund my attempts to write." He decided to become a physician, but once in college, soon realized that he had no gift for science; he changed his major to English: "I thought I could become a college professor and write on the weekends or at night."

Straub earned his BA at the University of Wisconsin at Madison in 1965. The following year, he married and took a master's degree in Contemporary Literature at Columbia University. He returned to his home town of Milwaukee to teach preparatory school English; after three years, he became bored and knew that he had to leave.

"I admire the people who teach all of their lives, because it takes a very special kind of human being to do that, one extremely dedicated to young people and to teaching. But I didn't have these specific dedications, and I knew that I would be ruined if I kept trying to teach. My fragile gifts for teaching were getting pretty tarnished and my character was beginning to dissipate. So we went to Ireland in 1969, and I became a graduate student again. Looking back, I had no notion of the dimensions of what I was doing."

While studying at University College, Dublin, he began to place occasional poems with such publications as *The New Statesman*, and eventually saw two poetry collections in print. He soon set aside a doctoral dissertation on D. H. Lawrence in favour of his first novel, *Marriages*, which, but for the prophetic appearance of a ghost, was decidedly non-horrific. A noble experiment in prose poetry, it was accepted by the first British publisher who saw it and was published in the United States in 1973. "Then I knew that I was never going to do another lick of work on my miserable thesis, and that I was going to write novels for the rest of my life."

Straub moved to London and spent the following two years writing *Under Venus*, a more plot-oriented novel tense with an underlying Gothic impulse; but he could find no willing publisher (and indeed, the book did not see print until 1984, in the retrospective omnibus, *Wild Animals*). "*Marriages* had the commercial fate that it asked for, which was death. It received good reviews and no sales, which is about what books of its type normally have. I spent a long time on *Under Venus*, and when it was rejected, I was deeply depressed."

His views of fiction, bred in an academic environment, were changing.

"My views at the time of *Marriages* had to do with the poetry I was reading and the sort of stuff that I had been learning in graduate school. Mainly, I was interested in the surfaces of literary works. I was interested in style and the way that different textures in a novel clashed and interacted. I viewed plot as anachronistic and unmodern. So my goals were to write something very akin to prose poetry, and my first novel incorporated a lot of that. It certainly did not incorporate a sequential, developing plot, which was the last thing I wanted.

"Right after that, my ideas changed, and I thought that novels were really stories and that you must have a narrative impulse. The reader should be actively curious about what is going to happen and keep reading just to see what this character is going to do or say."

Distraught by the rejection of *Under Venus*, he turned to one of his childhood pleasures, the tale of terror. Writing a new novel had become an act of survival.

"It was either make money writing or get a job, which sounded like 'write or die' to me. I wanted to write something that would appeal to a publisher, so that I would at least be able to get in at the door. I had an idea for a ghost story, and the idea scared me."

The result was *Julia* (1975), Straub's surrender to the Gothic impulse unfulfilled in his earlier writing; it was also his confirmation of supernatural fiction as a viable and venerable form.

"One of the things I was determined to do, from the first sentence of *Julia*, was to write books that would have readers, but that would nevertheless satisfy the demands I placed upon myself. I didn't see any reason why a book involving a supernatural occurrence couldn't be as good, in the conventional literary sense, as a novel about adultery. It struck me that these were just two different genres to which the merit is brought by the individual writer and is not inherent in the genre itself. So I wanted to bring whatever literary acumen and intelligence I could muster to a very attractive and quirky form.

"At the time, I was very conscious that it was an unregarded form—that it was ignored. This struck me as an enormous advantage, since it meant that I could try whatever I wanted and nobody important would notice. The only ones who would notice would be the kids who bought the books, who would presumably say to themselves, 'There might be something interesting in this guy.'

"I also saw that horror had, at one time, been quite serious and respectable. And I thought that it could be again, if simply treated the right way."

Julia was promptly purchased for publication both in England and the United States, and Straub's typecasting as a horror writer began. An editor soon told him that, with one successful horror novel, he would have to write more of the same.

"And I thought, 'Well, who says that? Why do I have to do it?' But it is simply a fact of life in the publishing world that if you have success with a book of any specific kind, the publisher is very interested in seeing you do another one.

"I certainly could have done another kind of book, but I wanted to increase the audience that I had. I was sure that I could write a horror novel that would be as well received as *Julia* but would be better artistically—and that was what I was mainly concerned about. I liked the idea that teenagers, housewives, all kinds of people would go out and buy these books. So I had no problem with thinking of myself as a horror writer; I just wanted to be thought of as a good one, one of unusual merit.

"If Steve King wrote a love story, the publishers would advertise it as 'a love story by the master of horror'. The reputation of being a horror writer is like wearing a long coat; it spreads out behind you and never quite catches up. I don't see anything wrong with that except for the obvious. People need convenient slots in their brains in which they can fit you. And I don't think people will object if they read a novel of mine and find it exciting or beautiful or moving but not a conventional horror novel."

His next novel, *If You Could See Me Now* (1977), represents Straub's taming of the supernatural idiom, tested and found worthy in *Julia*, and bending it to his own thematic concerns; indeed, it is his "lost" novel, *Under Venus*, recast as horror fiction—featuring a Wisconsin-born teacher grappling with a book about D. H. Lawrence while confronting a world of the supernatural. It was "a conscious attempt to get back to a landscape that I knew as a child. It was a wonderful experience to conjure all of that up in my head, to wander those little streets and look at the woods and the streams and the farmhouses in my mind, and then to try to work out their emotional nuances on paper."

"No story exists without its past," writes Straub in *If You Could See Me Now*, "and the past of a story is what enables us to understand it." Supernatural manifestations notwithstanding, the past is the ghost that haunts Straub's novels—and his life: "What happened to us twenty, thirty years ago is what makes us act as we do now. Even what happened to us last week explains what we do now."

He holds with Ramsey Campbell that we should look to the horror writer's childhood; but, he asks, "Are there happy childhoods? It seems impossible.

"There are degrees of happiness, and my childhood was often intensely happy. But I do think that most writing of any kind, certainly most imaginative writing, is a response to internal conflict and internal pain instilled in childhood.

Sometimes I think that ineffective horror writers might have had things too comfortable when they were children—they may never have been pushed enough by their own fears. You have to explain the intensity somehow—the intensity that marks good books of this kind—and one of the ways to explain it is to look back at the living room of the writer when he was about three or four years old and see what happened in that living room. Because that's where horror starts."

Straub's living room, shared by his mother, father, and two younger brothers, at times seemed "full of blood". He was born in Milwaukee on 2 March 1943; his mother, a nurse, worked throughout his childhood. "She was strong, hard-working, a Norwegian Protestant with a deep sense of duty. My father is a far more fantastic person—that is, he has a great imagination, a lot of playfulness and a lot of violence in him. He is very powerful emotionally, and also very charming in lots of ways. He has a big streak of irrationality and a big streak of fantasy. I get most of what makes me able to do what I am doing from him. But I got the ability to sit down and make it work from my mother—from the idea that life is, in large part, about work.

"What I am describing is a kind of union of irreconcilables. And I am quite aware that my own character is irreconcilable. The combination of those two people within my one skin is, I think, what has enabled me to do the things I do. My brothers weren't first on the firing line. They learned, from my bad example, how to accommodate themselves to the psychic reality in that living room by watching the way I attracted fire."

His religious upbringing as a Lutheran was strict and conservative.

"As a child, I was force-fed religion, made to go to Sunday School and church. I was raised in a kind of shielded Scandinavian Protestantism, which was pretty joyless and pretty well centred on the notion of human damnation and Original Sin. I remember my mother telling me that, when she was a child, she had a dream that the skies were on fire and that the world was going to end—and that kind of image comes right out of this kind of faith.

"I was an acolyte at age twelve; but by then, I was sufficiently dopey to take real delight in looking like the most bored, impertinent acolyte ever born. Fortunately, my rebellion went unnoticed—nobody noticed that I was always staring at the ceiling and crossing my legs and more or less acting up.

"Later, in my early twenties, I had a kind of intellectual interest in religion. I read a lot of theology, but almost out of agnosticism rather than out of religious impulse. I wanted to find out what it was really about, rather than being given another terrible sermon about how man is damned and how the Catholics were even more damned than the rest of us.

"I am not much aware of any outright and four-square religious impulses lurking within me now. I have a kind of provisional belief in supernatural matters, but these, by definition, are irrational; that is, I sometimes find myself believing in demons, but I always found angels sort of unimaginable."

When he was seven years old, Straub was hit by a car and nearly killed. Incapacitated for a year, he was "thrown back" on reading. "I already loved reading, but at this point, it was about all I could do. I experienced pain and helplessness, and I certainly learned to associate reading and writing with pleasure and with escape.

"Ever after, I read a lot—a conspicuous amount. Like most writers, I was truly terrible at most team sports. At least a dozen times, I was humiliated by being the last person picked for a team because everybody knew that if the ball came to me, there was no chance in the world that I was actually going to get it in my hands. But I always had an intense social life. I had many friends whom I saw all the time, as I do now. It's just that I always had a book with me, and when given the chance, I would go off by myself and read. I don't see that as a retreat. Reading is one way of being involved in the world."

Near the age of eleven, he discovered one of horror fiction's landmarks, the thick Modern Library anthology, *Great Tales of Terror and the Supernatural* it was his first exposure to the horror story. "As a child, I always carried a book with me, just as I always do as an adult. That book I carried with me for a long, long time."

He would not return to those stories, however, until the mid-1970s, when, with a burgeoning career as a horror writer, he determined to become better acquainted with the field. Guided by his friend Thomas Tessier (himself a talented writer of horror fiction), Straub's rediscovery of the pleasures of reading the tale of terror formed the basis of his breakthrough novel, *Ghost Story*.

"I was aware when I was writing *Ghost Story* that it was the most ambitious book I had ever tried. I took many, many chances. It may be that it took that long to recover from the blow of the rejection of *Under Venus*.

"I had, as anybody would, naturally improved by this point. If you do something long enough, you get better at it—even in brushing your teeth or driving a car, you improve with practice. And the imagination is like that, too. The more you use your imagination, the more muscular and adaptive it becomes. I know that I accomplished the novelist's job more successfully in *Ghost Story* than in the earlier novels, and part of it was due to the psychic effects of a kind of success. Even though I was largely unknown, *Julia* and *If You Could See Me Now* had actually sold very well by most writers' standards—enough so that I had a reasonable income for a normal human being and quite a healthy one for a writer. And this armoured my conscience."

Stephen King, whom he met and befriended when King visited England in 1977, also had a definite influence. "There was this overwhelming, undeniable impression that boiled off him that he was totally committed to what he was doing—and that he was unstoppable. It is a wonderful thing to see in a guy that age, and the authority and persuasiveness with which he did it was inspiring.

"Steve's example helped me simply to work harder—which

was a habit that I then took on—and with every book after that, I have worked harder and harder.

"As long as I write as closely as possible to the top of my bent—which means not being easy on myself and, in fact, investing more of myself every time out of the box—then the book will be as strong and effective as I can make it and will, I hope, satisfy first my editor, next the reviewers, and then the public. When I work at the top of my bent, I seem to be commercial. I am very happy about that, but it follows from my trying to find the widest possible audience as quickly as possible."

His relationship with King moved from the personal to the public when *Ghost Story* climbed the best-seller charts in 1979, and Straub became horror fiction's "number two" brand name. Even when writing in collaboration with King on *The Talisman*, the alphabetized credits placed his name second. Does he ever feel that he is working in the shadow of Stephen King?

"Certainly there is the feeling of being the number two man. I am frequently asked about Steve—and have been now for over a decade—and I have never really minded because I know that Steve is genuinely very, very good. And I have always thought that Steve deserved every success he has had. He is incredibly gifted. Back when nobody ever heard of him, I used to go around telling people, 'You really ought to read this guy, because he's great.' So I do sometimes feel as though ironic revenge has been visited upon me. But I don't think I envy Steve his success, because first, I think he more than deserves it, and second, the 'phenomenon' took over and it eventually began to have as much to do with celebrity as with books. I am just as happy that, when I walk down the street, people don't rush up to me for autographs. I don't think Steve likes that, and I *know* I wouldn't like that.

"I have always felt very close to Steve, and in fact, I have often felt as though he is one of the few people in the world I can always talk to, because he will understand why I am saying what I am saying. Steve and I have had remarkable things happen to us. Something drastic happened in our lives and changed them out of all recognition, and all because of something we did because we liked doing it. He is someone I can talk to very frankly about the whole circus that occasionally surrounds us."

The financial success of *Ghost Story* caused the Straubs to return to the United States in 1979 after ten years overseas, taking up residence in Westport, Connecticut, in order to avoid the bite of the onerous British tax system. Even today, he continues to be surprised by the magnitude of his success.

"It *is* astonishing, because anybody who writes a book would be astonished to suddenly have the skies open and uncountable amounts of dollars fall upon his shoulders. That isn't in your mind when you are writing a book.

"I thought I was successful with *Julia* and *If You Could See Me Now*. I made something like thirty or forty thousand dollars a year. I had my own house. For a writer, that is success. Then, when *Ghost Story* sold to Pocket Books and Universal Pictures on the same day, I thought I was deluged with money. And for a time, I was really thrown off track.

"But financial success of that kind is actually a massive vote of confidence. In personal terms, it is very nice to go into a bookstore and have the clerk recognize your name—and to have the guy know what you have done and be curious about what you're doing to do next. That's a little pat on the back, a little smile from heaven.

"On another level, popular success doesn't seem quite real to me. I know that I have to sit down and break my back to do anything of merit. I know that I am not rewarded for the wonderfulness of my character. I am rewarded for working very, very hard—painfully and to exhaustion. Not everybody would want that kind of success. On the other hand, most of the time I really *love* working. In case it isn't clear, I get real joy out of writing—out of invention at every level, every stage of the process. And I do get to have really good cars. I get to have nice houses. But I could perfectly well live in two rooms and work quite happily."

To what does he attribute the immense popularity of his books?

"If my books are enjoyed by large numbers of people, I think it must be because of a gift I have for writing narratives with a certain amount of emotional strength. Readers, I hope, find themselves personally involved, feel themselves at risk, and actually are carried ahead by the narrative pulse of the book. To attract readers in big numbers, you have to be able to hook them into your story. It isn't a consequence of going to graduate school and reading a million books. It's a consequence of discovering narrative muscle in yourself and the ability to construct scenes in such a way as to carry the reader through them."

How does he balance artistic and commercial impulses?

"The way I was taught to read novels never took into account randomness, chance, inspiration, or revision. It more or less presupposed that the object came out whole and entire and intricately linked in all of its parts—that it was born, or at least published, that way. But the experience of talking about literature that way is completely different from anybody's experience of writing it.

"There are no perfect masterpieces. Great ingenuity on the part of critics can create perfect masterpieces, but very few writers have ever done it. Things written one day would not be written the same way the next day, and in ten years you'll find things you'd be able to do better then.

"You should try to make each book as perfect as it can be, but you should not spend your whole lifetime working on one book, which seems, to me, to be a trap. You wind up accomplishing more in the long run if you decide to redress any imbalances in the next book and continue forward; it puts your vision forward, book by book, instead of pushing your vision always onto the same object. My model is more Dickensian, more exploratory, and more professional. That is, my job is to write books. It isn't to write a hundred books, but to write a number of books and to pursue my concerns throughout their course and to make each one as good as I can, but not to become so destructively obsessed with each one that I have to spend five or ten years on it. Yet I think it would be a lot of fun to rewrite every single book I've done, if I thought I was at last old enough.

"I hope that some of the books I have written will stay in print for a good time after my death. I would like to be seen as a serious worker in this field, who tried to contribute something of his own, who every now and then managed to pull off something pretty good and occasionally fell on his face."

Straub's ambition seems boundless. He followed *Ghost Story* with an entirely different kind of horror novel, *Shadowland* (1980), which explored fairy-tales and magic, searching for the root of supernatural fiction.

"There is no question about my being ambitious as a writer, but I think this is helpful. It's like having a cattle prod behind you—it keeps you moving. It would have been impossible for me, for example, to write a series of novels about the same character. To have been a series detective writer would have made me suicidal—to repeat myself over and over again with the same effects, the same voices, the same characters. Now some people manage to do a lot within that very constricting framework, but I would want to have taken in more territory, to get more of the world in my books."

Straub's mixed reactions to his return to suburban life in the United States formed the centre of *Floating Dragon* (1983), which saw an entire Connecticut town fall beneath the spell of evil. Now, with his wife, Susan, and their two children, Straub has moved from Westport to Manhattan—a move that also seemed to mark something of a transition away from writing about supernatural horror to tackling broader, more introspective themes in *Koko* (1988) and *Mystery* (1989).

"My view of horror had changed. I am a little bit dissatisfied now. I used to think that if you just swam far enough into horror, you would eventually find counterparts for everything in the world. Now I am not so sure. The field seems narrower to me, but that may be just my own response to *Floating Dragon*, where I tried to do everything I could think of.

"After *Floating Dragon*, I'm tired of using the typical materials of the genre. I don't want to write any more about animated corpses, about devils, about inexplicable fires, about loathsome diseases. I want to work with material closer to the human vein. I don't want to write John Updike novels, but I want to preserve what is good in me and use it in more general themes. I think that would be good for my writing, and I think it would lead to better books."

But as he talks about *Koko*, it is clear that Straub does not propose to leave the field entirely.

"*Koko* incorporates some of the motivations and imagery of horror and fantasy without indulging in the characteristic manoeuvres of horror and fantasy.

"I wanted to look at the emotional conditions that prevail in horror, which are striking and eccentric. Horror is very internal. It works with naked subconscious material. And it has a lot to do with fears of loss and fears of emptiness—with feelings of powerlessness. It also has to do with psychosis, with the embrace of madness, since it deals with things than cannot be, that never have been and never will be. So there's a kind of wilful suspension of rationality. *Koko* looks into that, but from the point of view of a madman instead of that of a sane man seeing monsters, because it is a truer perspective, I think.

"I would really like to see the horror novel move in the direction of literary accomplishment, which to a certain extent it already has—to the level of serious art and of involved, committed writing, of moral complexity. I would like to see more horror novels that can be read as serious novels—that are scary and enjoyable but which are also beautiful and moving. The other interesting thing would be to have more people come along who have genuinely strange, powerful minds and cannot help but see the world in odd, exotic patterns—provided they can actually write. Otherwise, the books would look like a series of wet dreams by amateurish high school writers."

On that note, we discuss the fact that most horror fiction

lacks explicit sexuality. Does he view horror as animated by elements of sexual repression?

"A lot of horror is, I think, a kind of unconscious flinching away from sex and death—and a way of dealing with the flinch. It is interesting that there are hardly any forthright sexual scenes in modern horror novels; and when they are a big feature in the work, they don't perform the way they should, so to speak.

"Explicit sexuality in a novel ought to be powerful—powerful enough, I always thought, to drain away the impact of horror. But if there is a bubbling, almost unacknowledged aura of sexual feeling in a book—trapped, unexpressed by the characters—it colours the horror. Repressed sexuality and misogyny are streams running straight through horror fiction.

"Now I personally do not feel at all misogynistic, nor do I feel at all afraid of sex. On the other hand, nor do I feel entirely interested in straightforward horror novels anymore."

The restless intricacies of Peter Straub seem symbolized by his avid enthusiasm for jazz. He has no doubt about what career he would choose if he could have the choice: "I would be a saxophone player." As the interview ends, he lovingly describes the classic Selmer Mark Six tenor saxophone, nearly forty years old, that he owns—as a piece of art, not as an instrument. In secret, special moments, however, he has tried to play it: "But you wouldn't call the noises that emit from it music. When I was a kid in school, I had trombone lessons. And when I quit, the teacher said, 'Peter, one day you are really going to be sorry that you quit.' And he was right."

I ask him to list his favourite jazz artists, but once started, he can't seem to stop. "What I like about these people is that they are purely expressive. Through these Rube Goldberg inventions that they stick in their mouths, they make delicate, passionate, exuberant, thoughtful, lyrical, expressive statements. My life would be a lot poorer without this kind of music, and I would be immeasurably poorer without what it has taught me, since a lot of what I think I know about art I got from listening to jazz records. I value virtuosity. I think it is a positive good—to be able to do undo-able things on your instrument, whether it be a word processor or a saxophone. I love the way music comes through jazz musicians. They don't think about it much when they are doing it, but within their minds are endless numbers of spontaneous patterns, and on good nights, they can create highly organized statements that are beautiful, passionate, charged with feeling. And I think it's the only thing better than words.

"I also like the immediacy of jazz—that someone plays and somebody else hears it right away. This is completely unlike writing a novel. I think that would be delightful, to be able to get instant feedback.

"I play jazz records all of the time when I work. It puts in the air a feeling of creation—of spontaneous, informed creativity. Half the time, I don't really hear it—it might as well not be on.

"But other times, I hear it and I hear a guy really doing something and I say to myself, 'Go, Peter, try to do that.'"

Stephen King

"I guess it's just my fate."

Stephen King stands at the far side of the kitchen, grilling the largest hamburgers I have ever seen. I'm sitting at the dinette table, staring out into a snowstorm that descended two nights before on Bangor, Maine, and that now, nearly thirty-six hours later, shows no signs of relenting. Snow is drifting up onto the windows of King's house, and we've been drinking a lot of beer and watching videotapes and talking into a tape machine, and slowly, ever so slowly, going stir-crazy.

"So you're putting together a book of interviews with horror writers," he says, shovelling the Godzillas of ground beef onto paper plates and walking over to join me.

"I dunno, Doug. I couldn't imagine a more ordinary group of guys. You're going to have to go out of your way to make this one interesting."

He sits down next to me and digs in. I'm still debating how to wrestle my burger off of my plate when I hear his muffled voice call to me.

"Doug."

I look up, and he shows me a mouthful of food.

Months later, the snow is gone; indeed, we're basking in the sun of southern Florida. It is the last day of spring training, and the only seats available in the small stadium are high atop its concrete bleachers. Armed with hot dogs and beer, we watch the Mets take on the Yankees in what wishful New

Yorkers might hope is a preview of the World Series six months away.

The game is barely underway when Yankee outfielder Steve Kemp, a barrel-torsoed lefthander, lumbers to the plate to bat. King elbows me, rising to a half-stand. "You bum!" he yells, then laughs. "This guy never fails to cream the Red Sox," he tells me before calling again: "Get outta here, Kemp, you bum!"

The fellow in front of us turns around. I expect the wrath of a Yankee fan, but he simply looks at King and says, "You hate him so much, you ought to put him in one of your books."

King is taken aback; he stares at him momentarily, then smiles. "I already did," he replies; but the man, no doubt having never read *Cujo*, shrugs and returns his attention to the game.

Stephen King leans toward me and whispers: "Jeez, Doug. Does *everybody* know me?"

One of the questions that I've come to learn to live with over the past few years is "What is Stephen King really like?" It's been asked of me by closest friends and total strangers, on the street, in classrooms, on radio talk shows, at cocktail parties—even twice in interviews for this book.

In searching for an answer, I've occasionally told amusing anecdotes like those above, which to me reveal important—and endearing—things about Stephen King and his career. But I've recently embraced the easy answer, which is to say that, if I could really sum him up in a few words, I wouldn't have had to write a book about him.

It is also, as are many easy answers, the truth.

He is, in one sense, the horror writer who needs no introduction. In little more than fifteen years, a hundred million copies of his books have been sold worldwide and eighteen motion pictures have been based on his work. His incredible popular success, coupled with an unassuming charisma, make him an ideal target for the cult of personality, and he is profiled regularly in such venues as *People* magazine and the

Entertainment Tonight television show. He has even succumbed to the irresistible invitation to parody himself for an American Express television commercial.

But it is precisely this visibility and popularity of Stephen King the horror writer that makes necessary a proper introduction—of the person, not the personality.

Here are the basic facts: Stephen Edwin King was born on 21 September 1947, in Portland, Maine. He was a midlife child, and something of a surprise—his older brother, David, had been adopted earlier when his mother was told by doctors that she could not bear a child. Even today, he lives his quiet and staggeringly productive life in Maine. His wife, Tabitha, is herself an accomplished writer, as witness her novels *Small World* (1981), *Caretakers* (1983), *The Trap* (1985) and *Pearl* (1988). With their three children, the Kings move seasonally between a contemporary summer home on Kezar Lake in Center Lovell and a large Victorian house in Bangor.

Stephen King is of Scots-Irish ancestry; he stands six feet four inches tall—hunching his shoulders slightly as if shy of showing his height—and weighs just over two hundred pounds. He is blue-eyed, fair-skinned, and has thick black hair; in winter, he usually grows a heavy beard. He has worn glasses since he was a young child, although he occasionally uses contact lenses. King plays tennis and softball in season, favouring the Boston Red Sox. He likes beer in quantity and loud rock-and-roll, does battle with a cigarette habit, and has been known to eat Excedrin dry when he has a headache. He tries to write every day except for his birthday, Christmas, and the fourth of July. His stories exist "because it occurred to me to write them. I have a marketable obsession".

That obsession has made Stephen King, in little more than a decade, the best-selling writer of horror fiction of all time—and, indeed, a publishing category unto himself. His meteoric rise began in 1976, with the release of Brian De Palma's motion picture adaptation of *Carrie* (1974) and the substantial sales of the paperback editions of that book and King's second novel, *'Salem's Lot* (1975). With the publication of his first hardcover bestseller, *The Shining* (1977), and of *The*

Stand (1978) and the short-story collection *Night Shift* (1978), his reputation as the modern master of the macabre was firmly established. *The Dead Zone* (1979) perched for more than six months on the *New York Times* bestseller lists and was followed by the similar popular successes of the novels *Firestarter* (1980) and *Cujo* (1981) a non-fictional reminiscence of the past three decades of horror, *Danse Macabre* (1981) and a collection of four novellas, *Different Seasons* (1982). In 1983, two King novels—*Christine* and *Pet Sematary*—saw print, and at the end of that year, they respectively occupied first positions in *Publishers Weekly*'s listings of bestselling paperback and hardcover books. His collaboration with Peter Straub, *The Talisman*, had hardcover sales of nearly one million copies in 1984; and a new collection of short stories, *Skeleton Crew*, appeared in 1985.

Then in less than sixteen months, his publishers released four new novels, *It* (1986); and *Misery*, *Eyes of the Dragon*, and *The Tommyknockers* (all 1987). They were followed in 1989 by *The Dark Half*, whose first American printing totalled a record 1.5 million copies.

In addition, King has published five novels—including two written while in college—under the pseudonym Richard Bachman: *Rage* (1977), *The Long Walk* (1979), *Roadwork* (1981), *The Running Man* (1982), and *Thinner* (1984). The pseudonym was used, he notes, "to publish stuff when I didn't want to be Stephen King. Paul McCartney used to talk about the idea of the Beatles going around to small clubs, playing gigs in masks or something—anything but as the Beatles. That's what Richard Bachman tried to do."

By the close of 1990, eleven of King's novels—and one of his short stories, "Children of the Corn"—had been produced as feature films, and 'Salem's Lot had been produced as a four-hour television mini-series. King himself had collaborated with director George A. Romero on an original film anthology, *Creepshow* (1982), and had also written the screenplays for the original motion picture *Cat's Eye* (1985), an adaptation of his novelette "Cycle of the Werewolf" entitled *Silver Bullet* (1985). He had also directed his first feature film, *Maximum Overdrive* (1986), based on his short story "Trucks".

Because Stephen King is so often the subject of personality journalism, and because I have written at length elsewhere about his life and work, it seemed a more fitting close to *The Faces of Fear* to let the most popular horror writer of all time simply speak for himself—about his life, his fiction, and the pleasures and perils of his success. I have selected the most telling excerpts from our many recorded conversations, and present them here in their original question-and-answer format.

It's now been some fifteen years since the publication of Carrie. *You've gone from writing in a little trailer in Hermon, Maine, when a short-story sale literally meant heat for the next month, to becoming one of the best-selling writers of our time. You've not only gained notoriety, but also security. Is it harder to find fear?*

"No, it's no harder to find fear than it used to be. In the years since *Carrie* was published, I have entered heart attack country—but nothing really changes inside, in the sense that I still feel vulnerable. Sometimes the objects of my fear change, and sometimes the quality of my fear changes—but I find too much fear, in a way.

"I can't go to sleep in a hotel without thinking, 'Who is in the room underneath me, dead drunk and smoking a cigarette and about to fall asleep so that the room catches fire? When was the last time that they changed the batteries in the smoke detector?'

"I worry about aeroplanes. I can remember being on a transcontinental flight and getting to the half-way point—which the stewardesses always announce with great cheer—although what they are actually saying is that you are now too far to turn back. You either have to go ahead or die. And I thought, what if somebody said, "I need a pillow," and the stewardess opened the overhead rack and all these rats came out into her face, and she started to scream, and the rats were biting off her nose and everything else, and one of the people in first class opened up a pouch to get an airsick bag because this was so gross, and rats came out of there, rats came out of everywhere. And the name of this story was going to be 'The Rats Are Loose on Flight 74'. I just haven't got around to writing it yet, but I probably will.

"I can still find fear. I can find more fear than I used to be able to find. Now, because I have some money, I can worry about whether bad guys are going to come and kidnap my kids and hold them for ransom. You're afraid of what it's doing to their lives. You're afraid of what it's doing to your own life. The last time I came home, the kids wanted to see my driver's licence to make sure I was their father. Yes, it's still possible to be afraid.

"I wish I could get away from horror for a while, and I do—or I think I do, and then suddenly I discover that I'm like the guy in the poem by Auden who runs and runs and finally ends up in a cheap, one-night hotel. He goes down a hallway and opens a door, and there he meets himself sitting under a naked light bulb, writing.

"And that's the way it's always been with me. If I try to write something else, sooner or later, it always comes back to the guy who is awake in the night and hears something getting closer and closer.

"I guess it's just my fate."

I asked Ramsey Campbell, who always seems to be smiling, why it was that horror writers were such a genial lot, and he replied, "It's a façade." You've read his introduction to The Face That Must Die, *where he talks of his childhood and its impact on his career as a horror writer. It's sometimes said that if you write horror fiction, you must have had a warped childhood. That's not your view, is it?*

"I don't think that it is. People who smile and laugh a lot—this is a sign of people who are *mad*. In Boulder, where we lived for a while, we used to go to a little park that, in *The Stand*, is right across from Harold Lauder's house, where he and Nadine make a do-it-yourself demolition kit. I realized, when we were going there on the bus, that there was something not right about the people on the bus because they were all laughing. Some of them would pick their noses and laugh, some would pick their seats and laugh, and I realized after a while that these people were all retarded. And when we got off the bus, I said to my kids, 'Did you make anything of those people?' And my daughter, who was six then, said, 'They were happy people, weren't they, Daddy?' And I said, 'Yes, they were happy people.'

"A lot of horror writers and fantasy writers I know do laugh and smile a lot. And it *is* a façade because most of us are half-way to being crazy—I would guess that, down underneath, a lot of us are really certifiable.

"There is this wonderful moment in 'The Cask of Amontillado' where a fellow is walling this guy up, and he's laughing. I always loved it. I used it in 'The Crate', which became part of *Creepshow*. Hal Holbrook played the guy who finally entices his wife down the stairs and she's asking him where this grad student is who is supposed to have got into trouble, and he says, laughing, 'She's under the stairs.' And she says, 'Your best friend is in trouble and you're laughing. What's the matter with you?' And he says, 'It is sort of funny, wait till you see.' And it *is*, really. That's the final level. And so we laugh and smile a lot because I would say we are tottering, most of us, on the brink."

But what about warped childhoods?

"Oh, warped childhood. That's all crap.

"People always want to know what happened in your childhood. The reason is because they have to separate 'them' from 'us'—to find some way of differentiating: 'There has to be some reason why all this shit is going down, why they're writing all these terrible things.' I think of myself as a fairly cheerful person. As far as my childhood being happy or unhappy, my memories are that it was quite happy, in a lonely or solitary way. But I could be mythologizing my own history—I know that people do that."

Did you have that sort of classic writer's childhood, where you felt alienated and retreated into books, into reading and telling stories, rather than interacting a great deal with others?

"Only to a degree. Inside, I felt different and unhappy a lot of times. I felt *violent* a lot of times. But not a whole lot of that came out, because in the family I came from, there was a high premium on keeping yourself to yourself—on maintaining a pleasant exterior—saying 'please' and 'thank you' and using your handkerchief even if you're on the *Titanic* and it's going down, because that's the way you were supposed to behave.

"But I hung out with the kids. I worked on cars, played sports as much as I could. I was a tuition kid, and it was a long way back and forth, so I wasn't involved in basketball and stuff like that. I had to play football, because I was big. If you didn't play football and you were big, it meant you were a fucking faggot, right? That's what it's like when you come from a small town.

"So I kept that other part of myself to myself. I never wanted to let anybody get at it. I figured that they'd steal it, if they knew what I thought about this or that or the other thing. It wasn't the same as being embarrassed about it, so much as wanting to keep it and sort of work it out for myself."

Many of your child characters—Carrie, Charlie McGee of Fire-starter, *Lard Ass Hogan of "The Body" in* Different Seasons—*are put upon by others, and forced to react in violent ways. You obviously identify a great deal with that sort of character.*

"Yeah, I have felt that way a lot. I have always felt tremendous feelings of aggression that I had to cover up, because it just seemed not cool to be going around always flying off the handle. And writing was a clear channel for that. I think that is why there is so much destruction in my books, because it is a way of getting rid of a lot of that energy that I can't get rid of in my day-to-day life. At the end of *Firestarter*—where Charlie McGee, who has been put upon so much, tears everything up—there's an effort, I think, to find ways of saying that this is justified destruction, because I have never been interested in destruction for the sake of destruction. But there's a great catharsis that turns it outward. It's me saying, 'Never mind my childhood.' I am doing this because there is a great catharsis in this for the reader. But that doesn't change the fact that it works for me personally.

"I have always felt a real dichotomy between the way that

I know that I am supposed to act and the way that I really feel a lot of the time. The way I feel a lot of the time is anarchic. It's shameful of me to even admit that, because you are not supposed to say that a lot of times you feel sort of crazy."

You had a fairly fundamentalist religious upbringing, which comes out in many of your books. How do you measure that upbringing against your current religious feelings?

"Well, my religious feelings have not changed much over the years; they are as traditional as the stuff that I write. They are not complete. I believe in God. I think there is a God. I suspect that Jesus Christ may have been divine. I believe what I write when I say that we live in the centre of a mystery. Believing that there is just life, and that's the end of it, seems to me as primitive as believing that the entire universe revolves around the earth.

"On the level of conservation, the idea offends me that you can spend sixty-five, seventy-five, eighty-five years of your life as a pilgrim storing up not just data and conclusions but some kind of wisdom, some kind of moral ability, and then one day you wake up dead, and that's the end—your brain is just so much useless clay and they can carve you up and put you in the fields. I don't believe that. On the other hand, it's very tough for me to believe in anything about organized religion. I think Jerry Falwell is a monster and I think Jimmy Swaggart is a monster.

"I was raised Methodist, fairly strict. We had Thursday night Bible School, and there was a big poster that read 'Methodists say, *No, thank you*'. We were allowed to dance, but the hips couldn't touch. We memorized Bible verses, for which we got little statues of the crucified Christ, which you could then paint. Blood from hands and feet was optional. And, of course, I listened to a lot of fire and brimstone as a child. My wife was raised fundamentalist Catholic—you know, deep-dyed, French Catholic Northern Maine as only they can be, with hell-fire on Sunday and Beano on Thursday. The nuns would say, 'Give them to me when they are five, and they'll be mine forever.' And that's true.

"Part of me will always be that Methodist kid who was told that you were not saved by work alone, and the hell-fire was very long—the idea that the pigeon comes to polish his beak on the top of the iron mountain once every ten thousand years, and by the time that mountain is worn down, that's the first second of your stay in Hell. When you are six or seven years old, that kind of stuff bends your mind a little. So it keeps coming back in my fiction. And the major reason, I think, is that I still believe that most of the ideas expressed by Christianity—particularly the progression from the Old Testament ideas to the New Testament ideas—are morally valid. And they make interesting sounding boards for a lot of supernatural fiction."

When did you actually start writing?

"I think I must have been seven or eight. I was sick, just constantly sick; there was one year I was sick all the time. I didn't go to school or anything, I just lay there in bed and wrote a lot of stories, and I really liked it. And I was very aware of how bad I was, and so sometimes I would copy stories. And then somebody told me, 'Oh, Stevie, that's wrong. You can go to *jail* for that!' So I stopped doing that; but I never stopped writing again.

"I can remember the first real horror story that I wrote. I was about seven years old, and I had internalized the idea from the movies that, when everything looked blackest, the scientists would come up with some off-the-wall solution that would take care of things. I wrote about this big dinosaur that was really ripping ass all over everything, and finally one guy said, 'Wait, I have a theory—the old dinosaurs used to be allergic to leather.' So they went out and they threw leather boots and leather shoes and leather vests at it, and it went away."

What other kinds of stories did you write?

"I was imitating everything that I liked. I would have short stories where I started off sounding like Ray Bradbury and ended up sounding like Clark Ashton Smith—or even worse, they would start off as James M. Cain and end as H.P. Lovecraft. I was just silly putty. And still today, there will be critical reviews that say, 'The kindest thing we can say about Steve King is that he doesn't have much of a style.'

"You know, I never have and I know that. Whatever it is, that stylistic thing, I can't isolate it in myself; and I'm not sure I even want to, because I think that there's a lot of critical interest in writing that is pretty rather than writing that is serviceable. I don't really want people to see my face in the book at all. If they want to look at the back and see my face on the book jacket, that's one thing, but I don't feel like I have to put my brand on a book."

When did you begin to think about actually selling what you wrote?

"I started to submit stuff when I was about twelve, to places like *Fantastic* and *Fantasy & Science Fiction*, mostly science-fiction and fantasy magazines. These stories had the trappings of science fiction—they were set in outer space—but they were really horror stories. One of the few good ones was about an asteroid miner who discovered a pink cube, and all this stuff started to come out of the cube and drive him back further and further into his little space hut, breaching the airlocks one after the other. And the thing got him in the end. All of the science-fiction magazines sent it back, because they knew goddamn well there was no science in it—there were no aliens trying to communicate using psionic talents, or anything like that. There was just this big pink thing that was going to eat someone, and it ate him."

Who was your major influence—the writer who had the truly significant impact upon the development of your writing?

"The guy who taught me to do what I am doing is Richard Matheson. Because I knew, instinctively, that I was trying to find a way to get back home, to where I belonged. I had read Poe and I had read a lot of Gothic novelists, and even with Lovecraft I felt as though I were in Europe somewhere. I loved the idea of the ghost story, and to a certain extent, I even loved the Gothic conventions that surround that kind of story. But I wanted to be at home, and I didn't know if it could be done. And then I read Richard Matheson's *I Am Legend*, where this fellow is blockading himself in his house every night—and it wasn't a castle, it was a tract house in Los Angeles. He was going out and staking vampires every day, finding them at the cold counter at Stop and Shop, laid out like lamb chops or something. And I realized then that horror didn't have to happen in a haunted castle; it could happen in the suburbs, on your street, maybe right next door."

You have worked right next door in most of your fiction—using Maine settings, even creating an entire fictional Maine landscape. Has life in Maine been an influence on your fiction?

"I don't really know, because I'm really too close to that thing. I am a part of that landscape, because I've lived in Maine almost all my life. I was born there and I've lived there full-time since 1958 or 1959, when we moved back after four years in Connecticut, which was the only urban experience we had until we moved to Bangor a few years ago. And Bangor is not exactly New York, with 35,000 people.

"All I can say is that Maine is a rural existence; and in that sense, it is universal, but only to rural people. The majority of our population lives in cities, and some of the success that I've enjoyed may be a longing for rural scenes.

"In a realistic sense—or in the sense that realism reflects myth in the story or idea in the story—I hate the country. I love Maine and I hate it. There's a bitter feel to the real country. When you think of Maine, you probably think of lobsters and the seacoast and Bar Harbor and sailboats and all that stuff. But the real country is poor people with no teeth. Junked-out cars in people's yards. Poverty. Food stamps. Hostility to the people who use food stamps. Indians who drink too much because it's expected of them. A kind of grotesque comedy of people who are so out of touch with the rest of the world that sometimes they live in their cars; they live in pup tents in the woods with great big colour TVs inside them. I could go on and on, and none of it really means anything, except to say that I also love it. I loved that guy Joe Camber in *Cujo*, but I also hated him because he was an asshole. But he was *my* asshole—not in the physiological sense, you understand. What I mean is that I know the guy and I love him because he's like me."

Before Carrie *sold, you had written five novels—more than fifteen hundred manuscript pages of work—that had not sold. What did it feel like when publishers not only bought* Carrie *but paid an incredible sum for it?*

"We were living in what really was a tenement in Bangor. It was a dreadful little hole, and we had a second-floor walkup. Our baby used to get up in the crib and eat the wallpaper. The couple upstairs fought every Friday night—it was very uplifting. So the phone rang one Sunday afternoon, and it was Bill Thompson from Doubleday, who said, 'We've got a paperback deal,' and I said, 'That's great.'

"My wife and I had sat down and talked about this, and she wanted to know what the possibilities were. And I said, 'Well, realistically, I think that it will sell to paperback, and I think we can look for a sum from $5,000 to $12,000, but that sums up to $60,000 might be in the ballpark.' And her eyes got big and round about $60,000, but we would have to split it fifty-fifty with Doubleday—which is where Doubleday and I finally came apart. But even $30,000 seemed unheard of. And my idea was that I could quit teaching for two years and actually get out from under the eight-ball and write two books, maybe even three if I wrote very, very fast.

"So when the phone rang and he said we had a deal, I said, 'How much is it?' and he said, 'Well, I think you better sit down.'

"I said again, 'How much?' And he said, 'Well, it's $400,000.' And I sat down on the floor. The strength went out of my legs and I fell right down on my ass on the linoleum in the kitchen. I said, 'You said $40,000?' and he said, 'Nope, $400,000.' I said, 'This is four hundred thousand *dollars*?' And he said, 'Yeah.'

"My wife was not at home. When that conversation was over, I hung up, and I walked around the house, running my hands through my hair, stopping, then sitting down for a minute and looking blankly out of the window. Then I would get up and walk around the house, running my hands through my hair some more. The thought going through my mind was that I had to do something—I had to mark this.

"After about twenty minutes, I finally decided that I was going to get Tabby a present. I was going to do it right now, and as I crossed the street, a drunk would come along in a car and he would kill me, and things would be put back in perspective. So I went downtown and bought her a hair dryer for twenty-nine dollars— and I scuttled across those streets, looking both ways."

What kind of impact did that sudden influx of money have upon you?

"Tabby and I argued more about money after *Carrie* than we ever had before, because before, we didn't have anything to argue over. She would say, 'Well, let's get a house now.' And I would say, 'No, I don't feel secure. What if I never sell anything else, and I've got this mortgage? No, no, no.' And she got very exasperated with me after a while, which she deserved to do. She was saying, 'You've made all this money. You *are* a success. Let's spend some of it.' And I was insecure—I was very insecure for a long time—and I was saying, 'Look, I don't trust this. Nobody can do this. You can't do this twice or three times.' So my idea was, let's keep it, and I'll be able to write for a much longer time, because it will never happen again, but I can trickle the money out. The kids will be eating Cheerios and peanut butter for dinner, but that's OK. Let them. I'll be writing.

"Today, my family is more important to me than the writing; it's been a gradual change. In 1975, if somebody had said, 'You have to pick one, the family or the writing,' I might very well have said, 'It's got to be the writing, because if I take the other, there won't be anything left for me.' But that isn't the way that I feel now. If somebody offered me that choice, I would say, 'Well, it's got to be the family.' I wouldn't even think twice about it."

Today, your writing has become a very public thing. You have become very public. People come to interview you constantly, to ask you to appear on talk shows, at lectures, in print—anywhere and everywhere. You've even written an article about becoming a "brand

*name", and I know you're very conscious of it. Has it changed the
way you look at writing?*

"Yeah, and I hate it. Being a 'brand name' has been a very
distressing thing. And yet, at the same time, it isn't anything
that I would change, because it got me all this. I mean, this
is a great place. My kid's out there with somebody to sort of
watch out for him and all of that, so I don't crap on it. And
it's always, in a way, what I wanted.

"In college, I would go around with a John D. MacDonald
book, or a collection of short stories by Robert Bloch, and
some asshole would always say, 'Why are you reading that?'
And I'd say, 'Hey, this man is a great writer.' And in fact,
MacDonald has written a novel called *The End of the Night*
which I would argue is one of the great American novels of
the twentieth century. It ranks with *Death of a Salesman*; it
ranks with *An American Tragedy*.

"But people would see the picture on the front, a Gold
Medal paperback with some lady with her cakes falling out
of her blouse, and they'd say, 'It's garbage.' So I'd say, 'Have
you read anything by this guy?' 'No, all I gotta do is look at
that book, and I know.' Which was my first experience with
critics—in this case, my teachers in college.

"I always liked that kind of fiction, and that's what I always
wanted to write. There ought to be a middle ground, where
you can do it with some nobility, instead of either (A) being
a schlockmeister, or (B) saying, 'Hey, everybody's just *saying*
that I'm only a popular writer. They don't understand how
sensitive my soul is.' There ought to be a place in the middle
where you can say, 'I'm trying to do the best I can with what
I've got, and create things that are at least as honest as
what any craftsman would make'—you know, what you would
expect from *physical* work."

*Is categorization part of the problem—that books can no longer
simply be books, but must be Type A or Type B or Type C, western
or romance or horror?*

"Properties. It has got to be a little bit like cereal, this urge
to make brand names.

"It bothers me now more than it used to, because there's

all this money riding on it. And it isn't that you're afraid that someone will say, 'I don't like this.' What I'm really afraid of now is that somebody will say, 'I think this is great because it fits the publication schedule.' I'm terrified of that. Every year I am on a faster track. For the publishers, it isn't a matter of creativity or trying to do the best book possible that's governing things right now. It's advertising. And that scares the hell out of me, because we'll fuck up really good one of these days, and then when people say 'Stephen King writes for money', at that point, they will be right.

"The product itself becomes very important. In the case of the last few books that Viking has done, the hardcover sales have been enormous—hundreds of thousands of copies in hardcover. So we're talking about a gross income that would be like $15.95 times hundreds of thousands. It's a huge gross, and just the amount of time that they're able to hold that money is important in terms of profit; it generates interest. I would not be willing to say that I'm the Viking franchise—that's ridiculous, they've got other writers who sell a lot of copies—but it's important enough so that, at this point, if there was a change suggested to me that I didn't like or I didn't want, I would simply have to say, 'No, I won't do that.' And it would never be a question of withdrawing the contract, would it? I mean, they'd just finally say, 'Well, OK. We won't do it.' Which means, in effect, that if I'm willing to be really intransigent, there's no editing at all; and that's a terrible position to be in. You just have to say to yourself, I will take editing and I will continue to do some things, even if I think they're wrong."

How do you face the age-old problem of balancing commercial and artistic impulses—of writing for the market or writing for yourself?

"Well, I always wrote for myself. There is no trick to balancing that off. I always wrote for myself, and then I looked for a market that was somewhere in the ballpark of what I was doing.

"I almost never think of an audience. I've got things so ridiculous that I *can't* be thinking of an audience. They amuse me and I don't have any idea whether they would amuse anyone else or not. I've got a novel-in-progress—I've put it aside now, because I've got a bunch of other stuff to do—but I've got about 450 pages done and it is all about these people who are trapped in an apartment building. Worst thing I could think of. And I thought, wouldn't it be funny if they all ended up eating each other? It's very, very bizarre, because it's all on one note. And who knows whether it will be published or not?

"And it really doesn't matter. I have got stuff piled up now so that I could continue to publish stuff that *I* think is commercial, so I don't give a fuck. I'll play around.

"Really, I am the only audience that I care about—and why not? I mean, I'm eating. Thousands aren't."

For you, what are the dangers of writing?

"There are manifold dangers in being successful, but I think that the real danger—the only danger that I know of—in the writing itself is that you tie up your self-image, your masculinity, whatever, in being able to do this. And you put it on the level of 'This is how I define myself'—by this function, by making these things up. And then, if you lose it, you have nothing—there is nothing left. I would like to be able to have some kind of meaningful life aside from writing; and I know that if it happened today, that I couldn't do it anymore, I wouldn't be able to find that. I would be able to find all the support that I needed in my family, but whatever it is that comes from inside, where you have to find some justification in yourself to go on, I wouldn't have it, because writing has been my aim for so long now.

"It was the way I defined myself, even as a kid. Maybe I couldn't put one past the centrefielder, and maybe all I was good for in football was left tackle. You know, I used to get cleat marks up my back.

"But I could write, so that was how I defined myself. And it is still how I define myself; and that's the danger that I see."

In Different Seasons, *in the story "Apt Pupil", the former Nazi death camp commandant who is hiding out in California*

*notes that there is apparently always an audience that is fascinated
with the kinds of stories that he has to tell. Does that fact ever
concern you, given the kinds of stories that you have to tell?*

. "Yeah. One of the things about *Pet Sematary*—and I think
it's a dirty, nasty book, and some of the fan mail reflects
that—is that it's a little bit disturbing to me to find that the
book not only went to number one, after *Christine* didn't, but
the sales were actually double in hard-cover over anything I
had ever done before.

"Twenty years ago, *Pet Sematary* would not have been a
publishable novel, not because of the language, but because
of its subject matter and theme. And the days of such equivo-
cations are gone. So, yet, it disturbs me that that taste is
there—in a sense, you can't gross people out, it's impossible
to do it. But I can't let it affect me. I try to do what I do,
and keep the morality of all situations in front of me, in the
sense that I want to tell the truth about what people would
do in these situations. Beyond that, somebody else has got
to figure this stuff out."

*One of a writer's most difficult problems is self-censorship. When
one is known as a horror writer—and particularly in your case,
where you are marketed as the "King of Horror" or whatever
hyperbole the copywriters choose—there must come a point at which
ideas, even if they are at first blush non-horrific, are transmuted,
consciously or unconsciously, into horror. Do you find that happening to you?*

"Yes. Your mind begins to go almost exclusively into that
vein. I don't really see it as a problem, as long as the idea is
good and it isn't just your mind fooling itself that an idea is
good just because it happens to be horror.

"There are a lot of people who are convinced that, as soon
as I have made enough money, I will just leave this silly
bullshit behind and go on to write *Brideshead Revisited* and
spy novels and things like that. I don't know *why* people think
that. This is all I've ever wanted to write; and if I go out and
I write a novel about baseball or about a plumber who's
having an affair with some other guy's wife—which I have
written, by the way—that is just because it occurred to me

at the time to write that story. And I don't think anybody would want me deliberately to reject an idea that really excited me.

"But you know, even the stories in *Different Seasons*, underneath, are really horror stories. They are like *Cujo* in the sense that we're getting a little close to the possible, and in this case it crosses over the line. The 'Apt Pupil' story, the one about the Nazi war criminal, is just dreadful. My publishers called and protested. They were very disturbed by the piece. Extremely disturbed. It was too *real*. If the same story had been set in outer space, it would have been OK, because then you would have had that comforting layer of 'Well, this is just make-believe, so we can dismiss it.'

"And I thought to myself, 'Gee, I've done it again. I've written something that has really got under someone's skin.' And I do like that. I like the feeling that I reached between somebody's legs like that. There has always been that primitive impulse as part of my writing.

"I don't really care for psychoanalysing myself. All I care about is when I find out what it is that scares me. That way, I can discover a theme, and then I can unify the story and magnify that effect and make the reader even more frightened than I am.

"I think I can really scare people, to the point where they will say, 'I'm really sorry I bought this.' It's as if I'm the dentist, and I'm uncovering a nerve—not to fix it, but to drill on it."

People constantly say how much they love *Stephen King, how much they* love *your books. Is there a dichotomy there, in terms of what you like to do, and what you are doing to the reader?*

"No, I don't think so. The response, the good response that comes that way, is to the openness of the stories, the accessibility of the stories, I think. And the fact that, in most cases, the characters seem very open and accessible, too. They seem like people that you would like to know, or even people that you *do* know. People respond to that, and there is very little of that in novels today. A lot of writers seem to want to stand very far away from their characters, and so the characters are kind of self-contained—it is tough to get inside of them. There's this feeling that they are moving around on little tracks, and that you are not moving with them.

"I believe that most people are all right. That's my experience. I don't believe that there is a middle-class, bourgeois experience that makes people bad, or an upper-class or lower-class experience that makes people bad. I am a guy who goes and eats at Wendy's, and I feel OK about most everybody. I don't feel bad about anybody, and that shows up. In most of the books, I think, there's a kind of Steve King hammock that you fall into—and you feel really comfortable in that hammock, because you know these people and you feel good about them. You don't have unease about who they are; you have unease about the circumstances that they find themselves in. And that's where the suspense comes from.

"I'll never forget the time when we were sitting around and bullshitting in college. This was the late '60s, and we were talking about Mr Middle Class, shitting all over the life-style and everything, and I said, 'Yeah, it's vinyl hoses and backyard barbecues.' And a girl said, 'Gee, I don't know. We used to have backyard barbecues a lot. I used to think they were really nice.' And I thought to myself, That's right. You had some, too, and liked them. So what the fuck are you talking about?"

What about the reaction to Cujo *and* Pet Sematary? *A lot of people were very disturbed by those books, and didn't like them for that reason. I was very disturbed by them, and I liked them for that reason.*

"Well, I know, but you are a more unusual case; that is to say, you have a tendency to read critically and to read for different values than I think a lot of people do.

"All I can say is that . . . I did it. I'm not entirely glad I did it, but they came out of such a dark time in my life. We thought Owen was hydrocephalic—and goddamnit, kids *do* die. You can't continue to write this kind of thing over and over again and finish up by saying, 'Oh, yes, and the kid was all right. God took care of him again, folks. Go to bed. Go to sleep. Don't worry.' Because they die. Kids get run over, they get knocked out of their cowboy boots. People pick them up and take them away forever. They get cot death, leukaemia. It isn't a large percentage—most of them do fine. But it has to be put into the equation: the possibility that there is no God and nothing works for the best. I don't necessarily subscribe to it, but I don't know what I do subscribe to. Why do I have to have a world view? I mean, shit, when I wrote those books, I wasn't even old enough to be President. Maybe I will when I'm forty, or when I'm forty-five, but I don't now. I'm just trying on all of these hats.

"And most of the books actually have had things in them that were pretty optimistic. There have been some cases where I felt things would turn out a lot worse than they did. In 'Salem's Lot, I wanted everybody to die at the end, because I thought that it would be the perfect balance to Dracula. But I just got to like the kid and the man and I let them get away."

There is an important political element in 'Salem's Lot, but not until The Stand, at least in your novels, were sociopolitical concerns explicitly at the forefront. During the 1984 presidential campaign, you went stumping for Gary Hart. How do the sociopolitical concerns voiced in your books tie in with your campaigning?

"Well, for me, the really critical line is in 'Salem's Lot, where Ben finally tells his girlfriend, Susan Norton, what he thinks is going on. And she begins to sputter and say, 'Well, you can't really mean this, vampires and everything.' And he says, 'The whole fucking world is coming down around your ears, and you're sticking at a few vampires.' And in most cases, that's how I feel about the stuff I write. Everything's falling down everywhere. Everything is turning to shit in a political sense and I've tried to say that in some of the books.

"The thing that I come back to since The Stand is that all of those things are laying around waiting for somebody to pick them up—you know, the gadgetry. And I get haunted by the idea of gadgets, because that's all it is—gadgets. It's all stuff hooked together with rubber bands and Elmer's

Glue; it's all insert Tab A into Tab B. And we *love* things like that . . .

"So now that we have nuclear bombs, we have stuff that can kill twenty million people in twelve seconds. CBW, nerve gas, the nukes, all of this stuff, it's just gadgets, that's all it is. Our technology has outraced our morality. And I don't think it's possible to stick the devil back in the box. I think that it will kill us all in the next twenty years.

"Every day, when I wake up and turn on the news, I wait for someone to say that Paris was obliterated last night . . . by a gadget. It's only the grace of God that has kept it from happening so far.

"But at the same time, I think that you have to try, so that if we do go on after we die, when we discorporate, we can look around at the spirits of our dead kids and say, 'Hey, I tried. My hands are clean.' You've got a kid who's twelve years old. What are you going to say to him after the big one goes up? Even if we don't go on, if you've got twelve minutes before the missiles land, you turn around and the kid says to you, 'I understand the world is ending, Dad. What did you do to stop this from happening?' And you say, 'Well, I played my Doors tapes.' It doesn't work. 'I gave to CARE. When the UNICEF volunteer came to my door, I gave what I could.' You can't say that, it's not sufficient.

"And particularly, it's not sufficient for me, because I own my own nuclear missile silo somewhere in Kansas, I think, with my taxes and all. That's mine. That's *my* Titan missile. I paid for it with my tax dollars over the years since *Carrie*. They are *my* cinderblocks; it's *my* liquid oxygen that's in the veins and in the fuel tank. It's *my* warhead, and I would like to do something about keeping it in that hole in the ground."

What do you see as the most essential element of a good horror story?

"Character. You've got to love the people. See, that's the real paradox. There has to be love involved, because the more you love—kids like Tad Trenton in *Cujo* or Danny Torrance in *The Shining*—then that allows horror to be possible. There is no horror without love and feeling. If you have that, then horror is possible, because horror is the contrasting emotion to our understanding of all the things that are good and normal. Without a concept of normality, there is no horror.

"So in that sense, I think that if you can bring on characters that people believe, that people accept as part of the normal spectrum, then you can write horror. It's the problem that a lot of the supermarket novels have. You don't believe the people, and therefore, you don't believe the horror and you're not scared."

Despite the millions of copies of books that you've published, the overwhelming number of people know you through the motion picture adaptations of your books — or indeed, the television advertisements for those movies — not realizing that you've had no real creative role in any of the films except Creepshow, Cat's Eye, Silver Bullet, *and, of course,* Maximum Overdrive. *How well do you think you have been treated in motion pictures?*

"I've never been hurt the way, for example, James Herbert and Peter Straub have been — at least not yet. The adaptation of horror fiction is not taken very seriously — all that the companies are looking for is the quick payoff, hoping for a five-week run and then good sales to foreign markets and to television. With some of the films from my novels, you could easily say that the people were just looking for that kind of payoff, knowing that as long as they stayed somewhere in the neighbourhood of the book, they couldn't go far wrong. I really don't believe that, since *The Shining*, there has been any conscious effort to make the film adaptations any better than the books.

"To me, John Updike said it all. He said that the best possible situation you could have with Hollywood is when they pay you huge amounts of money for your book and never make the film. Unless, as with *Creepshow*, I play an active part in the creative development of the film, I don't feel that I have any responsibility for what happens to a book when it goes on the screen. I send it off the way that I can imagine sending a child off to college. So the critical reaction to some of the films makes me feel a little bit like someone who has stumbled onto the scene of a murder and picked up a bloody knife, and the cops—in this case, the critics—come in. And I say, 'No, I didn't do it! it wasn't me!'

"An interviewer of James M. Cain once bemoaned the fact that Hollywood had ruined all of Cain's books. And Cain looked over to his bookshelf and said, 'No, they're still right there.' There is no movie that can ruin a book. They can embarrass the writer—sort of like showing up at a party with your fly open—but these things pass, while the books remain.

"At this point, I can't even explain why it seems so attractive to me to sell the books to the movie industry—it sure isn't the money. It seems to be something almost like exhibitionism—the same reason why I want to publish books."

In the early years, your novels were ignored, by and large, by the critical establishment. Have you found that the nature of reviews has changed with your growing popularity?

"Each new book seems to be received like *E.T.* or some of the things that Steven Spielberg has done lately, where it starts off having to prove itself all over again, simply because of the fact of previous success.

"In any other field, that sort of standard doesn't hold true; in fields other than the arts, if some guy does something again and again, you say that he is good, and the surprise is not that he has done something right—the surprise would occur if he did something wrong. But in our field, if you are popular and good at what you do, the more you succeed, the more you must prove yourself. People tend to think, 'Well, pretty soon he's going to stop working hard and start jacking off.' What this reflects more than anything else is an assumption from the critic's mind about what he would do if he were writing this stuff, which is something on the level of, 'As soon as I had enough money, I would just sit back and every once in a while sort of reach in my head for a little mindsnot and spread it on a few pages and make another bundle of money.'

"In other words, the mind-set is that this stuff really doesn't matter. Well, fuck that; rightly or wrongly, I'd like to believe that what we're doing is *important*. If we didn't believe that, I suppose we would go crazy."

Your work schedule only seems to grow each year—does it ever wear you down to the point that you would just like to stop?

"I don't feel tired in the sense of writing. I feel tired in the sense of having to be a writer.

"The commitments to things other than writing just keep growing . . . and it's a while before you see it as something less than benign. You justify things on the basis of your career: 'It's good for the career.' Or maybe, deep inside yourself, you say, 'Wow, think of that! They want *me* on TV, or they want *me* to make a speech at this thing.' And if you're young, or if you're not somehow freakish, with huge bumps growing out of your head, the celebrity machinery goes to work.

"But there is a real sense here of having to be careful that you're not eaten alive, because I sense more and more, particularly in the wake of things like the death of John Belushi, that celebrity is a little bit like being a turkey that's being fattened up in the pen for something you'd rather not contemplate—which might be front-page headlines for *The National Enquirer*. There is a real ominous feel about the life, as opposed to the work."

What really, deep down in your heart, scares you?

"Myself. I don't trust myself at all. I love my life, and I love my wife and kids, and I've remained sort of quasi-suicidal all the time. There's a real feeling of wanting to push things to the edge. You know, that it would be possible actually to continue to go out and do speeches and write books, and to continue to write at this breakneck pace until there is nothing left. And to go out and tour and do movies and continue to just take things on, not to be a good guy, but just so that I can say to myself, 'Look at all the stuff that you're juggling at once—isn't this amazing?' And, at the same time, to drink a lot every night, possibly take on a drug habit too—that might help.

"I'm scared of myself, mostly. And I like myself pretty

well, but I guess that's what scares me the most, because it's so perverse."

Where do you see yourself, ten years from now?

"I want to be alive. I would like the world to still be around. I would like to be able to play softball and goof around. I would like all my kids to be alive and fine. And I would like to write some more books, and not go dry. I would like not to go crazy.

"But I don't really plan ahead. In a rough sort of way, the only plan that I ever had was to get this stuff out of the way, and not take on any more commitments. I want to clear everything off, and I am going to just sit around. When I get up in the morning, I'll just grab hold of a book and go somewhere and sit in the corner and read all day long—except I'll take a walk in the morning, and I'll break at lunch for some hamburgers at McDonald's, and take another walk in the afternoon.

"And I would be bored shitless. I would be really unhappy if I were doing that. But that is the sort of goal that I always have in mind."

If you had the chance to talk with Edgar Allan Poe or H. P. Lovecraft, what would you say? What would you tell them?

"I wouldn't want to meet either of those guys."

Why is that?

"They seem like bores. I don't know. Of the two, I guess that if I had the chance to have dinner with Poe, I would go ahead and do it, but I'd say as little as possible. I'd listen, but there's nothing that I feel that I would want to ask either of these people—which isn't to say that I don't admire their work.

"But frankly, they both strike me as weirdos."

What do you think is the biggest myth, the biggest misconception about you?

"That *I'm* weird. That I must be weird. At least that's what most people seem to feel I'm going to be when they walk up to me at a convention or at a speech. There is this kind of careful approach: 'Are you all right? You're not going to bite me or anything like that?' That's one of the natural things that comes out of working in this field—people are going to think that, if you do this, then you must be a little bit strange."

Are they disappointed to learn that you aren't that weird?

"Yes. I think they are. I think they really want to see some red eyes and roaring. A lot of times I feel that I am disappointing people because I seem very mild-mannered and not very threatening. If I only had a little more of the Boris Karloff or Bela Lugosi charm or something . . . even Christopher Lee.

"And, of course, the other myth about any writer is that we must lead very glamorous lives, and that we live on the Riviera and all that; but here I am in Bangor, Maine. It's a nice house and it's a comfortable life, but it's not like—hell, I don't know, like something out of Rosemary Rodgers. It is not the glitterati . . ."

Douglas E. Winter

Douglas Winter was born on 30 October 1950, in St Louis, Missouri; he grew up, with his older brother, in the smoke-clouded steel town of Granite City, Illinois. His first encounters with the faces of fear came in apocryphal tales told by his grandfather, the hellfire of his Southern Baptist upbringing, and, ultimately, in comic books, 35 cent paperbacks, and films like *Invasion of the Body Snatchers* and *Psycho*.

His family was very close. His mother, a schoolteacher, encouraged him to read and write, even if it meant buying him subscriptions to *Famous Monsters of Filmland*. His father, a self-made businessman who rose from a boyhood job loading cases of Seven-Up onto a truck to the presidency of the Seven-Up Company, taught him the virtue of persistence.

After a confused '60s adolescence (he was an honour student by day, rock-and-roll drummer by night, a campus activist who nevertheless felt obliged to serve in the Army when drafted), he dabbled with careers in journalism and advertising, taking a graduate degree in communications at the University of Illinois. In pursuit of vague ideals, he decided instead to attend Harvard Law School, from which he graduated *cum laude* in 1975.

Today, Winter works with one of the nation's leading law firms in Washington, DC. When he is not engaged in the travails of federal court litigation, he may be found nights at home in a book-crowded office, hunched over a word processor. There, beneath lurid posters from films by his favourite horror directors—Dario Argento, Lucio Fulci, and George A. Romero—he writes to the accompaniment of

European rock-and-roll and his ever-growing collection of obscure motion picture soundtracks.

His criticism, reviews, and interviews have appeared in publications ranging from the *Washington Post*, *Gallery* and *Harper's Bazaar* to *Twilight Zone* and *Fantasy Review*, and have been translated into twelve languages. Among his seven published books are the definitive and critical study *Stephen King: The Art of Darkness* (1984), and his guide to contemporary horror fiction and film, *Shadowings* (1983). He edited the best-selling horror anthology *Prime Evil* (1988), and his own short stories have seen print with increasing regularity, most recently in the anthologies *Silver Scream*, *The Book of the Dead* and *Splatterpunks*.

Winter lives in Alexandria, Virginia, with his wife, two stepsons, and a black cat named Red. His few free moments are spent trying to coax music from an array of electronic keyboards and synthesizers, or watching professional wrestling on television. He is comfortable in his dual career as lawyer and writer, although he is usually very tired. In his secret heart of hearts he would probably rather be writing the screenplays and musical scores for low-budget Italian horror films.

Appendix A

A horror fiction buying guide

Speciality booksellers

Although many general-purpose bookstores are devoting increasingly substantial shelf space to horror fiction, speciality booksellers remain the ideal sources for devoted horror readers, as well as for inquisitive newcomers who wish to locate some of the more obscure or out-of-print titles mentioned in this book. The following speciality stores have both excellent selections and reputations:

A Change of Hobbit
1853 Lincoln Boulevard
Santa Monica, CA 90409

Andromeda Bookshop
84 Suffolk Street
Birmingham BI 1TA

Fantasy Centre
157 Holloway Road
London N7 8LX

Forbidden Planet
71 New Oxford Street
London WC1A 1DJ

Forbidden Planet
821 Broadway
New York, NY 10003

Moonstone Bookcellars
2145 Pennsylvania Avenue, N.W.
Washington, D.C. 20037

Except for Andromeda Bookshop and Fantasy Centre, which publish regular mail-order catalogues, the retailers listed above engage only in limited mail-order services. The premier mail-order outlet in the United States for horror fiction (as well as for fantasy and science fiction), and a source for many in-print British paperback editions, is:

Robert & Phillis Weinberg
15145 Oxford Drive
Oak Forest, IL 60452

For out-of-print horror and fantasy titles, including rare first editions, and for many in-print American and British hardcover editions, the most reliable and well-stocked source is:

L. W. Currey, Inc.
Elizabethtown, NY 12932

Monthly catalogues are available from these mail order dealers at a minimal price.

Speciality presses

A growing number of small press operations have played an increasingly crucial role in contemporary horror fiction, particularly in the past few years, either by producing deluxe limited editions of books (usually signed by the author and illustrated) or, more importantly, by publishing types of horror fiction, such as short story collections and form-breaking novels, that lack the apparent mass commercial potential demanded by New York publishers. The best of these small presses are Donald M. Grant, whose books are literally treasures of design and construction, and Scream/Press, which has mounted an ambitious publication schedule devoted entirely to contemporary horror fiction. Other long-established small presses are Arkham House, Underwood-Miller, Dark Harvest and Starmont House — the latter devoted solely to non-fiction. Catalogues or price lists are available on request from each of the following recommended speciality publishers:

Arkham House
Sauk City, W1 53583

Dark Harvest
P.O. Box 48134
Niles, IL 60648

Donald M. Grant, Publisher
West Kingston, RI 02892

Scream/Press
P.O. Box 8531
Santa Cruz, CA 95061

Starmont House
P.O. Box 851
Mercer Island, WA 98040

Underwood-Miller
651 Chestnut Street
Columbia, PA 17512

Weirdbook Press
P.O. Box 149
Buffalo, NY 14226

Whispers Press
70 Highland Avenue
Binghamton, NY 13905

Magazines

The only newsstand magazine currently devoted to horror fiction and news is *Fear*. Subscription inquiries should be mailed to:

FEAR
P.O. Box 20
Ludlow, Shropshire SY8 1DB

Three major "little magazines" of horror fiction, not

regularly available at newsstands or bookstores, are worth the attention of any horror reader:

Fantasy Tales
130 Park View
Wembley, Middlesex HA9 6JU

Weirdbook
P.O. Box 149
Buffalo, NY 14226

Whispers
70 Highland Avenue
Binghamton, NY 13905

In addition, a variety of semi-professional magazines are published regularly as part of the horror fiction "underground". In their pages, new writers, artists, and critics are testing their talents, and the results are sometimes crude, occasionally brilliant, and always entertaining. By nature, these magazines are often ephemeral, living or dying at the whim of a single person who may serve as editor, publisher, writer, and illustrator, but readers are urged to seek them out and support them. For news and commentary about motion pictures, two newsstand magazines, although often oriented to the special effects aspect of contemporary horror and fantasy film, are recommended:

Cinefantastique
P.O. Box 270
Oak Park, IL 60303

Fangoria
475 Park Avenue South
New York, NY 10016

Shock Express
26 Stanley Road
Chingford
London E4 7DB

News and reviews from the British publishing and film-making scenes are readily available through the British Fantasy Society, which publishes both a regular newsletter and a fiction and review magazine, *Dark Horizons*. Information about membership in the Society may be obtained by sending two International Postal Reply coupons to:

British Fantasy Society
46 Oxford Road
Acocks Green
Birmingham B27 6DT

Reference books

The following volumes, generally the best and most entertaining of the growing number of contemporary critical and reference sources, were consulted during the writing of this book:

Ashley, Mike. *Who's Who in Horror & Fantasy Fiction*. New York: Taplinger, 1977.

Bleiler, Everett F. *The Guide to Supernatural Fiction*. Kent, OH: Kent State University Press, 1983.

Clarens, Carlos. *An Illustrated History of the Horror Film*. New York: Putnam, 1967.

Daniels, Les. *Living in Fear: A History of Horror in the Mass Media*. New York: Scribner, 1975.

Hogan, David J. *Dark Romance: Sex and Death in the Horror Film*. Jefferson, NC: McFarland & Co., 1986.

Jones, Stephen, and Newman, Kim. *Horror: 100 Best Books*. London: Xanadu, 1988.

King, Stephen. *Danse Macabre*. New York: Everest House, 1981.

Meyers, Rick. *For One Week Only: The World of Exploitation Films*. Piscataway, NJ: New Dimensions, 1983.

Newman, Kim. *Nightmare Movies*. New York and London: Proteus Books, 1984; New York: Harmony Books, 1988 (revised edition).

Nicholls, Peter. *The World of Fantastic Films: An Illustrated Survey.* New York: Dodd Mead, 1984.

Prawer, S. S. *Caligari's Children: The Film as Tale of Terror.* Oxford: Oxford University Press, 1980.

Punter, David. *The Literature of Terror.* London: Longman, 1980.

Stanley, John. *The Creature Features Movie Guide.* Pacifica, CA: Creatures at Large, 1981.

Tymn, Marshall B., ed. *Horror Literature: A Core Collection and Reference Guide.* New York: Bowker, 1981.

Weldon, Michael. *The Psychotronic Encyclopedia of Film.* New York: Ballantine, 1983.

Winter, Douglas E. *Shadowings: The Reader's Guide to Horror Fiction, 1981–1982.* Mercer Island, WA: Starmont House, 1983.

_____ *Stephen King: The Art of Darkness.* New York: New American Library, 1984.

Zicree, Marc Scott. *The Twilight Zone Companion.* New York: Bantam, 1982.

Appendix B
The best of horror fiction 1951–1990

The following list of approximately 150 books is intended to provide a comprehensive, if occasionally idiosyncratic, reader's guide to the best of the modern generation of horror fiction. My definition of horror—which, like Supreme Court Justice Potter Stewart's definition of obscenity, is to know it when I see it—embraces authors and titles that some readers may identify with other genres. The only limitation I have observed is to restrict my selections to no more than five titles from any individual author.

Author	Title	Year
Peter Ackroyd	*Chatterton*	1987
	First Light	1989
Robert Aickman	*Cold Hand in Mine*	1975
	Tales of Love and Death	1977
	Painted Devils: Strange Stories	1979
V. C. Andrews	*Flowers in the Attic*	1979
	My Sweet Audrina	1982
J. G. Ballard	*The Atrocity Exhibition (Love and Napalm: Export U.S.A.)*	1969
	Crash	1973
	Concrete Island	1973
	High Rise	1975
Iain Banks	*The Wasp Factory*	1983
Clive Barker	*The Books of Blood*	1984–85
	The Damnation Game	1985
	Weaveworld	1987

James Herbert	*The Fog*	1975
	The Survivor	1976
	Shrine	1983
	Domain	1984
	Sepulchre	1987
Shirley Jackson	*The Sundial*	1958
	The Haunting of Hill House	1959
	We Have Always Lived in the Castle	1962
Gerald Kersh	*The Brighton Monster*	1953
	Men Without Bones	1955
Jack Ketchum	*Off Season*	1981
Stephen King	*'Salem's Lot*	1975
	The Shining	1977
	The Dead Zone	1979
	Different Seasons	1982
	Misery	1987
Russell Kirk	*Old House of Fear*	1961
	The Surly Sullen Bell	1962
	The Princess of All Lands	1979
T. E. D. Klein	*The Ceremonies*	1984
	Dark Gods	1985
William Kotzwinkle	*Doctor Rat*	1976
Tommaso Landolfi	*Words in Commotion*	1986
Joe R Lansdale	*By Bizarre Hands*	1989
Fritz Leiber	*Conjure Wife*	1953
	Our Lady of Darkness	1977
	The Leiber Chronicles	1990
Ira Levin	*Rosemary's Baby*	1976
	The Stepford Wives	1972
Joan Lindsay	*Picnic at Hanging Rock*	1967
Thomas Ligotti	*Songs of a Dead Dreamer*	1985
Frank Belknap Long	*The Horror from the Hills*	1963

	The Early Long	1976
Richard Lortz	*Dracula's Children*	1974
Robert R. McCammon	*They Thirst*	1981
	Blue World	1989
Michael McDowell	*Cold Moon Over Babylon*	1980
	The Elementals	1981
	Blackwater	1982
	Toplin	1985
Ian McEwan	*The Cement Garden*	1978
Robert Marasco	*Burnt Offerings*	1973
William March	*The Bad Seed*	1954
George R. R. Martin	*Songs the Dead Men Sing*	1983
Richard Matheson	*I am Legend*	1954
	The Shrinking Man	1956
	Shock!	1961
	Hell House	1971
	The Collected Stories of Richard Matheson	1989
Peter Matthiessen	*Far Tortuga*	1975
Thomas F. Monteleone	*Night Things*	1980
	Night Trains	1985
Brian Moore	*Cold Heaven*	1983
David Morrell	*First Blood*	1972
	Testament	1975
	The Totem	1979
Joyce Carol Oates	*Night-Side*	1977
Herman Raucher	*Maynard's House*	1980
Anne Rice	*Interview with the Vampire*	1976
Ray Russell	*Unholy Trinity*	1967

Alan Ryan	Cast a Cold Eye	1984
	The Bones Wizard and Other Stories	1988
Joan Samson	The Auctioneer	1975
Sarban	The Sound of His Horn	1960
David J. Schow	Seeing Red	1989
Anne Rivers Siddons	The House Next Door	1978
Dan Simmons	Carrion Comfort	1989
John Skip and Craig Spector	The Light at the End	1986
Fred Mustard Stewart	The Mephisto Waltz	1969
Peter Straub	If You Could See Me Now	1977
	Ghost Story	1979
	Shadowland	1980
	Floating Dragon	1983
	Koko	1989
Whitley Strieber	The Hunger	1981
	The Night Church	1983
Theodore Sturgeon	Some of Your Blood	1961
Bernard Taylor	The Godsend	1976
	Sweetheart, Sweetheart	1977
Thomas Tessier	The Nightwalker	1979
	Phantom	1983
	Finishing Touches	1986
	Rapture	1988
Jim Thompson	The Killer Inside Me	1952
	Savage Night	1953
Roland Topor	Le Locataire Chimérique (The Tenant)	1964
Thomas Tryon	The Other	1971
	Harvest Home	1973
Karl Edward Wagner	In a Lonely Place	1984

Appendix C
The best of horror films 1951–1990

The following list of approximately 150 motion pictures is intended to provide a comprehensive, if occasionally idiosyncratic, viewer's guide to the best of the modern generation of horror cinema. Unlike the preceding survey of horror fiction, this listing indulges in certain manifestations of tacky brilliance whose questionable merits as film are overcome resoundingly by their power to entertain. Again, the only limitation I have observed is to restrict my selections to no more than five titles from any individual director. Where films have been released under more than one title, I have indicated the alternative names in parentheses.

Director	Title	Year
Robert Aldrich	*Whatever Happened to Baby Jane?*	1962
	Hush, Hush, Sweet Charlotte	1964
Dario Argento	*The Bird with the Crystal Plumage*	1970
	Deep Red	1976
	Suspiria	1977
	Inferno	1980
	Tenebrae	1982
Jack Arnold	*The Creature from the Black Lagoon*	1954
	The Incredible Shrinking Man	1957
Clive Barker	*Hellraiser*	1987
Lamberto Bava	*Demons*	1985

Mario Bava	*Black Sunday*	1960
	Black Sabbath	1964
	Blood and Black Lace	1964
	Planet of the Vampires	1965
	Kill, Baby, Kill	1967
Ingmar Bergman	*The Seventh Seal*	1956
	Hour of the Wolf	1968
Kathryn Bigelow	*Near Dark*	1987
Peter Bogdanovich	*Targets*	1968
Tim Burton	*Beetlejuice*	1988
James Cameron	*Aliens*	1987
Marcel Camus	*Black Orpheus*	1959
Rene Cardona	*The Wrestling Women vs. the Aztec Mummy*	1965
John Carpenter	*Assault on Precinct 13*	1976
	Halloween	1978
	The Thing	1982
	Prince of Darkness	1988
William Castle	*Homicidal*	1961
	Strait-Jacket	1964
Roger Christian	*The Sender*	1982
Bob Clark	*Black Christmas (Silent Night, Evil Night)*	1974
Jack Clayton	*The Innocents*	1961
Brian Clemens	*Captain Kronos, Vampire Hunter*	1973
Henri-Georges Clouzot	*Diabolique*	1955
Francis Ford Coppola	*Dementia 13*	1963
Roger Corman	*The Little Shop of Horrors*	1960
	The Haunted Palace	1963
	The Masque of the Red Death	1964

Don Coscarelli	*Phantasm*	1979
Wes Craven	*The Hills Have Eyes*	1977
David Cronenberg	*They Came from Within (Shivers)*	1975
	The Brood	1979
	Scanners	1981
	Videodrome	1982
	The Fly	1986
Dan Curtis	*Trilogy of Terror*	1975
	Burnt Offerings	1976
Joe Dante	*The Howling*	1981
Steve de Jarnatt	*Miracle Mile*	1989
Armand de Ossorio	*The Blind Dead*	1972
Brian De Palma	*Sisters*	1973
	Phantom of the Paradise	1974
	Carrie	1976
	The Fury	1978
	Dressed to Kill	1980
Andre de Toth	*House of Wax*	1953
Ruggero Deodato	*Cannibal Holocaust*	1979
Martin Donovan	*Apartment Zero*	1989
Gordon Douglas	*Them!*	1954
Clint Eastwood	*High Plains Drifter*	1973
Abel Ferrara	*Ms. 45*	1981
Michael Findley	*Shriek of the Mutilated*	1974
Terence Fisher	*The Curse of Frankenstein*	1957
	Horror of Dracula	1958
	The Curse of the Werewolf	1961
	The Devil's Bride (The Devil Rides Out)	1968
Gene Fowler	*I Was a Teenage Werewolf*	1957
	I Married a Monster from Outer Space	1958

Freddie Francis	*Dr. Terror's House of Horrors*	1965
Georges Franju	*Yeux sans Visage (Horror Chamber of Dr. Faustus)*	1959
William Friedkin	*The Exorcist*	1973
	Sorcerer	1976
Robert Fuest	*The Abominable Dr. Phibes*	1971
Lucio Fulci	*Zombie (Zombie Flesheaters)*	1980
	The Gates of Hell (City of the Living Dead)	1980
	The Beyond (The Seven Doors of Death)	1981
	The House by the Cemetery	1982
	Apoteosi del Mistero	1987
John Gilling	*The Plague of the Zombies*	1966
Jorge Grau	*The Living Dead at Manchester Morgue (Don't Open the Window)*	1974
Val Guest	*The Creeping Unknown*	1956
	Enemy from Space	1957
Howard Hawks	*The Thing*	1951
Douglas Hickok	*Theatre of Blood*	1973
Alfred Hitchcock	*Strangers on a Train*	1951
	Psycho	1960
	The Birds	1963
Inoshiro Honda	*Godzilla, King of the Monsters*	1954
	Rodan	1957
	The H-Man	1958
	The Attack of the Mushroom People	1963
	Destroy All Monsters	1968
Tobe Hooper	*The Texas Chainsaw Massacre*	1974
	Eaten Alive	1976
Alexandro Jodorowsky	*El Topo*	1970

Philip Kaufman	*Invasion of the Body Snatchers*	1978
Masuki Kobayashi	*Kwaidan*	1963
Stanley Kubrick	*The Shining*	1980
Harry Kumel	*Daughters of Darkness*	1971
Akira Kurosawa	*Throne of Blood*	1957
Umberto Lenzi	*City of the Walking Dead (Nightmare City)*	1980
Richard Loncraine	*The Haunting of Julia (Full Circle)*	1977
David Lynch	*Eraserhead*	1976
	Blue Velvet	1986
John McNaughton	*Henry: Portrait of a Serial Killer*	1988
Michael Mann	*Manhunter*	1986
John Moxley	*Horror Hotel*	1960
	The Night Stalker	1971
Kurt Neumann	*The Fly*	1958
Sam Peckinpah	*The Wild Bunch*	1969
	Straw Dogs	1971
Roman Polanski	*Repulsion*	1965
	The Fearless Vampire Killers	1967
	Rosemary's Baby	1968
	Macbeth	1971
	The Tenant	1976
Michael Powell	*Peeping Tom*	1960
Sam Raimi	*The Evil Dead*	1982
Michael Reeves	*The Witchfinder General (The Conqueror Worm)*	1968
Alain Resnais	*Last Year at Marienbad*	1961
Wolf Rilla	*Village of the Damned*	1960
Nicholas Roeg	*Don't Look Now*	1973
George A. Romero	*Night of the Living Dead*	1968

	Martin	1977
	Dawn of the Dead	1979
	Creepshow	1982
	Day of the Dead	1985
Joseph Ruben	The Stepfather	1987
Peter Sasdy	Hands of the Ripper	1971
Ridley Scott	Alien	1979
Steve Sekely	Day of the Triffids	1963
Jim Sharman	The Rocky Horror Picture Show	1975
Kaneto Shindo	Onibaba	1964
Don Siegel	Invasion of the Body Snatchers	1956
Jerzy Skolimowski	The Shout	1979
Michel Soave	Aquarius (Bloody Bird, Stage Fright)	1986
Alfred Sole	Alice, Sweet Alice	1976
Steven Spielberg	Duel	1971
	Jaws	1975
	Raiders of the Lost Ark	1981
Lewis Teague	Cujo	1983
Jacques Tourneur	Curse of the Demon (Night of the Demon)	1956
Vincent Ward	The Navigator	1989
Peter Weir	Picnic at Hanging Rock	1978
	The Last Wave	1978
Ken Wiederhorn	Shock Waves (Death Corps)	1977
Robert Wise	The Haunting	1963

All Pan books are available at your local bookshop or newsagent, or can be ordered direct from the publisher. Indicate the number of copies required and fill in the form below.

Send to: **CS Department, Pan Books Ltd., P.O. Box 40, Basingstoke, Hants.   RG21 2YT.**

or phone: 0256 469551 (Ansaphone), quoting title, author and Credit Card number.

Please enclose a remittance* to the value of the cover price plus: 60p for the first book plus 30p per copy for each additional book ordered to a maximum charge of £2.40 to cover postage and packing.

*Payment may be made in sterling by UK personal cheque, postal order, sterling draft or international money order, made payable to Pan Books Ltd.

Alternatively by Barclaycard/Access:

Card No.

Signature:

Applicable only in the UK and Republic of Ireland.

While every effort is made to keep prices low, it is sometimes necessary to increase prices at short notice. Pan Books reserve the right to show on covers and charge new retail prices which may differ from those advertised in the text or elsewhere.

NAME AND ADDRESS IN BLOCK LETTERS PLEASE:

Name

Address

3/87